Eating the Elephant and Other Plays

By Julia Darling

New Writing North Plays

First Published in 2005 by
New Writing North
2 School Lane
Whickham
Newcastle upon Tyne
NE16 4SL
www.newwritingnorth.com

New Writing North Limited 3166037
Registered Charity Number 1062729

ISBN 0-9541456-4-X

Series editor: Claire Malcolm
Publications manager: John Adair
Proofreader: Will Mackie
Printed by Cromwell Press

Front cover photo: Sharon Bailey
The image is taken from a photography and creative writing project that took place in conjunction with Tak Tent, Cancer Support Scotland, which accompanied the first production of *Eating the Elephant*. For more information, see their website at www.taktent.org.uk.

Back cover portrait: Sasa Savic

New Writing North acknowledges the support of

Contents

Also by Julia Darling

Fiction
Bloodlines
Crocodile Soup
The Taxi Driver's Daughter

Poetry
Sudden Collapses in Public Places
Apology for Absence
The Poetry Cure (edited with Cynthia Fuller)

Plays
Live Theatre: Six Plays from the North East

Introduction

By Julia Darling

I fell into writing theatre. I never wanted to be a playwright, but theatre was a world I naturally leant towards, and which appealed to my love of the oral tradition in poetry, of working with others, of rooms full of laughter or emotion.

In the 1980s I was in a poetry performance group called The Poetry Virgins, which was a troupe of raucous women who liked a wild night out, and who 'took poetry to the places that least expected it' (and probably didn't want it either!) like housing co-op AGMs and women's refuge coffee mornings, and political rallies, and sometimes cabarets and poetry venues. At the time I had two small daughters, and was just beginning to try to be a writer. I wrote poems about the condition of motherhood, and relationships, and the chaotic life I was living. The Poetry Virgins were mainly unemployed actors, apart from the poet Ellen Phethean, who also wrote material. We had a grand time and our foot-stamping, sociable type of performance led easily to theatre.

I was first commissioned to write plays for youth theatres and theatre in education companies. These plays were often for large casts, and were devised as much as written. The atmosphere at that time was very issue-based and politically correct. Language was changing. Many playwrights in the North East worked in this way, and I am proud to be in the same tradition as CP Taylor, Tom Hadaway, Steve Chambers, Peter Mortimer, Michael Wilcox and many others. I did seem to be one of the only women on the landscape, which was odd.

My early plays were all rather worthy. I wrote about patriarchy, single mothers, bad capitalists and nice socialists, rotten men and brave women trying to find themselves. Plays, especially youth theatre plays, were often in a state of change right up until the opening night, and they had no shelflife at all. It was all about the process, not the product.

At that time in the North East there was an organisation called Northern Playwrights, who held very serious monthly meetings in dark libraries. It was a good way to meet other writers, but I think of the meetings as being rather embittered and competitive. Also, everyone else seemed like proper playwrights in leather jackets, carrying briefcases. I wasn't sure if I belonged to this club.

I was lucky with commissions. One play led to another. This was a mixed blessing, as commissions can take you in the opposite direction to where the heart is, and the older I get, the more I believe in following one's passions and intuition, rather than writing what others think you should. I don't really see writing as a job. It's lots of other things; a means of surviving, of understanding this confusing world, of telling people what you think, of celebrating the complexity of human beings, but I am not a 'jobbing' writer. This is probably why I have never written for television or film, and will never be rich.

I wrote three plays for a Cumbrian theatre company called Quondam, each play taking a year, and involving much research, reading and plodding about gloriously surreal towns like Maryport or Whitehaven, meeting and interviewing extraordinary local people, and piecing together hidden, often uncomfortable histories. I wrote about an infamous communist called Johny Rafferty from Maryport, the building of the Settle to Carlisle railway line by navvies, and the Whitehaven slave trade. These were essentially history plays, written for small-scale touring, which travelled the village halls of Cumbria and beyond. I developed a real love of small-scale touring, and the idea of taking such epic stories into such small communities. Working for Quondam was uncomplicated and I could write what I wanted given the boundaries of budget, and although the subject matter was prescribed, it was always fascinating.

Eating the Elephant was a departure for me in terms of theatre. In 1995 I was diagnosed with breast cancer, and this changed my life and writing. The Ashton Group commissioned me to write the play, and for the first time I wrote about my own experience, using the writing of the play to exorcise my own demons. The cast was all female, and the whole process was both challenging and healing. I have called this collection *Eating the Elephant and Other Plays* because it is a pivotal piece of work for me. The play was produced twice by the Ashton Group, and has been used extensively by voluntary groups, both as entertainment and as a basis for discussion.

The first play I wrote for Live Theatre was *The Women Who Painted Ships*, and since then I have been closely involved with that theatre. I have always believed in the ethos of Live, with its informal close theatre space and intelligent local audience. It has remained loyal to its political beginnings and still is for me the voice of the North East, and certainly the best place for a writer to develop. Max Roberts, the artistic director, asked me to be writer in residence with the poet and playwright Sean O'Brien, and we both produced a number of plays in that time, working with Live directors Jeremy Herrin and Max Roberts. It was a privilege to be in a situation where one could develop theatrical ideas and also work with actors who had so much to offer. It's funny how you start out trying to learn the craft of theatre, but somehow you just have to do it for long enough to gain confidence to just be yourself, and I think Live helped me do this. Through them I built up an audience for my theatre work. It's hard to say what one's work aims to achieve, but I suppose I write for and about the invisible, for all the ordinary people, particularly women, who don't have guns, or even do particularly dramatic things, but whose everyday lives are still incredible, filled with poetry, pathos and small explosions.

I have been hugely encouraged and inspired by the actors of the North East region, many of whom I have written specifically for: Charlie Hardwick, Zoe Lambert, Madeleine Moffat (who is my quintessential older woman), Trevor Fox, Jez Casey, Judi Earl and Carol McGuigan and many others. Not only have they taught me a great deal about theatre, but they have also given me all kinds of insights into other worlds. My happiest moments in theatre are working with actors, hearing the range of possibilities that an actor can give to a script, and delving deeper into a character's motivations and pre-occupations.

Also a full house at Live Theatre has a wonderfully Elizabethan feeling about it, with bright faces leaning over the balconies, and the place alive with a rapt, engaged, sometimes unruly audience.

As Newcastle becomes more corporate, glossier and up-market (on the surface anyway) Live is still a beacon in the midst of this development. Although the building is expanding, it is still a theatre for new writing, a voice for the region. I hope it never changes.

This book also includes some of my radio work, much of which came from plays that originated as stage plays at Live.

Compiling this anthology of plays has been an opportunity to reflect on twenty years of theatre work. Like all theatre, my work has been of its time, depending on the spirit and the possibilities of the moment. It has benefited from the ideas of actors, directors, and friends, or it has had to comply with restrictions of budget, time or space. Often plays have been altered in rehearsal, so that finding final versions of each script has been quite hard.

I am delighted that all my characters, my Venetia Loves, my Ednas, my Maureens, and all the others have been given a safe home within these pages.

Spring 2005

Editor's note

*'It is perhaps rather arrogant to think that one's history is important, but
I like to reflect upon my life's correspondence in much the same way as I like
to shake snow-storms.'*

From Venetia Love Goes Netting

Eating the Elephant and Other Plays was a project that we began in
the last few months of Julia Darling's life. Julia selected all of the
plays for the collection and we agreed to order the plays by form,
separating the theatre work from the plays for radio. As you will
see there is a great deal of synergy between the work and many
stage plays went on to become, or directly influence, radio plays.

When we started to discuss doing the book, Julia referred to it as her
'bitty bob book' as we were bringing together lots of work from
different places. As I began to read through her work, some of which
I'd seen or heard in original productions, some of which I had never
seen or read before, I began to realise that this book would in fact be
very important. I began this process wanting to produce a book
which would enable Julia to reflect on her script work and present the
work that she liked best for posterity and because I both personally
and professionally greatly admired her writing. I've ended the process
feeling that her gift for comedy and characterisation, her deceptive
lightness of touch and her inherent grasp of dramatic form are
actually rather exceptional. I feel that this book should go some way
to establishing her reputation as a serious dramatist.

I would encourage anyone who is reading this book without
knowing Julia's other work to also explore her novels, poetry and
song collections as you will find many of the same concerns and
ideas at play in her work across the genres that she excelled in.

Finally, I would like to thank all of the people who have helped to
bring this book together and who have been kind enough to give
the project their time or advice, especially Bev Robinson, Sue
Roberts, Jeremy Herrin, Max Roberts, Sarah McPhail, Sean
O'Brien, John Adair and photographer Sharon Bailey, who
worked with Julia prior to her death to ensure that we chose a
cover image for the book that Julia felt was right.

Claire Malcolm, New Writing North
July 2005

Julia Darling's theatre plays

By Jeremy Herrin, Live Theatre, Newcastle

Julia Darling is a generous person. This is demonstrated in all her work, and particularly in her plays. These plays were written as gifts: always offerings for an unsuspecting but invariably charmed audience; often specific treats for particular performers or companies; and always given with an almost casual kindness. Having worked with her on a number of projects, I've never had a sense of Julia writing in order to receive anything in return. Not for her a take on the world that is cluttered by petty ego or a thin definition of what success really is. This wisdom is never far from her work.

Her relationship with Live Theatre has been an effortlessly favourable one: the inclusive feeling of the auditorium perfectly reflects the warm give in her writing. I have enjoyed many memorable nights with her plays: *Venetia Love Goes Netting*, as performed by Madeleine Moffat and presented as part of an epic two evenings of monologues titled *NE1*, was the start of Julia's interest in all things postal. The story was so strong that it quickly became repositioned to be the climax of the first evening. Literally, no one could follow it. This obsession with mail continued with a tour around County Durham and back to Live Theatre with *The Last Post. Personal Belongings* was written for the actress Zoe Lambert to show off her crazy talent and delightful voice. Also *Attachments* was written with Charlie Hardwick and Trevor Fox in mind and Julia beautifully harnessed their consummate skills for high comedy and sweet pathos. To me these shows are as definitive of the theatre's work as any of the plays by Live's most celebrated writers.

Her creation of character is an enduring example of her generosity. Characters are presented with humour, they all have surprises under their wrapping and they always reveal their better natures sooner or later. The people in her plays usually undergo some process of self-realisation and they (and we, their audience) end the evening happily more often than not. This defiantly unfashionable approach is typical of Julia and the feeling of seeing her plays is equivalent to working with her or even spending any time with her at all: audiences leave the theatre in the same buoyant, heartened mood as any number of writing students, taxi drivers or slightly pushy young directors who have had the genuine pleasure of her company.

I am delighted that New Writing North has chosen to collect all of this work: it is fantastic that it is available and I am hopeful that Julia's work will be presented again and again. It's a gift.

Spring 2005

Eating the Elephant

This was an important play for me. It was the first play that I wrote based on personal experience, and in many ways it was the first time I used writing as a way of making sense of my illness. In 1995 I was diagnosed with breast cancer, and I wrote the play the following year, almost as a discussion with myself. I always thought that the four characters were parts of me, all in conflict, but trying to find common ground. The play tells of four women's journey through breast cancer, and how class, race, culture and sexuality affect how one copes with a cancer diagnosis.

It was great when the play opened. I loved the cast, and the way the play was presented. Theatres seemed to be full of groups of one-breasted laughing women, and I felt the play spoke to our experience.

Since its first tour the script has been used by many voluntary and professional health groups, many of whom found it a useful vehicle for facilitating discussions with women about cancer.

Julia Darling

Eating the Elephant was first presented by the Ashton Group Contemporary Theatre at Forum 28, Barrow in Furness, on 16 April 1997. It was directed by Rachel Ashton and designed by Mandy Dike with music by Nicky Rushton.

CAST

Carol	Janet Dye
Miranda	Vari Sylvester
Laura/Joyce/Danny	Monica Gibb
Zimmy/St Agatha	Kay Purcell

Various doctors, nurses and the talking liver and lungs were played by members of the company.

ACT ONE

SCENE ONE

Laura's diary

Laura's diary lies somewhere on the set, and is returned to throughout the play.

I was in the shower when I first felt the second lump. It was small and definite. I kept feeling it over and over again, not wanting to believe that it was there. Graham was downstairs putting weedkiller on the lawn. Wrapped in my towel I waved at him and he waved back. He had huge red rubber gloves on. I said the word LUMP at him, just made the shape with my mouth, and he went pale. Came running in the house. Trod dirt all over the sitting room carpet.

I went to the doctor that day. I wasn't wasting any time. I got an appointment at the clinic straight away. I practically ran t here. Don't come, I said to Graham, you just get on with your exterminations. For the first time I didn't really want him there. I don't like the way he breathes.

SCENE TWO

The waiting room

We are in the waiting room of a busy hospital, waiting to see the breast specialist. Two women come in and sit down. They pick up magazines and look around. We get the impression that the waiting room is full. They both look up as someone else's name is called.

Carol   You could die and be cremated before you got seen in this place.

Laura   They're very busy. The consultant's off.

Carol   I'll be off in a minute.

Awkward silence.

Laura   Are you just having a check-up?

Carol   Yeah, I've got a lump. I've had it for years. It started off like a bit of gristle, just here. Never changed or anything, that is until recently. You can see it through my clothes. Look! Big as a lemon.

Laura looks away.

Carol   What's yours like?

Laura   Er, more like a pea.

Carol   Doctor saw mine. I only went for my athlete's foot. He nearly fainted. Thought I'd have to give him the kiss of life.

Laura   You should have got it checked straight away!

Carol   I know. My whole foot was a mushroom farm...

Laura   Actually, I meant the breast.

Carol   I just didn't have time that's all.

She sighs, bored with Laura. Zimmy walks in and looks at the waiting room. She seems annoyed. She sits down and picks up a magazine, turning the pages angrily. Carol brightens up.

Pause.

Carol   Is that *Hello*?

Zimmy   Hello?

Laura   She means the magazine.

Zimmy   Do you want to read it? Have it. I can't be bothered.

Carol   Give it over here.

Zimmy   I can't stand hospitals.

Carol   Neither can I. The way the nurses and doctors clip about as if they know something that we don't.

Zimmy   Nobody tells you anything.

Laura   They're doing their best. They're busy, that's all.

Zimmy/Carol So are we! We're busy.

Carol   Very busy.

Laura   So am I. Extremely busy. But you have to be patient, don't you?

Zimmy   Do we?

Laura   It's only a routine check-up after all. It's always best to check. My husband usually comes with me but he's trying to get rid of a rat.

Carol and Zimmy stare at Laura.

Zimmy   I beg your pardon?

Laura   It's just that there's a rat infestation in our area. It's nothing to be ashamed of. I live in Coniston Avenue. Apparently, wherever you are there's a rat within ten yards.

Everyone looks round nervously.

Zimmy   You should be careful of the chemicals they use. Why not try asking the rat to leave before you nuke it?

Laura   I don't think Graham would want to do that kind of thing.

Carol   I can't see any sign of a rat round here.

Zimmy   Hospitals! They're full of disease.

Laura   You mean ill people.

Zimmy   No, germs, rats, plagues, mites...

Carol   It's lovely and clean!

Zimmy   On the surface, maybe. It's all so depersonalised, isn't it? They should have information on the walls, not flowers.

Carol   That's a wonderful picture, that. (*Pointing at a picture of pink flowers*) Mantel Pinks.

Zimmy   Pictures of bodies, for instance.

Carol   What, boobs?

Laura   I don't think so. It wouldn't be very suitable, would it? It's a hospital, not a brothel.

Zimmy   What's wrong with breasts? They're not dirty, are they? I mean informative pictures.

Carol   Like pictures of lumps?

Zimmy   Maybe!

She huffily gets a magazine and turns the pages crossly.

Laura tuts and looks away in disgust.

Carol   Where's your lump?

Zimmy   (*Soft and furious*) I haven't got a lump. It's just a sensation. A pricking sensation. A swollen gland maybe. I know when something's wrong with me, that's all.

Carol   So do I! Usually I fall over.

Zimmy   In the most subtle way, I know. I just wanted to make sure. I'm about to leave the country.

Carol   Going back home, are you?

Zimmy   I was born here actually. I've got family in Jamaica.

Carol   Close family?

Zimmy   My mother.

Laura   I bet it's lovely there, is it? Climate-wise?

Zimmy   Beautiful. I haven't got the money for the ticket yet. Bank won't lend me any.

Laura   Well they wouldn't. How do they know you're coming back?

Zimmy looks at Laura curiously.

Carol   Borrow it off your mother. That's what most people do.

Zimmy   I can't.

Miranda walks in, interrupting.

Miranda Is this the... (*Looks at a bit of paper*) breast clinic? (*Pause*) Have you been here long?

Carol   Yes. This is section F. F for Fucking ages. Excuse me, everyone.

Laura   Since ten o'clock.

They all look curiously at the newcomer. Eyebrows raised.

Carol   We're having a bit of a chinwag here, aren't we? Sit yourself down. Is this your first time?

Miranda Yes.

Laura   Were you sent by the doctor?

Miranda I had a mammogram.

Carol   I've heard about those mammograms, squeezing you flat. Like squeezing your titties with your grandmother's flat iron.

Miranda That's a very accurate description.

Carol   What do you do then?

Miranda I teach, at the university.

Carol   I clean. I do the university sometimes. Contract. See the bleach stains on my trousers? It's a grimy place that university. Stains everywhere.

Laura   What do you teach?

Miranda Art history.

Carol   Ooh, art. What kind of pictures?

Miranda Catholic iconography.

Carol/Laura Lovely.

They look at the ceiling and at the floor.

Carol   It's enough to bore the tits off you!

Everyone looks horrified. Carol shrugs.

Carol   Let's read the horoscopes!

Laura   Libra.

Carol   Pluto is in the ascension. I wish they'd leave out all that jargon. Who cares if it's coming up or going down? Prepare yourself for a big surprise involving friends and family. Don't stint on the treats. All Librans need their perks and you're no exception.

Laura   I might have my legs waxed.

Carol   What's your sign, dear?

Zimmy   Don't I know you? (*To Laura*) You look very familiar.

Laura   I don't think so.

Zimmy   I do. I know. You work in the bank on the corner.

Laura   Yes.

Zimmy   Doesn't matter. You probably see people like me all day.

Laura I'm afraid I... (*She suddenly recognises Zimmy*) Oh yes. (*Pause*) I just have to follow the bank's policies. I don't make the rules.

Zimmy It's funny, isn't it? Me shouting my head off in a bank and then I meet you here.

Laura It's just my job.

Zimmy Of course. Sorry about the wastepaper basket. I mean, it didn't hit you or anything, did it? Did you actually call the police or was that just a bluff?

Laura The glass is bullet-proof.

Zimmy It was a wastepaper basket, not a gun.

Laura I didn't call the police.

Zimmy You didn't have to. I left!

Laura Let's not mention it again. Forget it.

Zimmy I just lost my temper. It's my spleen. It needs attention.

Carol (*To Miranda*) What's your sign?

Miranda Er, Pisces.

Carol You might feel as if you're going against the current, but the ocean and all its wonders are not far away. That's nice. Be prepared for some opposition. Stand up to those who keep trying to put you down. Lucky day, November 21st. Today!

Miranda Lucky me.

Carol Can I get anyone a cup of tea while I'm going up?

Miranda Would you mind? I'll have a black coffee.

Carol Hey, one lump or two? Geddit?

Miranda One. (*She hastily gets an academic book from her bag and buries her nose in it*)

Everyone looks really embarrassed.

Zimmy Get us a herb tea. I presume they do herb tea. Anything, camomile, hibiscus.

Carol I fancy a biscuit too.

She goes off.

Laura It's certainly changed since I was last here.

Zimmy In what way?

Laura It's been painted pink. New curtains.

Miranda How feminine!

Zimmy I beg your pardon?

Miranda Pink for little girls.

Zimmy Speak for yourself.

Miranda I meant their clothes, historically anyway.

Laura Well, I think it's a nice colour. I dressed both my girls in pink, but that was some time ago. One's in Woking. The other's in Birmingham.

Miranda How interesting.

Zimmy When were you last here anyway?

Laura Fifteen years ago. I had a, you know...

Carol overhears as she comes back with the tea.

Carol (*Shouts*) You had the bust off, did you? Three teas. They didn't serve herbs.

Laura   I had a (*Whispers*) mastectomy. You know how they say your chances get better as time goes on.

Carol   Chances of what? Getting off with someone?

Laura   Of course not. Chances of... chances of...

Miranda Survival?

Laura   Yes.

Carol   *Staying alive. Staying alive, whup, whup, whup, whup... STAYING ALIVE!*

Laura   That's right.

Carol   They hire me to break the ice at parties, you know!

Laura   As I was saying, I thought it was all over. That I was clear.

Carol   I bet it will be nothing, love.

Laura   I'm not worried. Could just be a cyst. It's only a check-up.

Miranda It's one in twelve, isn't it?

Zimmy   What?

Miranda One in twelve will be positive. So, let's hope we all walk away.

Carol   That's good, because we're only four, so there you go! I mean, even if one of us was, you know, had it, the rest of us wouldn't have. At least it would be a daft coincidence if we were all, you know, positive. Very unlikely.

Freezing moment.

Carol   Isn't it?

Miranda I have always loved the sound of the word 'cyst'.

Carol   'Fibroids'. That's nice too. I tell you what, let's swap phone numbers. I mean, you never know.

Miranda What for?

Carol   You might want someone to... talk to.

Laura   You can have mine.

Zimmy   I told you, I'm leaving the country. You can have my temporary number.

Laura   If you give me your addresses I'll put you all on my Christmas card list.

Reluctantly, the other two exchange numbers

Carol   I've just thought. We don't even know each other's names.

SCENE THREE

Diagnosis

They all stop. Step out of naturalism. We hear the following sequence on tape and watch their faces as they listen.

Zimmy   Zimmy Jarret.

Laura   Laura Goodchild.

Miranda Miranda Hurt.

Carol   Carol Proudfoot.

They each stand up. Take off their tops and sit in their vests, listening to the doctor giving them his diagnosis.

Zimmy   There is no easy way to

Laura   tell you this, and I know

Miranda that it will come as a shock

They lean forward, sympathetic looks on their faces.

Carol   I'm afraid that your test has been

Zimmy   positive, and that the

Laura   cells are malignant.

Break. Intake of breath. Back to direct speech.

Miranda Cancer. Remember Mother. The white smell of the bedroom. Bloody Clarissa at the university, she'll take over my teaching. Look at the doctor's mouth – it's like a fish. Mother's hand on the bed. And Sister Frost.

Carol   I knew I knew I knew... Don't say any more. Just give me the good news. Hear no evil, see no evil. It's as if the doctor has said something to me that was already there. I knew what he was going to say. I've always known. I mean, that's why I didn't go to the doctor. Because I knew. I just put it off.

Laura   But I've done everything right. I've eaten well. I exercise. I don't drink or smoke. I enjoy myself. I go to quiltmaking classes. It can't have come back! Not now.

Zimmy   Which door did I leave unlocked? How did it get in? Was it that time I swum in the sea on the West Coast. Is it stress? Is it the pylon near my house, the fat in my diet, Chernobyl, anxiety, or just me?

SCENE FOUR

Conversations with doctors

Zimmy becomes The Doctor. Laura starts putting on her clothes, although she is clearly distressed.

Laura   I'm fine. It's alright. It's just the shock, that's all. One thing on top of another. Telling Graham. All the trouble that everyone will have to go to.

Doctor   Laura, Laura, Laura.

Laura   It's not as if I've got young children or anything. It's just me and Graham now. Oh, Graham. He'll be so upset.

Doctor   What was he like when you were ill before?

Laura   Marvellous. He's always marvellous. But he doesn't like any upheaval. Why has it come back. Why now? Why not before?

Doctor   That's a good question. It could be due to a number of factors. It could be hormonal.

Laura   But you must know something. After all this time.

Doctor   There have been developments.

Laura   What?

Doctor   Tamoxifen, for instance.

Laura   I know about that. Makes you fat. You lose your sex drive.

Doctor   That's not actually accurate. Some women find that they put on...

Laura   Long nighties. Sorry. Is that it?

Doctor   We are refining the treatments all the time.

Pause. The doctor shrugs and grins. Laura stares at her.

Laura   Oh well. I expect you've got other people to see.

Doctor   I've got plenty of time. You're the one that matters here. You don't have to be brave.

Laura buttons up her blouse carefully and wipes her eyes. The Doctor examines the notes.

Doctor   Let's see. You had a mastectomy fifteen years ago. I'm afraid that you'll need to have another one.

Laura   Oh. (*Pause*) How many from the waiting room were positive this morning?

Doctor   Out of the whole clinic? Six or seven, I think. Of course it varies enormously. You're not the only one.

Laura   Who were they?

Doctor   I can't tell you that, I'm afraid. December 15th I can fit you in.

Laura   What for?

Doctor   The mastectomy.

Laura   Did you say that before? I didn't really hear properly.

Doctor   I'll expect you'll want to talk to the breast nurse. You can phone her up any time. There's more support than there was in the old days.

Laura   Is there?

Doctor   We've got better at communicating.

Laura   But no one's found a cure, have they?

Doctor   It's a complicated illness. Look, ask me anything you want. Write a list of questions and I'll do my best to answer them...

Laura   Why did you paint the waiting room pink?

Doctor   Is it pink? It wasn't my decision.

Laura   I just wondered. Why not blue? Or yellow? And why do you have pictures of flowers on the walls?

SCENE FIVE

Talking to the jolly doctor

Laura stands up and becomes The Jolly Doctor, while Carol becomes the patient. She is being ridiculously cheerful.

Doctor   The operation really isn't too bad.

Carol   (*Cheery*) Well, my granny had it. It's in the family, so I'm not surprised. How long did you say I'd have to be off work?

Doctor   Six weeks perhaps. Some people take longer to recover. I can see you're a strong lass!

Carol   I haven't had a day off work for years.

Doctor   We'll get you back to work as soon as we can, but you have to rest.

Carol   Aye. I know. Linda McCartney's got it, hasn't she?

Doctor   Yes, so I hear.

Carol   And Olivia Newton John. You reckon that will be that, after the op? I won't have to wear a wig and all that.

Doctor   We can't really say until we've done further tests. I'll put you on a drug, it's called Tamoxifen.

Carol   Tamoxxy what? Oh, doesn't matter. Do I get one of them free breasts?

Doctor   You certainly do.

Carol   What a carry on!

Doctor   You should have come before. The tumour is quite advanced.

Carol   You know how it is...

Doctor   It doesn't matter now. You're here.

Carol   The operation. It'll have to be next month. It's my eldest son's wedding.

Doctor   Carol. I'm afraid this is serious. More serious than your son's wedding. You'll have to come first this time.

Carol   Me?

SCENE SIX

Miranda meets Saint Agatha in the hospital corridors

Miranda   I'm gliding along. Giddy with shock. A scan? To me they are all death words. Scan, cell, malignant, metastases. It is at this point I first see her. Imagine my surprise. I knew her at once from the paintings... Saint Agatha. She is in front of me in the corridor. She turns and there's the plate. Her breasts upon it, just like in the painting. Imagine how I felt? The patron saint of breasts, here, in the Royal Victoria Infirmary on a normal weekday!

Zimmy is playing Saint Agatha, holding a plate with two prostheses on it. Miranda behaves as if she's meeting a film star she's always admired.

Miranda   Excuse me, but... I hope you don't mind. Did you know that I'm writing a book about you?

Agatha   You must be Professor Hurt. Of course I know of your work. I enjoyed your last book very much, *Venus, Cupid, Folly and Time*. Oh yes. Fantastic.

Miranda   That was published ages ago.

Agatha   But you've written articles in magazines. And don't forget that the book about me has taken many years to write. Of course, my case was so extreme and interesting.

Miranda   Burning tongs! It couldn't have been worse really!

Agatha spits.

Agatha   Cut off my breasts because I wouldn't lie with Quintianus.

Miranda That's right. This is so exciting!

Agatha But I had faith. I was healed. Saint Peter healed me, with his lotions and embalmings. As you know, I was too modest at first. Wouldn't let him touch me. I was fine in the morning though. At least until they burnt me at the stake.

Miranda How did you stand it?

Agatha I can't remember that bit very well. It was so smokey. I went to heaven. There are plenty of breasts there, Miranda. Angels kissing you all day.

Miranda I bet!

Agatha I didn't make much of a fuss. I just said...

Miranda O thou tyrant! Shamest thou not to treat me so, thou who hast been nourished and fed from the breast of a mother.

Agatha That's what I said! Otherwise, I just put up with it. That's my point.

Miranda I would have done the same in your situation. Absolutely. Where are you staying?

Agatha I was wondering if I could stay with you. I might be quite helpful in the months to come.

Miranda With me? I'd be delighted.

Agatha I'll just get my icons then. See you later.

Miranda And I'll get the prayer mats out!

She rushes off.

SCENE SEVEN

Laura's diary

The first skill you need is patience.

Having breast cancer is an activity that will fill hours, days and months.

I sit in a green waiting room outside mammography and laugh. There is no one else anywhere. The hospital is strangely deserted. Laughter tears roll down my cheeks and drip down onto my chest, marking my silk blouse with greasy tears. Biotex, I think.

The stupid, stupid thing is that we'd just started having (*Whispers*) sex again.

Can you believe it? After fifteen years. It started after the rat came. I heard it scratching in my room at night and I had to go and get in with Graham. Now I'm thinking, perhaps the sex was the thing that started it. That's ridiculous. I don't mean that. Cross it out.

SCENE EIGHT

Miranda comes home to Joyce

Miranda comes into a room, all alone. Wrapped up in a coat against the obviously cold weather, carrying a bunch of very red flowers. Laura becomes Joyce, Miranda's girlfriend.

Miranda Joyce!

Joyce   Are they for me?

Miranda Who else.

Joyce   I let myself in.

Miranda It's getting quite icy out there.

Joyce   I'll light the gas fire.

Miranda I walked through the market. It was very bright, beautiful in fact. After the university. Big melons, turnips, huge oranges. Lots of natural things are round, aren't they?

Joyce rubs Miranda's shoulders.

Miranda Don't do that!

The phone rings. Joyce picks it up.

Joyce   It's for you. Someone called Laura.

Miranda Laura?

She takes the phone.

Miranda Miranda Hurt speaking. Oh, it's you. I'm afraid so, yes. You too? Look, could you phone back in half an hour?

Joyce   Who is Laura?

Miranda A woman I met.

Joyce   She sounded like she worked in a bank.

Miranda She does. And she's a Libran.

Joyce   I see. You seem to know her rather well.

Miranda Her husband's called Graham. She's the kind of person who has doilies in her biscuit tins, and her dog wears a knitted coat.

Joyce   Where have you been again?

Miranda I told you, I went to the market. All that colour. People.

Joyce   Dead grinning pigs. Heaps of pink mince.

Miranda Life and death. Better than staring at dusty old paintings.

Joyce   I think you've been somewhere else. You seem different.

What's up?

Pause.

Miranda Sit down, Joyce. I want to talk to you.

Joyce I've got to put these in water.

Miranda Wait a moment.

Joyce Well? Did you hear from Madrid?

Miranda Not yet.

Joyce You'd better. I got my passport today.

Miranda We're not going to Spain.

Joyce What are you talking about? Why are you being so serious? You're scaring me!

Miranda There was this nun at the convent. Sister Frost. Nobody liked her. She smelt of catfood. She was very ample. We used to make fun of her the way that they stuck out in front. Mimic her.

But nuns have always got hidden underneaths, haven't they? Their bodies are such a long way from the outside. It seemed terrible when she got ill. Being convent girls we all felt guilty. She was sort of whisked away and only talked about in hushed tones. Apparently they hardly ever get cervical cancer, nuns.

Joyce Is somebody ill?

Miranda I went to the hospital.

Joyce You? What for?

Miranda Tests. I was referred. I had a mammogram. I hate all the bloody words. Mammogram! As if we're all mammals with big milky tits.

Joyce Miranda! What are you talking about?

Miranda I didn't want to say anything. As far as I was concerned it was just a routine test. I don't tell you when I go to the dentist.

Joyce   But I would have come with you. You know I would.

Miranda I had a needle test at the clinic.

Joyce   And?

Miranda It's cancer. They told me straight away.

Awful pause.

Joyce   Are you sure? What are you going to do?

Miranda Take the medicine. What else can I do?

Joyce   What is the medicine?

Miranda They want to remove the lump.

Joyce   Not the whole breast?

Miranda No.

Joyce   Oh well! That's alright, isn't it? You'll have a little scar.

Miranda shrugs. Joyce tries to kiss her but she backs off.

Miranda It's still cancer.

Joyce   Can I get you anything?

Miranda I just keep thinking about everything I should have done. It doesn't matter now, does it?

Joyce   Of course it does. Lots of women have breast cancer. It doesn't mean you're going to die. What did the doctor say?

Miranda I didn't hear most of it. Is there any food in the fridge. I'm starving. Do you think I should give up meat?

Joyce   It's obviously not advanced. Probably stage one, less than a centimetre. That's about seventy percent chance of non-recurrence.

Miranda You're such a text book. Anyway, that's not so cheering for the other thirty percent. Today I was one in twelve.

Joyce It's not the end of the...

Miranda Roll out the clichés, Joyce.

Joyce I'll get onto the internet. I'll find out everything there is to know.

Miranda Go ahead, surf off!

Joyce We can handle it.

Miranda That's what I wanted to talk to you about. I need to be on my own.

Joyce That's the last thing you need.

Miranda But I do. I really do. Just for a few days. Why don't you go back to your own place? Like *now*.

She turns to the audience, in a saintly pose. Joyce freezes.

Miranda Do you smell frying martyr?

Then back to Joyce.

Joyce I can't leave you on your own. Don't be bloody stupid.

Miranda Just walk away. No one's looking.

Joyce puts on her coat and leaves. Miranda pours out another drink.

Joyce I'll phone you later. How can someone as clever as you be so stupid?

Joyce leaves. The phone rings again in the distance, but Miranda doesn't answer. Saint Agatha appears, carrying her plate and a small suitcase.

Agatha   Where shall I put my things?

Miranda   Anywhere you like. Treat the place as your own. I'll open a bottle of vino tinto.

SCENE NINE

People reacting

Zimmy, Miranda and Monica become a concerned friend or relative. There is Agnes from the university wearing a strange hat, and Danny the 12-year-old and a hippy-looking woman dangling a crystal. They are all on telephones.

A string of greetings cards appear, and a bowl of bright fruit, cut flowers, Lucozade.

Hippy lady   How are you dealing with it all, Zimmy? We're centring on you, Zimmy, and thinking of you every day. Here's the list. Have you got a pen? Selenium, Iscador, Vitamin C, Zinc. The list is rather long. Shall I send it instead? You should be juicing carrots, broccoli, kiwi and orange. You will be alright, we know you will. Because you're a strong woman and I know you can do it. Mandy's sending over some seaweed soup, and Hilary's got you some shiitake mushrooms.

Agnes   She's having the op next week. No, she's not dealing with it very well. She won't speak to anyone in the department and we sent a huge bouquet. Humanities have offered to clean her house and everything, but she won't have it. Mind you, she's always lived in squalor. And of course there's (*Whispered*) the alcohol problem.

Hippy lady I've got you some relaxation tapes, and Gregorian chants. Put garlic under your pillow. Rub your breasts with onions. Get up at dawn. Climb mountains. Give up cheese and eggs and red wine. Are you listening, Zimmy? Your anger can also be the source of your strength. Have you tried circle dancing?

Agnes   I went round to see her. She got your card. Didn't look at it. She sits there, rummaging through old family photographs. Apparently her mother had it. I offered to cook her a meal but she looked at me as if I was dog poo on a white carpet. And don't worry about the Dean's dinner, I said. We'll all miss you, of course, but we'll quite understand. Clarissa is taking over your teaching, I said. That got a reaction. A bad one. No, she's not a good patient. I just keep phoning.

Danny lollops in.

Danny Who, mam? She's asleep. Yeah. Hospital? I don't know. Next week, I think. Oh, she's alright. Same as usual. There's lots of cards. From the school mainly. Dunno. I'm just going to stay with my friend. Yeah, I'll tell her, Auntie May. What? What have I got to tell her? I've forgotten. Oh yeah, I'll tell her she's a very brave person and that you love her. What? Me? Yeah alright. I'll clean up. It's alright, you don't need to come round, yeah I'll be considerate. Oh, bye.

(*She yells*) It's just Auntie May. Nothin'.

She looks down her knickers, bursts into tears.

Mum. I've started. Mum!

SCENE TEN

Laura's diary

The fortnight before my operation I spend at home. I'm making a quilt. I'm sewing bits of my life into it. Scraps of the children's clothes, letters from my mother, and now I thought I might sew bits of my diary in, or shreds of useless brassieres. I won't tell Graham that. He thinks it's best not to dwell. I agree in a way, it's just that I can't stop dwelling.

I'm going to take the quilt in with me, when I go to hospital. Graham is very attentive. The breast care nurse calls round. Inwardly, I think she needs to condition her hair, although she's a very sweet person. Of course I know it all. It's like watching an old film that you half remembered again. People tiptoe in. The house is full of flowers and cards. But I keep thinking about the women I met.

She gets out the scrap of paper with their names on.

I mean, they weren't my kind of person. None of them were. But I just keep wondering what happened to them. Are they like me? Are they sitting at home staring out of the window. Is anyone looking after them?

She sews the scrap into the quilt.

SCENE ELEVEN

Miranda has a body scan

Miranda is in an imaginary scan, a huge machine which is looking at all her body parts. A disembodied voice calls instructions from somewhere else in the room.

Voice   Hello, Mrs Hurt. Come in please.

Miranda How long is this going to take exactly?

Voice   Turn on your left side. Arms above your head.

Miranda follows the instructions.

Liver   Hello, Miranda.

Miranda Who's that?

Liver   It's me, your liver, can you see me?

She looks up.

Miranda My liver? You look blurred, but yes, I can see the shape. How are you?

Liver   Blurred. Thanks for the lifestyle. I mean, I'm barely functioning here. If your mother hadn't been a teetotaller then I might not have lasted this long.

Miranda Leave my mother out of this. I don't drink much.

Liver   Couple of bottles of wine a night. You and that Agatha!

Miranda You look alright, anyway. Better than I expected.

Liver I'm holding up, yes. Just.

Voice Turn over. Arms by your side please.

Miranda What's that?

Lungs Your old friend. Lungs.

Miranda You look rather primitive. A tree in a sandstorm.

Lungs I am. Dry and decaying. Don't worry. I'm functioning. There's no shadows here. I'm knee deep in tar, but the top twigs are OK. Just tell me something – did you really imagine that you were immortal?

Miranda Of course not. You know I think about death all the time. As Freud said, the aim of life...

Liver Is death. Not if you're an organ.

Miranda Please don't get moralistic with me. I'm not in the mood. I've got breast cancer.

Liver We just wondered why you drink so much. I mean, we know you're a depressive.

Lungs And have you ever thought about giving up the Woodbines?

Miranda I don't drink all the time. I've been under pressure. I like the taste. Damn it. I like being drunk.

Lungs It's something we often discuss. Why, we ask ourselves, is Miranda such a mess?

Miranda Watch it!

Liver Perhaps it's to do with breast feeding?

Miranda Oh don't be ridiculous. I haven't got any children.

Lungs   Your mother breast-fed you.

Miranda You know, my mother died of breast cancer.

Lungs   So you keep sucking the nipple over and over again, just like a dry old cigarette.

Miranda I don't. I resent you bringing my mother into this dialogue.

Lungs   We're just passing the time.

Miranda You're supposed to be on my side.

Liver   You were weaned too early, that's my theory. Either that or it's straight alcoholism. Have you considered AA? Did you know drink is a risk factor?

Miranda Are you blaming me? For getting cancer? You are! Everyone is. You think I'm a dry, cancerous person who drinks and smokes too much, and who is repressed, with no children. That's what you think. Well. why me? Why not all the other drunken depressed academics? It's not as if there's a shortage.

Voice   That will be all, Mrs Hurt.

Miranda My mother was a swimmer, a really good swimmer. She never drank. She laughed a lot. She died when I was twelve, not two. I had plenty of breast milk, and a good diet.

Voice   It's alright, you can go now.

Miranda She was good fun. She was in her bloody prime!

Liver   You could try therapy?

Miranda I would rather die.

Liver   Literally?

Lungs   At least try breathing exercises.

Miranda Just leave it. I can't change now. It's too late.

SCENE TWELVE

In the ward following the mastectomy

The hospital ward. Two beds are divided by a screen. Carol wakes up suddenly. Both women are attached to drains coming out from under their armpits. Next to her Laura is still sewing her quilt. A nurse whisks in and removes the screen. Carol announces the first line to the 'ward' in general.

Carol   The way I see it, nothing is as bad as having all your teeth pulled out, is it?

Laura   I beg your pardon?

Carol   Hey! It's me, Carol. You're the lady from the bank. Remember me? What's your name again?

Laura   Laura Goodchild. Of course I remember you. In fact, I phoned you. I think I spoke to your daughter.

Carol   Danny, she never tells me anything. You as well. That's bad luck. I don't feel too bad, do you?

Laura   It's certainly not as bad as you think. You recover quite quickly. From the operation at least.

Carol   I forgot. You've been through it before. I'm hoping I'll be out in a few days.

Laura   Well, nobody needs to know if you don't tell them.

Carol   I've told everyone. Have you had a look yet?

Laura   Oh no. I'll wait until I get home.

Carol   Are you married?

Laura   Yes, I am. To Graham.

Carol   That's right! Graham! Did he catch the rat?

Laura   Yes, it was dead when I got home. Lying in the back yard. Chemicals.

Carol   Is he coping?

Laura   Graham? He's a saint. Does everything for me.

Carol   Wish I had someone to do everything for me.

Pause.

Laura   I phoned up everyone. You, Zimmy and Miranda. No one phoned me back. I spoke to Miranda, briefly, but when I phoned again she never answered. And I got Zimmy's answerphone. Left a message. I just wanted to talk to someone and Graham isn't like that. He likes to do things, not listen.

She's holding back tears.

Carol   That's right, get it off your chest!

Realises the awful pun and hits herself on the head.

What is it you wanted to talk about?

Laura   Last time it happened.

Carol   What?

Laura   The cancer.

Carol   Don't say that word! Just whisper it. It's stupid I know, but...

Laura   Sorry. After I'd had the, you know, I went home and it wasn't the same. I mean, I got over it, but, in the bedroom...

Carol   Did he not fancy you, like? Bloody cheek.

Laura   It was just awkward. He was rather shy about it. Didn't know where to touch me. Treated me as if I was fragile. I was.

Carol   Did it get better?

Laura   No, worse. Things were just picking up recently.

Carol   That's a sin. Perhaps you should have an affair.

Laura   I couldn't. Look at me!

Carol   Are you worried that he might not be able to tell your front from your back? Ha ha. Keep your bra on.

Laura looks aghast.

You're only young! I'm not past it myself! You could pick somebody up at Coping With (*Whispers*) Cancer. I've heard you get all sorts there!

Laura   I don't think so. I'm not interested in those kinds of groups.

Carol   Oh well. You asked for my advice! Do you mind me asking you something. What did you think, when you saw the scar?

Laura   Me?

Carol   Never mind Graham.

Laura   I didn't think anything. The prosthesis is very good. No one can tell.

Carol   But underneath the prosthesis. It's not as bad as it used to be though, is it, the scars?

Laura   I don't know. I've never seen anyone else's.

Carol   I mean, what's yours like?

Laura   I don't look very often. It's just flat.

Carol   I'll just have to go and see for myself, I suppose. Strange. Like getting a new body. Did you find out what happened to the other two? That one who was into saints.

Laura   Miranda, she was positive.

Carol   No! Her as well! What a shame! And the other one?

Laura   I don't know. I just heard her voice on the answerphone. I don't think she liked me, being from the bank and everything.

We hear Zimmy's voice from off stage. Laura and Carol immediately recognise it.

SCENE THIRTEEN

Zimmy in hospital

Zimmy sits up furiously, dressed in a white nightie. Miranda enters as a female doctor, holding a large felt-tip pen.

Zimmy   Get your hands off me! What are you doing, marking me up with a felt-tip like that? I'm not a leg of lamb.

Doctor   In our opinion...

Zimmy   Our? Or *your*?

Doctor   You're going to have to have a mastectomy. You don't want us to remove the wrong breast, do you?

Zimmy   Hang on. I thought I was having a lumpectomy.

Doctor   After discussions with my colleagues, we think it would be better if you had the whole breast off. Your tests show...

Zimmy   You've been discussing me with men?

Doctor   We have to discuss each case carefully and...

Zimmy   Don't give me that crap. How would you feel if you got breast cancer?

Doctor   How do you know I haven't?

Zimmy   Well, have you?

Doctor   No, but I understand your feelings. Other women often feel the same.

Zimmy   I was just about to go away when this happened.

Doctor   Anywhere nice?

She approaches with the felt-tip again.

Zimmy   Jamaica. Oh, what do you care?

Doctor   I care very much. It's my job.

Zimmy   I know what your job is. You want to give me the slash, poison and burn treatment. That's all you've got. There is nothing else. Listen, everyone, it's the same brutal treatment they were doling out fifty years ago!

Doctor   Please don't upset the other patients. You'll be getting the best treatment available in the whole world at this hospital.

Zimmy   Lucky me. I'd rather be anywhere else than here.

Doctor   Of course you would.

Zimmy   I know what you think of me. I know the kind of things you say when we're lying on the operating table.

Doctor   I don't know what you mean. Listen. We're working together on this.

Zimmy   I'm not working with you.

Doctor   Maybe you'd rather see another doctor?

Zimmy   As far as I can see you're all the same. A box of chocolates, soft ones, hard ones, fruity ones, nutty ones, all types, all wrappings, but you're all made in the same factory.

Doctor   Zimmy...

Zimmy   Ms Jarret to you.

Doctor   Breast cancer is a serious condition. It doesn't react to softer treatments, which is why we must attack it with the very best weapons we have.

Zimmy   Like men fighting a war.

Doctor   It's a powerful enemy.

Zimmy   And you'll be playing *Land of Hope and Glory* in a minute.

Doctor   Just give me a chance, will you!

Zimmy   I'm not stupid. I am fighting back, but not in the same way as you. It's my body. I can believe what I like, can't I?

Doctor   What is it that you want?

Zimmy   I want to be sure that a mastectomy is the right thing. Maybe it's not. I want to know more about the cancer I have, why I've got it. Is it aggressive? How long has it been there?

Doctor   I'll let you have any information you want. Just ask.

Zimmy   And I'll discuss it with my other doctor.

Doctor   Which doctor?

Zimmy   I've got a Chinese doctor.

Doctor   (*Pause*) That's fair enough. I have many patients who swallow all kinds of odd concoctions. I mean, my own husband goes to a homeopath, for God's sake. Believe me, it is your choice, but you can't fight cancer with herbal tea and a couple of acupuncture needles. I'm sorry, Zimmy.

Zimmy   Ms Jarret.

Doctor   Anyway, you can do both. Complementary treatments won't do you any harm.

Zimmy   Alternative. You can't bear to be turned down, can you?

Doctor   I don't think you're thinking very clearly.

Zimmy   I know what you think. It's what I think that counts.

Doctor   You're still a young woman.

Zimmy   Does that make me different? More worth saving?

Doctor   Of course not.

Zimmy   Give me an hour.

Doctor   Hospital beds are precious. Don't think too long, Ms Jarret.

The doctor moves away.

Zimmy   (*To audience*) In trying to be in control, I end up out of control. It feels as if everything pulls me in circles. Powered by fury. I think, is this fury in me the cause of the cancer in the first place?

But I don't feel powerful. I feel tired and weak. At the last possible moment I will agree to the mastectomy, and I agree because when it comes down to it I can't take the chance that they might be right.

She lies down to sleep.

SCENE FOURTEEN

Carol, Laura and Zimmy

Carol and Laura tiptoe over to Zimmy's bed. They are holding drainage bottles above their heads, with tubes to their armpits, and wearing long nighties.

Carol   Zimmer! It's us.

Zimmy   Who?

Carol   Don't you remember me? You'll-have-to-see-the-manager-Laura. Graham and the rat? Carol the good-looking one!

Zimmy   Oh my God.

Carol   From the breast clinic!

Zimmy   Oh, yes! There's a rat within ten yards, no matter where you stand. One lump or two. I remember. How's it going?

Laura   We've both got (*Whispers*) cancer, but we're alright.

Carol   We had the busts off yesterday.

Zimmy   I got your message. I should have phoned. I've been in a bit of a state.

Laura   It doesn't matter.

Zimmy   But it does matter.

Carol   So what's the verdict?

Zimmy   Verdict?

Carol   What are you having?

Zimmy   A mastectomy.

Laura   We thought you weren't having one. We heard you, er, shouting.

Carol   Have you ever thought of a career in shouting?

Zimmy   They make me so mad. But I feel... well, I can live without a breast. How are you feeling?

Carol   Not bad. The doctor says I've got to have chemo and that.

Zimmy   Did you ask why?

Carol   No. I'm not like you.

Laura   No one's like you!

Zimmy   There's no need to rub it in. (*She smiles*)

Carol   Laura's had hers off too, haven't you?

Laura   Yes. I'm symmetrical again.

Zimmy   Are you going to have chemotherapy too?

Laura   They haven't said. I suppose I will if they advise it.

Zimmy   You'd let them do anything, wouldn't you? I tell you something. I'm not having it. They can go to hell.

Laura   Are you sure?

Zimmy   Absolutely.

Laura   I think you're very brave.

Zimmy   Brave. Do you mean stupid?

Laura   No!

Zimmy   You're the one they call brave. You don't complain, you put up with it. I make a fuss. That's not brave, it's the opposite.

Carol   Stroppy?

Zimmy   Look, only you know your own body. Nobody else knows what it needs better than you do.

Carol   It needs a bloody holiday.

Laura   They do have qualifications. It takes an awfully long time to train to be a doctor.

Zimmy looks really grumpy.

Zimmy   So what about the other woman? From the clinic. The weird one?

Laura   Her too!

Zimmy   That's bizarre.

Sound of a tea trolley rattling.

Carol   Here comes the cavalry! We'll see you later.

Zimmy   Wait. Was it alright? The operation.

Carol   It's over so quickly. Morphine at the press of a button. Fantastic.

Laura   Don't worry. We're here! Perhaps the four of us could meet up some time?

SCENE FIFTEEN

Carol goes to have a look

Carol wakes up on another part of the stage.

Carol   (*Opens her eyes*) I woke up in the night. Couldn't get back to sleep. All around me there were women whimpering and snuffling. I thought, why not have a bath? I mean, I hadn't had a proper wash or anything. I felt alright. Quite perky actually. And I couldn't stop thinking about the wedding. The shape of the sausage rolls and that kind of thing, and money. I was thinking about Danny too. She's only twelve, but she looks older, and I was wishing I could help her grow up a bit more gently than all the other women in our family.

Carol gets up. Zimmy opens her eyes again.

Zimmy   Carol?

Carol   Yes.

Zimmy   Where are you going?

Carol   I can't sleep. I'm going to get a bath.

Zimmy   Isn't it a bit soon?

Carol   That's never worried us in the past.

Zimmy   Wait, I'm coming with you.

Carol   Are you planning to get in the bath with us, like?

Zimmy   No, I'll just sit. I can't sleep either.

Together they get to the 'bathroom'. There is a large mirror. Carol pulls a screen around herself as she undresses. She pretends to turn on a tap.

Carol   Water's boiling. Nice not to have to pay for it.

Zimmy   You'd better put some more cold in. The stitches might melt and come undone.

Carol   I'm sitting up. I'm going to look.

Zimmy   Are you sure?

Carol   It can't be so bad. Anyway, I might have reconstruction.

Zimmy   What for? More operations? You must be crazy!

Carol   (*Popping her head round the screen*) It's free, isn't it? I'll have a Dolly Parton. Or a Pamela Anderson. Why not? Wouldn't you fancy a new pair?

Zimmy   No. Of course I wouldn't.

Carol   I bet you would really. I think you're all hot air!

Zimmy   Imagine, when you die, your breasts wouldn't decay. They'd lie there in the coffin like two pink jellies...

Carol   Not if you were cremated. Will you help me with these buttons? You really know your mind, don't you, Ms Jarret?

She gets into the water.

Zimmy   Zimmy. I just don't like being told what to do.

Carol   What do you do?

Zimmy   I teach tai chi. And I do yoga, and aromatherapy.

Carol   That's lovely, that tai chi. I've seen them in the park in the summer.

Zimmy   It's only part-time work. I'm skint. I keep on making plans, but they never come off, and now this...

Carol   At least you've got plans. I'm just living day to day.

She sloshes about a bit.

Being a woman, it's like eating an elephant, isn't it?

Zimmy   I don't get you.

Carol   One bite at a time. That's the only way we get through the days.

Zimmy   Sometimes I feel I can't even find the elephant, let alone eat it. I don't think my kind of elephant lives in this part of England.

Carol gives out a bloodcurdling scream.

Carol   Oh my God! I've been massacred!

Zimmy   What? What have they done!

Carol   It looks like they've been at my breast with a bloody spade!

Zimmy   Is it bad?

Carol   It's just... like I've been in a battle!

Zimmy   Shall I call someone?

Carol   No.

Zimmy   Are you sure?

Carol   It's just not me. It's somebody else. A different shape, you know.

Zimmy   Do you want me to look?

Carol   Will you? Wait, do you think it's a good idea? You haven't had yours yet.

Zimmy   I'm not afraid.

Carol   Are you sure about that?

Zimmy   Do you want me to look or what?

Zimmy steps behind the screen.

Zimmy   God...

Carol   What do you think?

Zimmy   (*Slowly*) It's fine. No problem. It's going to be a neat scar. It just hasn't healed up yet.

Carol   D'you think they've done a good job?

Zimmy   Yes, I do. It's really not as bad as...

Carol   Zimmy? Are you still there?

Zimmy faints. Two nurses come in and drag her off, while Carol watches from over the screen.

SCENE SIXTEEN

Laura's diary

Now I'm out of hospital. I just had the results of tests this morning. I've got to have a course of chemotherapy, because the cancer has spread into four of my lymph nodes. Apparently it's a window of opportunity. Zap the cells while they are feeling weak. It took a while for this to sink in. It's not quite the same film that I remembered. In the hospital, Zimmy and Carol and me got quite close. Zimmy had her operation. In the end she was quiet about it. Not how we expected at all. I even saw her crying once. It made me cry.

We agreed to get together in a few weeks' time. I've been crossing off the days. Everyone else I meet is so respectful and polite. It tires me out. Zimmy said she'd phone Miranda. I don't expect she'll come. No sign of any rats, but there are a lot of ants on the patio. Graham says he'll put insecticide down the cracks but I'd rather he didn't. I feel a bit like an ant myself.

SCENE SEVENTEEN

Miranda accepts an invitation

Miranda speaks from her spotlit place. She's typing. Agatha lounges about, looking on approvingly.

Miranda The atrocious subject of Agatha's martyrdom is rarely shown in English churches, as it is often deemed upsetting to women. Agatha is usually bound to a pillar, undraped to the waist, and on each side there is a slave or executioner with a pair of shears.

The phone rings. She looks at it dubiously, then hesitantly picks it up.

Miranda Who are you? Who? Zimmy Jarret, from the waiting room. I know who you are. What, me, go out? I don't think so. I'm ill. All four of us! That's extraordinary. Sorry, it's not my type of thing.

We hear Zimmy shouting through the receiver.

There's no need to shout. I'm quite alright. I'm just a very quiet person. Look, I hardly know you. Why on earth would I want to talk to strangers?

She has a drink of whisky from a bottle.

Alright. Why don't you tell me where you're meeting? I'm not going there. It's where my students go. If I go anywhere it will have to be The Angel.

(Whispers so Agatha can't hear)

I've written it down. I'll see. I might come, and I might not.

Bring up music.

SCENE EIGHTEEN

Meeting in The Angel

Music.

Laura walks in, unsuitably dressed in bank-type clothes, carrying a small non-alcoholic drink. She sits down nervously. Zimmy strides in, waving at some people in the bar. Sits down with a pint of Guinness.

Zimmy   You found it alright then?

Laura   Graham drove me. We had to look in the A to Z.

Zimmy   Not really your part of town, is it? Aren't you drinking?

Laura   No. I'm on a diet.

Zimmy   Fat-free?

Laura   Weightwatchers.

Zimmy   *(Sarky)* I bet you'll be slimmer of the month.

Laura   Hopefully! They say you can put on weight on the hormone drug, that Tamoxifen, and I wanted to nip it in the bud.

Zimmy   Well, I'm not taking that either. And I'm not wearing a falsie either, thank you very much.

Laura   Well, it's up to you. I think clothes look odd when you've only got the one. And people stare.

Zimmy   They don't. No one ever seems to notice. Unfortunately. I mean, who am I wearing it for?

Laura   It saves embarrassment. For everybody.

Enter Carol.

Carol   Hiya! It's me! Is everyone OK for a drink?

They both shake their heads.

Carol   Pint of lager! Chemo begins next week. Might as well make the most of it. How are you doing?

Laura   We were just discussing our prostheses.

Carol   Aaah, guess what happened? The dog chewed mine up. It all spewed out. The silicone. I'm going to have to have that reconstruction. Do you think they'll give me another one?

Laura   I suppose if you explained, they might. They're very expensive.

Carol   Wasn't my fault. It was on the settee. Must have thought it was a bit of chicken, or something.

Zimmy   I haven't got one.

Carol   Why not? Didn't you get a chitty? For the surgical appliance shop?

Zimmy   Why hide the fact we've had breast cancer? I mean, I can understand choosing to have no breasts, but they won't remove healthy breasts, will they? Oh no! You have to be a proper two-breasted woman who keeps her mouth shut.

The other two cover their ears.

Carol   Is it that they don't do ones in your colour?

Zimmy   Are you serious?

Carol   I'm only asking.

Zimmy   Nothing would surprise me, but apparently you can get appropriate skin colours. Now.

Carol   Keep your hair on! Sorry, I forgot you're not having the chemo, are you? So Saint Miranda hasn't shown up?

Zimmy   She was really snotty on the phone.

Laura is looking around, suddenly aware of her environment.

Laura   What kind of a bar is this?

Enter Miranda. She looks a mess. She's carrying a large gin.

Miranda It's a women-only bar.

All   Miranda!

Carol   Saints alive!

Miranda My local.

Zimmy   I thought you lived by the park.

Miranda I do, I mean in the spiritual sense.

Laura   I don't get it.

Miranda I was coming here anyway. That's my corner over there.

Laura   You mean you come here on your own?

Carol   What's wrong with that?

Laura   It's not my usual kind of place, hard to put your finger on it.

Miranda Not really.

Zimmy   No men!

Carol   That's a shame. Laura here fancies a bit of a shag.

Laura   Carol! It's nice to see you again, Miranda.

Miranda Thank you. How are you all?

Carol   Do you want the short and happy or the long and sad answer?

Miranda Start with the short.

Carol   We've all had the bust off, even Zimmer here.

Zimmy   ZIMMY!

Carol   Laura is completely flat, but currently browsing through brochures of busts available on the NHS. Me too, incidentally. But we have to wait a year, don't we? And we're fine! The best of mates! Dare I say it, bosom pals!

Laura   What about you, Miranda?

Miranda   I just had a lumpectomy, that's all. I suppose I got off quite lightly.

Zimmy   So what are you doing for yourselves?

They look at her with puzzled expressions.

I mean, I'm on a fat-free diet, and I do tai chi every day.

Carol   Like slow-motion aerobics, isn't it?

Laura   Well I do keep fit.

Zimmy   I take Iscador.

Carol   What door? I sleep a lot.

Zimmy   And I meditate.

Laura   I do relaxation sometimes. I've had my legs waxed.

They all look at Laura, then sip their drinks.

Miranda   Well, well. What bad luck we've had. The rat must have been an omen.

Zimmy   So what have you been doing, Miranda?

Miranda   Working. I've been concentrating on Saint Agatha.

Carol   Who?

Miranda   The patron saint of breasts. I'm writing a book about her.

Zimmy   Never heard of her.

Miranda Well, she's modest, beautiful, capable of miracles. The subject of some incredibly delicate paintings, even though the subject matter is somewhat harsh.

Laura   Why's that?

Miranda She had her breasts torn off with tongs because she wouldn't sleep with this man.

All look uncomfortable.

Carol   And you think about her all day?

Miranda Yes. It takes my mind off other things.

Laura   I prefer Van Gogh myself.

Carol   We didn't think you'd come out tonight.

Miranda The diagnosis has brought up a lot of things for me. I had a relationship that's broken up. I'm thinking of going back to Catholicism, actually.

They all stare at her, nonplussed.

Zimmy   You must be in a really bad way.

Carol   Hits you smack in the face, doesn't it?

Zimmy   I thought you were a feminist.

Miranda Look, I don't want to talk about it. It's just something I've been considering.

Zimmy   I went to a Catholic boarding school. I've been trying to forget it ever since.

Laura   How old were you?

Zimmy   Nine.

Carol   Your mother sent you to boarding school? No wonder you're the way you are.

Laura   Are you looking forward to seeing your mother, Zimmy?

Zimmy   Yes. I think so. I mean, I haven't seen her since my parents divorced, so it's quite exciting really.

Zimmy turns away. Miranda starts to smoke, offering them round. Carol eagerly accepts. The other two waft the smoke away.

Laura   Why us?

Zimmy   That's what I keep thinking.

Miranda Why not us?

Carol   I suppose there would never be a good time. Drinks, everyone? Go on, Laura! Who cares about your figure? You might be dead this time next year! You said yourself that Graham's not up to...

Laura   Alright! Alright! I'll have a vodka.

Later. All four are drunk and in tears.

Miranda You know, they never really told me what was the matter with her. I was only twelve. I'd just started my period. They just took her away. I was supposed to pray.

Zimmy   The bastards! How could they have done that? Your own mother!

Carol   My Danny's only twelve. She can't do anything for herself.

Laura   You need to make provision. That's what Graham says. Get your affairs straight. Stupid git!

Zimmy   But he's got a point. No one ever made any provision for me. I haven't seen my own mother for over twenty years. Christmas cards, that's all I get!

Carol   Some people shouldn't be allowed to have children.

Miranda My mum made provision. She just got it wrong, that's all. How was she to know that my father's second wife would be a religious fanatic? You can make all the provision you like but...

Zimmy   Stop it. Stop talking about death! Stop smoking. I think I might be sick.

Miranda Why? That's what it's all about, isn't it. Being sick.

Zimmy   Don't be so maudlin, all of you!

Carol   Why not? Don't be such a stroppy cow.

Zimmy   I'm not stroppy. I'm just frustrated. Everything in here is blocked. I can't move on.

Carol   Is it your bowels?

Zimmy   Don't give me that crap. It's not my bowels. It's me!

Laura   All those lesbians are looking at us. I think we should keep quiet.

Miranda Really? (*She waves flirtatiously across the bar*)

Zimmy   Why aren't people marching down the streets?

Carol   There's just too much to do. Too much washing. Too many floors with dirty marks on. Too many sausage rolls to make. That's why. We can't. We have to hoover.

Laura   We could form a united front.

Miranda What?

Carol   That's a good line, Laura! The united front! Or maybe the knitted front?

Zimmy   Call it BUST UP.

All hoot with laughter.

Miranda Burn our bras AGAIN!

No one laughs, they all look puzzled.

Carol What shall we unite about?

Laura Coffee mornings?

Zimmy Coffee mornings? Oooh. Milk or cream? Pass the sugar!

Laura Mmmm. We could fund-raise, sell biscuits. Have a fashion show?

Carol Of single-breasted jackets!

Zimmy Why don't we form a radical wing! Let's chain ourselves to the bra department in Marks and Spencers.

Laura What for?

Zimmy One-cup bras. I don't know.

Miranda I'm too old for that caper. I'd rather get drunk.

Zimmy We could get drunk at the same time.

Laura I could raffle a patchwork quilt.

Carol I'm not doing any raffles. Can't we, er, just enjoy ourselves?

Miranda What?

Carol Like now. Enjoy ourselves. Have a laugh.

Zimmy A laugh?

Laura Not even have a secretary, or a treasurer or anything?

Miranda Drink to it! We have nothing to lose but our...

All BUSTS!

Carol lurches up onto the table and breaks into a rowdy song. Everyone claps and joins in, the song ends with Carol falling and being caught by the others.

Interval

ACT TWO

SCENE ONE

Laura's diary

Of course it was a ridiculous name. I had a terrible headache afterwards. I wondered if I might be going through some kind of crisis. I was sick on the lawn when I came home. It's left a stain that will always be there. I really felt that I was somehow letting myself go. I went back to work today. Everyone said how well I looked, which was obviously a lie because I had breath like a skunk and my neck was blotchy.

I sat and worked on the counters. Stamping and counting, being courteous.

I started thinking about all the money going back and forth across the counter. Piling up, then draining away. Tides of money.

The manager kept on looking at me. I think he was worried that I might not be capable of dealing with the public. He's right in a way. I couldn't stop staring at ladies' fronts, wondering if they were real or not. At the end of the day he asked me if I would like to work on the cashpoints, loading and unloading. It's quieter, he said. Just you and the machines.

SCENE TWO

Carol on chemo

Carol sits there passively. We hear the recorded voices.

Carol   Drip drip drip. At first it's alright. What's all the fuss about? I wonder why the woman opposite me is green?

Voice   Nurse, I need the toilet.

Carol   It's not like the place where we had the operation. That was full of...

Voice   It's gone again, nurse.

Carol   Fresh-cut flowers and everything was bright clean. And we were all getting better all the time, sitting up and looking around; here people are sinking down.

Voice   I need somebody to talk to me! Please somebody come!

Carol   Over there, a woman milky white. Her face heavy and sad. Her family come and wheel her along to the visitors' room and she lies and smokes menthol cigarettes in long slow draws. They stand around her silently.

Voice   I'm going to be sick.

Carol   And the nurses run from bed to bed. Kind, laughing nurses, but you can see how tired they are.

Voice   Bleep, bleep.

Nurse   Cup of tea, anyone? Magazine? Anyone want to see the vicar?

Carol   I don't like Danny coming here.

Nurse   Isn't your daughter coming today, Carol?

Carol   No, pet, she's with her Auntie May. Nurse, how much longer?

Nurse   Another four hours. Shut your eyes. Try and sleep.

Carol   But I can't. My hair begins to fall out. I start to feel nauseous.

Enter Zimmy.

Zimmy   Carol. Visualise the poison rushing through you. See it as men on horses, women with Hoovers, mopping up the cancer cells.

Carol   Zimmer! You came here of your own accord! My God! What was that about women with Hoovers?

Zimmy   You've got to see the cancer cells as weak and vulnerable.

Carol   I'm weak and vulnerable.

Zimmy   Or a wave rushing through you, sweeping away the debris, leaving you clean and fresh.

Carol   I feel sick.

Zimmy rubs some oil on Carol's forehead.

Zimmy   Carol, can you hear me.

Carol   Yes. I can't go on with this.

Zimmy   Try Carol. Imagine a house. The house of health. See what it looks like.

Carol   I can't. All I can see is my front door in the rain.

Zimmy   Keep looking.

Carol   Wait, I see it. It's golden. It's a detached house with new carpets. A house with clean windows. Fitted kitchen. Parquet flooring. I've got it. There's the cleaning lady! Hi, Miranda... ha ha.

Zimmy   And where are you in it?

Carol   Sitting in a red leather recliner by the window.

Zimmy   And what can you see?

Carol   I can see you, Zimmy. You're in the garden. Doing cartwheels.

She opens her eyes abruptly.

And there you are.

Zimmy   I've brought you a little elephant. It's only tiny.

Carol   I could eat that in one bite.

Zimmy   I wouldn't. It's not edible. Just put it under your pillow.

Carol   I will.

She closes her eyes again. Zimmy drifts away.

Carol   It helps, you know. I put the elephant under my pillow and I sit in the chair by the window, and that's how I get through the worst months. Months of feeling nauseous, of half sleeps. By the end of it, I knew every part of my house of health as well as I knew my own body.

SCENE THREE

Miranda goes to confession

Miranda is in the confession box. On the other side of the screen is Saint Agatha, grinning maliciously, and nodding wisely.

Miranda Holy father, I have sinned.

Agatha   Tell me your sins, child.

Miranda There are so many I don't know where to begin.

Agatha   Start at the beginning.

Miranda I was awful to my mother when she was dying of breast cancer. I blamed her. I stole money from her. I spent it on drugs.

Agatha   Yes, that was very wicked.

Miranda Then, after she died, when I got sent to live with my father...

Agatha   Who was a convert, I believe.

Miranda Yes, and his wife, Pope Joan.

Agatha   That's not funny.

Miranda Sorry. I planned to kill her. I once nearly pushed her over a cliff, and another time I put crushed-up paracetamol in her coffee. When she died from a bee sting, I couldn't have cared less.

Agatha Carry on.

Miranda After I left home I drank heavily and was cruel to good Catholic girls. I bullied them, and I lost my faith. I slept with everyone I could lay my hands on.

Agatha Men?

Miranda No. Good Catholic girls.

Agatha You corrupted them?

Miranda If possible, yes. Then when I became a professor I slept with students in my tutorial room, and did improper things with objects.

Agatha Holy objects?

Miranda Sometimes. And I drank very heavily.

Agatha And now?

Miranda I am being punished. I have breast cancer and I think I'm having a nervous breakdown.

Agatha You must pray to Saint Agatha. Your sins are very grave. Are you prepared to renounce your former life and live again in grace?

Miranda I think so. I feel very close to Saint Agatha.

Agatha closes her eyes happily and nods.

Agatha Pray with me, and to the Virgin Mary.

Miranda One more thing...

Agatha What, my child?

Miranda I've met some other women with breast cancer.

Agatha Are they good Catholic girls?

Miranda No. It's not that sort of thing at all.

Agatha Be careful. Now you have made this first step, don't fall into the arms of heathens.

Miranda I'll try not to.

Agatha I'll be waiting for you, and praying.

Miranda I know. I can feel that you're with me all the time. Incense, candles, and all the heavy aromas of church. Terrifyingly secure.

Agatha Safe.

Miranda The door is still open, just a crack. I'll come back. I just need some fresh air.

She runs out.

SCENE FOUR

Laura's diary

She's quilting again.

The four of us started going swimming every day. Graham bought me a new bathing costume especially. It cost sixty pounds. I was a bit embarrassed about getting changed, and I never went into the communal showers, although everyone else did. I saw everyone else's scars. Each was different. Miranda's was just a little pucker. Zimmy's was a small neat line, and Carol's was rougher. Her skin looked sore. She was losing all her hair by now. I'd just started the chemotherapy. I envied the other two, not having it. I got myself a wig, but I'd already bought a special hat which stopped your hair falling out. The swimming was good. I did it right through my chemo. You'd feel really fresh afterwards, and my arms got stronger.

On the whole we didn't speak much.

SCENE FIVE

Swimming

The four women take off their clothes and put on rubber bathing hats. Waving at each other, they climb into an imaginary pool and start swimming lengths, each doing breast stroke.

Miranda Twenty lengths a day, that's one hundred and forty lengths a week. You know what I think about when I'm swimming? My mother. I let myself see her pushing through the water. I have memories of her holding me up in her arms, teaching me to swim. I try and imagine that I'm swimming back to her.

Laura   I think about quilts. The shapes of patches, squares and diamonds. And what's left. Time. How far? How long?

Miranda I think of the university as a stagnant pool with me an old crocodile, cogitating in it!

Zimmy   When I'm swimming that's the only time I let myself think about the future. I consider the letter I will write to my mother in Jamaica. And I even try and see myself on a plane. I have to breathe long and deep. Breast cancer has jeopardised my future tense. I always believed I had all the time in the world.

Carol   Up and down for hours. And it's for me. I'm not working. I'm not sleeping. I'm doing something I enjoy. I just shut off all the other stuff.

Laura   Sometimes I feel I could swim forever. I'm sure we came from fishes, not monkeys.

Carol   I might try water aerobics after this. Bring Danny. Hey, watch it! Bloody crawler. Nineteen.

Laura   Twenty!

They get out of the pool.

Zimmy   I imagine that I'm swimming an ocean, from the country of illness to the country of health.

Miranda Are you sure that they're different places?

They step out of the water. Rub down with towels. Laura puts on a short mousey wig and Carol puts on a long blonde one. Miranda puts on dark glasses. They pose for a photograph.

SCENE SIX

Carol has radiotherapy

Carol sits in another waiting room.

Carol   No swimming while you're having radiotherapy. The waiting room is like an airport, wide and impersonal, with plenty of delays, but today I'm finally taking off. It's my last day! I know all the other passengers, him with a big nose and a five-year-old with a brain tumour who runs about laughing. That woman in a turban reading *The Times*, the tea ladies, the receptionists. (*Pause*) And I've read every bloody magazine in the place. Stupid, because most of them are about things I'll never do. Upholster a chaise longue, invent a patio, entertain a party of twenty...

She listens, hears her name being called, steps into a different space.

What's it doing to me? I don't feel anything. Just tired. I shut my eyes and try and sit in the house of health, but that could do with some bloody interior decor, and the windows are filthy.

She's in the machine now. We can hear it buzzing.

The machines are so big and I'm so small. Tiny. Powerless. I'm a little squeak in a forest of vast machines. When I see the doctor – and it's always a different doctor – I can hardly be heard at all. Just a little squeak. The machines know everything. I know nothing. It's all in the file. And the file is too high to reach. Smaller and smaller. Quieter and quieter.

SCENE SEVEN

Zimmy and Laura in the park

Zimmy is doing tai chi in the park. It looks beautiful and elegant. Laura enters, in her short smart wig and raincoat. She sees Zimmy and looks as if she might avoid her, but is drawn to her. She sits and watches. Zimmy finishes the movement and stops.

Zimmy   It's you!

Laura   Sorry, shall I go?

Zimmy   No, it's OK.

Laura   I've finished the treatment. Carol finished today, and I finished last week.

Zimmy   So how is it?

Laura   I feel in a bit of a fog. Can't think straight. Graham has to follow me round the house, turning off fires and lights. But I'm alright. The anti-sickness drugs are really good. I mean, it's not what you, what people, think these days.

Zimmy   You look alright.

Laura   Everyone says that.

Zimmy   Yes. I get sick of being told how well I look. (*Pause*) You just always end up managing, don't you?

Laura   Managing?

Zimmy   Coping with everything. You don't complain.

Laura   I wasn't brought up to complain...

Zimmy   I'm not getting at you. We all have our ways of coping.

Laura   I wish I could do that. Whatever you're doing.

Zimmy   Tai chi?

Laura   It's like dancing, isn't it? Christ, I don't know how you've got the nerve to do it, here in the park.

Zimmy   Nearly got bitten by a dog last week. Come here.

Laura   Me?

Zimmy   Yes, you.

Laura   What for?

Zimmy   I'll show you. Copy me.

Zimmy shows her the movement. Laura copies and soon they are both moving together. It looks fantastic. They finish the movement.

Zimmy   You're good at it!

Laura   I might take it up. I need to get some cotton trousers.

Zimmy   (*Sarky*) Oh yes, you need the right equipment.

Pause.

Laura   How are you?

Zimmy   The doctor won't speak to me, he's so annoyed, about me not having the treatments. Doctors are like children sometimes, don't you think? They can't bear it if you turn against them. They take it personally and sulk and won't speak to you.

Laura   I wish someone would say to me, Mrs Goodchild, we pronounce you cured!

Zimmy   They can't say anything for definite, because they don't know.

Laura   Are you scared of death, Zimmy?

Zimmy   Of dying, not of death. Scared of ill health. It feels like a failure. Tell you the truth, I'm scared of lots of things. That's why I shout so loud. It isn't just money that stops me going away. It's fear of flying, fear of strangers. Fear of seeing my mother again. Why do you think I do this? It calms me down, that's why.

Laura   But you can't control everything.

Beat.

Zimmy   Why do you think you got cancer?

Laura looks at her, aghast.

Laura   No one's ever asked me that.

Zimmy   Well?

Laura   Bad luck, I suppose.

Zimmy   You're not happy, are you?

Laura   I am, sort of. Happy as anyone ever is.

Zimmy   You know what they say. You only live once!

Laura   That's what Graham says when he opens a bottle of wine.

Zimmy   What are we frightened of?

Laura   Of being alone.

Zimmy   But you are alone. You die alone. Graham won't go with you there.

Laura   I don't think about that.

Zimmy   But it's true.

Laura   So what about you?

Zimmy   I'm terrified that the cancer is going to come back, and that I made the wrong decision. Scared of being emaciated and diseased and off my head on morphine. The only thing that keeps me going is a slender thread of control that I hold on to desperately... trying to remember what I know. I cry myself to sleep most nights.

Laura   So do I.

The two women embrace.

Laura   Zimmy? If I gave you a present, would you accept it?

Zimmy   What is it?

Laura   Just something I made.

Zimmy   What have I done to deserve it?

Laura   Told the truth.

SCENE EIGHT

Laura's diary

She's quilting again.

I mean, what do they need all that money for in the bank? Most of it just sits there, and it's dirty stuff. What's the point of money unless it's being used?

Now I've got no breasts I feel very light. I feel as if I could be anyone, male or female. This sounds strange, but I feel as if I've got no strings attaching me to the ground. I feel flighty. Of course I still wear the prosthesis. It protects me. I couldn't possibly go out without it, but sometimes at home I stand in front of the mirror, turning this way and that, sometimes naked, sometimes in a tight vest. I put my arms above my head and my whole body is a straight line, like being a child again.

SCENE NINE

Danny and Carol

Carol lies on a sofa. She isn't wearing her wig. She stares into space listlessly. Danny clumps in irritably, looking for something.

Danny   Mam, what are you doing? I wish you'd wear your wig.

You look really stupid lying there like that. People can see
through the curtains.

Carol   I can't find it, pet.

Danny   You're lying on it. Look!

*She pulls it out from under Carol and plonks it on her head. Carol looks
even worse.*

Carol   Would you rather I wore me woolly hat?

Danny   No! That's even worse.

Pause while Danny makes odd faces in a hand mirror and plays with her hair.

Danny   It's so stuffy in here.

Carol   I was cold.

Danny   Mam, you know my birthday?

Carol   How could I forget?

Danny   I've seen some high-heeled silver platforms.

Carol   Oh?

Danny   But they're eighty pounds.

Carol   Well, that's out then, isn't it? I've got nothing, Danny.

Danny   Just don't pay the rent.

Carol   I don't. And didn't you notice the phone's cut off?

Danny   Of course I noticed. I'm not stupid.

Carol   You could get a Saturday job.

Danny   Eighty pounds. I couldn't earn that kind of money.

Carol   Neither could I.

Danny   What's the matter with you?

Carol   I just don't feel too good. Back ache.

Danny   You should go to the doctor.

Carol   I know.

Danny   When are you going back to work? And you haven't been swimming for ages.

Carol   Don't know.

Danny   You can't just lie there for the rest of your life. You've got responsibilities.

Carol   You.

Danny   Yes, me.

Carol   Danny, if anything happened to me...

Danny   Oh no, not that again. (*Mimics*) If anything happened to me...

Carol   It's just your Auntie May offered...

Danny   I'm not living with Auntie. Anyway, shut up.

Carol   Don't tell me to shut up.

Danny   Well, don't go on about it then.

Carol   I've got to make provision.

Danny   No, you haven't. You've just got to get up and do something, you lazy cow.

Carol   Hey!

She slaps Danny.

Danny   Ow, ow, ow, that really hurt. I'm going to phone ChildLine.

Carol   On you go! The phone's been cut off.

Danny   You're not allowed to hit me.

Carol   Stop being like this then. How do you think I feel?

Danny   Well, get up then. Make me something to eat. Just be like you were before.

Carol   I just was. I'm tired.

Danny   Always. You're always tired.

Carol   I don't want to be tired.

Danny   Is it the cancer? (*Pause*) Don't you know?

Carol   I don't want to know.

Danny hurls herself at Carol and cuddles into her. She's suddenly like a child.

Carol   It's alright, Danny. I'm fine. Here, take the money from my purse and get us some fish and chips and I'll put the kettle on.

Danny jumps up and finds the purse, rattles through it greedily.

Danny   I'll just put my make-up on.

Carol   What, to go to the chip shop?

Danny   Yeah? Why not? Here, there was a note for you. Came through the door.

Danny rushes out with Carol's purse.

Carol   A balloon ride? Who's organised this? Bust Up? It's tomorrow, for God's sake!

SCENE TEN

Miranda

Spotlight on Miranda reading a similar note.

Miranda Agatha!

Agatha appears with a candle.

Agatha You called?

Miranda Would you mind if I went out tomorrow?

Agatha Out, you're always out! It's those women, isn't it?

Miranda It's a balloon ride. I've always wanted to go up in a balloon.

Agatha How frivolous.

Miranda Don't be like that.

Agatha You leave me all alone. Just me and my awful memories.

Miranda I've nearly finished the book.

Agatha Don't go, Miranda.

Miranda You'll be alright. Have a rest.

Agatha Of course I can't have a rest. I have to worry about you day and night. You are so easy to tempt.

Miranda I'm not, am I?

Agatha You have to do your work. You may die and you've got to finish it or no one will remember you. Or me!

Miranda I'll really get down to it tomorrow.

Agatha You've been swimming too much.

Miranda OK, no more swimming this week.

Agatha   Remember the prize at the end.

Miranda Right. I will. Heaven.

SCENE ELEVEN

Laura's diary

I hadn't seen the others for some weeks, not since we had all finished our treatments. I was trying to think of how we might celebrate.

I was really busy, sewing quilts for Carol and Zimmy. Luckily, Graham was also busy at this time on a plague of pigeons that had been nesting in the outhouse. He spent whole nights out there with his air gun.

I finished the quilts and it was then that I suddenly had the bright idea. Balloons!

I found this balloon club in the *Yellow Pages*, Cloud Nine, and phoned them up straight away. Money is immaterial, I said. I want your best balloon. I'm paying cash!

SCENE TWELVE

The balloon ride

Miranda strides in wearing flying gear and looking very excited. She sees the balloon. Zimmy appears, looking nervous.

Zimmy   What is this?

Miranda It's an unattended balloon.

Zimmy   But who had the idea?

Miranda Don't look at me.

Zimmy   Well, it certainly wasn't me.

Laura runs on.

Laura   Cooee! Isn't this fantastic!

Zimmy   It's a joke. You know I'm scared of flying.

Laura   This isn't flying!

Zimmy   No it's... dangling.

Miranda   You'll be alright. Let's get going.

Laura   We've got to wait for Carol. And the man's just gone off to get parachutes. He said to stand here.

Zimmy   I beg your pardon? Did you say parachutes?

Laura   It's just for safety purposes. Like life jackets on a boat.

Zimmy is backing away.

Miranda   It's a rather small basket for four women and a man.

Zimmy   You're right. I'm going home.

Laura   Just a minute. Can't you think of it as a magic carpet?

Miranda   We'll let you be captain if you like.

Zimmy   I don't want to be captain.

Laura   Trust us, Zimmy!

Zimmy   I feel completely sick.

Laura   Look, we're going to have to get on.

Miranda   What's the hurry? You know Carol. She's always late.

Laura   It's just that someone's coming.

Zimmy   The man?

Laura   No, over by the hut. It's the police.

Zimmy   What have you done, Miranda?

Miranda Me? I haven't done anything.

Laura   I just don't want to see them right now.

Zimmy and Miranda You?

Miranda You haven't poisoned Graham?

Laura   No. Don't ask questions. Just get in.

Zimmy   I can't.

Laura   You must.

Zimmy   Go without me.

Pause.

Laura   For me. Please, Zimmy.

Reluctantly, Zimmy allows herself to be pulled into the basket.

Miranda Just tell me something. Are we stealing this balloon?

Laura   Oh no. I've paid for everything. Cash.

They look at her suspiciously. Carol appears, breathless.

Carol   Wait, wait for me! Wait!

Miranda Get in!

Laura   Zimmy, let go of that rope.

Zimmy   We can't. The man's not...

Miranda Forget him!

Laura   Just let go of it. You're the only thing keeping us stuck to the ground.

Zimmy   I'd rather die.

Miranda Chicken!

This really gets to Zimmy. Glaring at Miranda she throws the rope over the side and they take off. We sense that they are really in the sky.

Miranda This is better than kneeling on a prayer mat!

Carol   It's hot, isn't it? Is my wig steaming?

Laura   No, its fine.

Miranda We're going up, that's the main thing. That's all you do in a balloon, go up!

Zimmy   But we don't know how to come down. Laura, if I die, I blame you.

Laura   I thought it would be fun. I didn't mean...

Carol   Fun!? It's bloody amazing!

Miranda Fantastic! Don't listen to her. We're all alone! Together.

Zimmy   Heads in the bloody clouds.

Miranda Look, you can see right into people's lives. Almost as if you could pick them up and move them around. Look, dogs, children...

Zimmy   Angry balloon club proprietors.

Carol   I'm bigger than they are for once!

Zimmy   Am I really here?

Miranda Stop! Peace. Listen to it!

Pause.

Zimmy It's so green. Green and blue. Smell the sea. THE SEA!
We might come down in the North Sea!

Laura We won't.

Carol We can swim, can't we?

Zimmy Twenty lengths in a heated swimming pool.

Miranda Don't be so negative. I feel like I'm in heaven.

Zimmy Make the most of it. We probably will be in heaven in a
couple of hours' time.

Laura It's obvious what you do. You just mess around with
the air vents.

She does and they all lurch about.

Carol Anyone mind if I take my wig off? My head's really
itchy.

Miranda Won't you be cold?

Carol I just hate the feel of it, and my bloody prosthesis.

Zimmy Why don't you throw it over the side?

Carol Might kill someone.

Miranda Oh well, the police are already after us so...

Zimmy Why not throw it at that man shouting at us?

Carol Alright.

Laura Two can play at that game!

She chucks her two prostheses over the side.

Zimmy I think you've maimed him.

Miranda He was a right tithead anyway.

Laura rips off her wig.

Laura   Hair today, gone tomorrow.

Carol   Anyone got a drink?

Laura   Oooh, yes. A bottle of champagne in my handbag.

Zimmy   She never fails.

Carol   I tell you, I feel like royalty. This is bloody magic.

Miranda A miracle.

They toast.

Zimmy   To letting go.

Miranda To heaven.

Laura   Friends.

They all look at Carol as she searches for an appropriate toast.

Carol   To... ME!

SCENE THIRTEEN

Miranda and Agatha

Miranda storms in, still in her flying gear from the balloon ride.

Miranda Agatha!

Silence

Miranda Agatha, I know you're there. I've got something to tell you.

Agatha appears sheepishly. She is still carrying the plate.

Agatha   You've been enjoying yourself!

Miranda What if I have? I've been up in a balloon.

Agatha Is that all you had to tell me?

Miranda No.

Agatha What then?

Miranda I've finished with the book.

Agatha The one about me?

Miranda The one about the Virgin Martyrs, yes.

Agatha So you've sent it to the publishers?

Miranda No, I've put it under the bed. My friend Laura says she'll use the back for patchwork scraps.

Agatha The back for scraps? But you've only got to write the summary.

Miranda I'm the summary.

Agatha You? You can't just cast it aside.

Miranda And I want you out of here.

Agatha You can't get rid of me that easily.

Miranda Out!

Agatha Have you been drinking?

Miranda Only champagne. You know, Agatha, when I was younger I used to make things.

Agatha Things? What things?

Miranda Sculptures, sand castles, food.

Agatha So what?

Miranda Why don't you put that tray down?

Agatha I can't. I have to carry it around all the time.

Miranda Who says?

Agatha That's what being a saint is all about. Anyway. You weren't very successful at making things. You're much better at writing about things, and people, like me. All those long words you use, like emancipatory and construct. I've seen them lying around, very impressive.

Miranda Only because you don't know what they mean. No, it was much better when I was making the things. And another thing. I miss Joyce.

Agatha Joyce? Who's Joyce?

Miranda She was living here before you appeared.

Agatha Her. She's just a simple-minded girl.

Miranda I'm very fond of her. She's really nice.

Agatha I don't know what's got into you. You're frighteningly airy.

Miranda It's just not going to work, Agatha.

Agatha slowly puts the tray down.

Agatha You know that you're being selfish, don't you.

Miranda Yes. That's the idea.

Agatha What would your mother say?

Miranda puts up her hand. She is pushing Agatha out of the door.

Miranda My mother would approve.

Agatha You'll go to hell. You'll lose all your power. No one will be interested in you. You'll just be an ordinary...

Miranda shoves her out and from off stage we hear the word.

... woman.

Miranda Joyce! Come back! JOYCE!

Joyce appears. Miranda bounds up to her. They dance.

SCENE FOURTEEN

Carol's funeral

Funereal music. The flowers appear again. Miranda, Laura and Zimmy stand in the pew. There are daffodils on the stage.

Carol appears and speaks directly to the audience. She is wrapped in Laura's quilt.

Carol   I wish I'd made more of my funeral. Left some provision, as Laura would have said. As it was, it was a small, quiet do. Death is not as bad as they make out. I accepted it when I got there. I died at home. I had all my family round me. Zimmy brought her herbs and bells and crystals and I pity the person who has to clean out my room because it's full of her junk. Miranda sat with me for hours, reading and listening to music. Just being. She seemed to be incredibly calm, as if she really wanted to be there. She got on very well with Danny. They both liked Madonna and smoking. Laura made sure I had every cancer accessory on the market... neck rests, invalid tables, a foot spa, and an endless supply of flowers from her garden, and of course the beautiful quilt she made, which I have left to Danny, knowing that sooner or later she'll unpick the seams. I've had a lot to be thankful for. I've got a wonderful family and good friends, and I've really enjoyed my life, even though I was only forty-two.

SCENE FIFTEEN

Laura's diary

She picks up the daffodils left from the funeral.

These remind me of Carol. Isn't it funny? Do you know it's a year since the first time we met? Such a lot has happened. Zimmy eventually got on that plane, you know, which was unbelievable, considering the fuss she made that day.

You should have seen us. The balloon gradually deflated and down we sank, Zimmy screaming her head off. We landed in the hospital grounds. Can you believe it? Doctors, nurses and patients came out to watch. They even clapped. What did we look like! Two of us were bald, no boobs, and we were all drunk. Zimmy was escorted to outpatients and treated for shock, and me, I was arrested! Miranda and Carol couldn't believe their eyes. They kept telling the police that there must have been a terrible mistake.

My case was in all the papers. WIFE NEVER THE SAME AFTER CANCER STRIKES TWICE. Graham blamed it on the cancer, and so did I. Anyway, the judge was very understanding, nice man, and apparently chemotherapy does cause memory loss.

Do you know, I've become a bit of a feminist icon?

Anyway, Graham's given up killing vermin and I have stopped quilting, so we have plenty of time to spend together. I even saw a live mouse and a couple of slugs yesterday.

They keep asking me where the money is, but I'm not going to tell them. I just hope it keeps the others warm for a long, long time.

She puts down her pen and does some tai chi steps in the fading light.

The End

Head of Steel

Strangely, considering the subject matter, I wrote *Head of Steel* while staying on the Isle of Wight over the course of a beautiful English summer, wearing a pair of shorts and a floppy hat while my daughters splashed about in a paddling pool.

The play was commissioned by Quondam Arts Trust and like the other plays I wrote for this company (*Rafferty's Café*, *Black Diamonds*, *Doughnuts Like Fanny's*) it involved a long period of research, of talking to local historians and absorbing myself in the fascinating history of the area where the play takes place. I never think of the Lake District as lovely any more, although it is. I know so much about the suffering dead buried in that landscape, and the story of the building of the Settle to Carlisle railway line is quite shocking. It was the last railway to be built by navvies, using shovel and pick, not machinery. Navvies and their families lived in shanty towns with names like Jericho and Jerusalem, in a kind of John Martinesque hell, suffering terrible winters and unbearable working conditions. They drank themselves to oblivion, and were pursued by missionaries and the temperance movement.
I plodded around graveyards reading the sad epitaphs of children who died from the various epidemics. I found the book *The Railway Navvies* by Terry Coleman incredibly useful.

The play did the usual small-scale tour, with three actors, some boxes, and a gallant stage manager. The actors played all the parts, and were on their feet for most of the play. I love the smell and ambience of a packed village hall, the cups and saucers with a ginger biscuit, the idea of a troupe of players bringing a huge and epic story to a community. *Head of Steel* was a great success on this kind of circuit. It was produced twice, directed by Rachel Ashton and secondly by Fine Time Fontayne. Both productions used acoustic live music, and the play had a great liveliness and vivacity.

Julia Darling

Head of Steel was produced by Quondam Theatre Company and was first performed at Ullswater Community College, Penrith, Cumbria on Tuesday 19 October 1993.

It was directed by Rachel Ashton.

The actors Michael Derrington, Jo Law and Paul Morrow played all of the parts.

CHARACTERS

James Allport (representing the Midland Railway)
Old Blackbird (a navvy, English)
Rainbow Ratty (A navvy, English)
Sore (a navvy, English)
Mr Tiplady (a scripture reader)
Jimmy Armstrong (who later becomes **Sad John**)
Jack The Lip (a navvy, Irish)
Alice (a navvy and landlady)
Mr Crossley (an engineer)
Various society voices
Man with eyeglass
Missionary
Scottish navvy in tunnel
Hannah (a navvy's wife)
Elizabeth Garnett (a missionary lady)
Isabella's friend

ACT ONE

SCENE ONE

Head of Steel *starts with a song, sung unaccompanied.*

As the song ends, James Allport stands, with a glass of red wine, at a dinner party.

James Allport The arms of iron are long, sirs. The railways have flexed and stretched their sinews all over England. We of the Midland Railway have pushed the rails of progress on through this century. Our objective now is to push on with this new, additional route between England and Scotland.

(*To himself*) If the Midland Railway could have abandoned it, we would. My engineer and I, Mr Crossley, walked – prospected if you like – the length and breadth of that terrible country. Never have I seen such terrain, such wild, changeable conditions. Once I had seen those barren wastes, those deep marshes, felt the wind tear the words from my mouth as I spoke, I tell you, progress didn't seem such an important matter. I am not a young man, my heart nearly failed me. Even the names make me shudder... Blea Moor... Blea Moor... (*He shudders*)

(*To assembled company*) After many discussions, we are ploughing forth with this great pioneering adventure, creating a line that will become an economic necessity. A line that future generations shall marvel at. A cathedral of engineering.

(*To himself*) If we could have abandoned this foolish scheme, we would. It will nearly break the company. Nothing, nothing in my whole career has caused me so much anxiety as this, the building of the damn Settle to Carlisle railway line.

Gentlemen, a toast! To progress, to railways, to the spirit of the Victorian age!

SCENE TWO

Three navvies sitting on the ground, with drink. They are telling stories. We have the feeling they have been here for some time.

Blackbird I'm heading north. For Settle.

Ratty You said Bristol.

Sore There's work for sure in the north.

Blackbird The wages are higher in the north.

Ratty So are the hills.

Sore I've seen them coming back. They say it's unbearable work, even for a navvy.

Blackbird North it is.

Ratty I'll be coming with you.

Sore Then I'll be coming with you, Blackbird.

Pause. Sore knows that they'll only let him come if he amuses them. This is his saving grace, the telling of tall tales.

Do you know the tale about the navvy working in the south?

Blackbird Is it bloody?

Ratty It's the one about a murderer. Tell it again, Sore. It makes me feel like a good man.

Sore There was a man. His name was Sad John, but I shall call him Sad.

Ratty It's not a likely name for a navvy.

Sore Sure, I made it up, it will have to do. Sad fell in love with a woman, who lived with another navvy. She was very beautiful, with long black hair, and a face like a dark angel. And they say she had a terrible temper, but that's not important.

He was delirious with love for this girl. He couldn't sleep or eat, or look after himself and nothing brought him any comfort but to be with her. Needless to say, she couldn't stand the sight of him. She was well attached to her own man and showed no signs of wanting to leave him.

Ratty   He sounds a fool.

Sore   He was. But then who can say when such an affliction might occur? Why tomorrow, Ratty, you could be tramping along the road and suddenly see a girl, and that could be that.

Ratty   Oh aye!

Sore   He so loved this girl, Catherine, that he decided to murder her man. And one day he was working high above the other man, swinging buckets down to him, and he cut the rope, so the heavy bucket crashed down onto the other's head, and down he went.

Blackbird Was he seen?

Sore   Of course he was seen, otherwise how could I tell you the tale? It was a mate of mine who was there, who saw every little thing. But that's not the end of it. As the man fell, he pulled another four men down with him, so five men died that day. Then the navvies turned against him and reported him to the law and Sad was charged with murder. Before they caught him he ran to Catherine and begged her for just one kiss... and she spat in his face.

Blackbird That was the end of him. Was he hung?

Sore   He must have been hung. Sure, all the navvies would have gone to the hanging. There was a court case, but I lost the thread of the story, I was in Norfolk by then.

Ratty   I heard that story, but the man's name was Pegleg, and the woman was Grace, and the place was Manchester. Are we tramping or not? Whoever he was, he deserved all he got. To turn against a mate for the sake of a woman, that's a sin. If I came across him I would stick a knife in his ribs.

They rise to their feet and exit.

SCENE THREE

Mr Tiplady sits painting a watercolour. His clothes are shabby, but he has a poor respectability.

Enter Jimmy, holding a letter.

Mr Tiplady   Shut the door. The wind gets in and dampens everything. A new man? And where are you from?

Jimmy   Bradford, sir. I've walked from Ingleton. It's very cold. I've brought a letter, from the mission.

Mr Tiplady   The mission? I am very pleased to meet you... ah, Jimmy. So you know who I am?

Jimmy   Mr Tiplady.

Mr Tiplady   So, Jimmy Armstrong, they think well of you in Bradford. It says here you are a fine upstanding man who works hard. Do you drink?

Jimmy   No, sir. Not for some years.

Mr Tiplady   So you have been a drinker?

Jimmy   I soon realised that drink can ruin a man.

Mr Tiplady   And you've come to seek work... as a navvy. You have no other trade?

Jimmy   No. Before, I was tunnelling, and blasting, and earth moving.

Mr Tiplady   So the letter says. You understand the nature of this place. This is no soft southern railway. Do you see what I am painting? It's an attempt, a poor attempt at the settlement. The trouble is, there is so much snow that I have quite run out of white paint! Oh well, it amuses me. I can take you to meet the contractor in the morning. There is, you understand, a minority – a minority – of men here who like to drink and be unruly. I very much hope you won't be one of them.

Jimmy   No. I'm here to work.

Mr Tiplady   I take it you'll be attending scripture evenings on Saturday nights? There are refreshments. Sometimes I think it is the bread rolls and hot tea that attract the audience, but never mind, at least they come, eh? Here there is no work on a Sunday, unlike other railway constructions. That at least is a bonus. Well, Jimmy, I am very pleased to meet you. I must confide in you, there are not many Christian men on the works and I do miss discussing some matters of faith, as I once did in the old days at the mission, so I hope we can have many talks together.

Jimmy   Of course, sir. I would like that very much, to have an opportunity to talk to an educated man such as yourself. I would be honoured.

Mr Tiplady   The work is exceedingly difficult here. Often the weather defeats even the navvy, hence long periods of idleness and of course the temptation to drink. I try my best to be of spiritual use to the men. That's my job.

Jimmy   Men have told me what a difference it has made having readers, such as yourself, living among working men. In Bradford they spoke of you very highly.

Mr Tiplady   Did they really? Why, that is good news! Come, Jimmy, we must find you a bed and a fire to warm yourself at. Good man. Old Alice has lodgings, very basic, you understand. When you are settled – settled in Settle! – you can tell me all about yourself. Good!

Jimmy   I sing sir. I am happy to sing at scripture readings.

Mr Tiplady   A singer! What an offer. Jimmy, that is splendid! A good voice will greatly enrich our rather weary choir. That is good news!

Outside, in the distance, we hear a drunken singer, singing a bawdy song. Jimmy and Mr Tiplady stand, embarrassed.

Mr Tiplady   Now, Jack, that's enough!

Voice in distance   Pardon, Mr Tiplady, sir. (*Burps*)

*Mr Tiplady shrugs, woefully. Jimmy looks sympathetic. Jack the Lip appears,
drunk and swigging from a bottle and freezing cold. He falls about the stage
drunkenly. He thinks he's with a crowd of people, who have evidently left him.*

Jack The Lip   *(Shouts/sings)*

I've navvied up in Scotland, I've navvied in the south
Without a drink to cheer me or a crust to cross me mouth
I fed when I was working and starved out on the tramp
And the stone has been me pillow and the moon has been me
lamp

Jack looks round laughing, but there's no one there.

That's right, leave a man when he's down! It's the same wherever
you go, the poor Irish bastard has to fend for himself. Are you
hiding? Shadow and Bones! Where's the beer money you promised me? May you rot... may your bones sink into the slurry and
stay there! Ireland's a wonderful country, praise God for Ireland.
Can you hear me? Long live the Irish!

You're hiding in the gorse bushes. I can hear you, rustling and
murmurin'. What kind of place is this anyhow? It's a penance.
What have I done to end up here? In Ireland we don't have
climate, we have weather. But here, it's not even weather, it's hell.
A living hell. Nothing but sulky sheep to keep a man company.
Clouds that come down like cloaks of death and swaddle you in
them, rains that get into your orifices and soak your heart until it
nearly stops. Roaring blizzards that blind a man! Snows that
deceive you into believing you're lying on soft silk coverlets and
kill you with coldness, sleet that cuts your skin to shreds! And you
can't trust the ground you walk on. One minute you're standing
on your feet, the next you're waist deep in green bog. Now, if I
was describing hell, it wouldn't be as bad as that... Christ be
Jesus, it would be hot! There would be coals to warm your blue
toes at... and other wickedness.

He crosses himself.

What kind of fool thought to put a train up here? He must be a
devil to have even considered it.

He lies down.

I saw a horse tear its hoof off in the mud today. It's like soup one minute and granite the next. Dear God, when do we get paid?

He closes his eyes and lies down.

Enter Alice with a lamp. She carries a barrel or a pot. Jimmy follows her.

Alice   You can have the bunk at the end, that's fourpence a night, or a penny to sleep on the table, or a halfpenny on the floor. Well?

Jimmy   I'll take the bunk.

Alice   You pay me in advance. Buy your own meat and I'll boil it in the pot for you. I'll do your washing, but you have to pay.

There's twelve men in this hut. Keep your voice down, there's five sleeping and the rest are drinking. If you pay your way and behave properly you'll not have no trouble from me. That's why Mr Tiplady brings the new men here. Some of the other huts aren't fit for rats, though the men that sleep in them don't deserve better. Has the cat got your tongue?

Jimmy   I've come a long way. You keep a cosy lodging house, Alice. Would you have some broth?

Alice   It's watery, but it's hot. Here you are, laddie. Where are you from?

Jimmy   South.

Alice   Is it very different, the south? I've never been further than Manchester myself.

Jimmy   Aye.

Alice   I lived with a navvy. That's how I came to be here. Before that I was a farming girl. I curse the day I met him.

Jimmy   I'm sorry to hear that.

Alice   And I wish I'd never left the farm. I would like to have a farm again.

Jimmy   Where did you say I would sleep?

Alice   The far end. You're not fat, are you? Have you seen the contractor? Mr Tiplady will take you down in the morning, to the contractor's hotel. They'll take you on for certain. They're desperate for men, to meet the deadlines. And there's not many that stay for long. You'll see. You've got no wife? That's a good thing. What woman would want to live here?

Jimmy   Navvy women have hearts of steel, Alice... Women like yourself.

Alice   (*Pleased*) It's true, we're not feeble, but neither are we content. It's pleasant to meet a navvy man who is sober and has manners.

Jack The Lip   (*He is outside, singing*)
I fed when I was working and starved when on the tramp
And the stone has been me pillow, and the moon has been me lamp

Alice   Keep your noise down, you drunken sot. I'll be putting him out – he can't find his own bed, let alone sleep in it.

How old do you think I am?

Jimmy   Missus, I wouldn't like to say.

Alice   I'm not forty yet.

Jimmy   Ah.

Alice   I know you're thinking, she's all gristle. I was a good-looking girl when I lived on the farm. The wind has blown me good looks away and left me with an old woman's face before I deserve it. I went to a fairground once, a travelling fair. There was a gypsy there who made a living guessing women's ages. You paid him a halfpenny and he looked at you in the eyes, as if he looked into your past, and then he guessed your age. I was thirty-five and he guessed ten years younger. You're twenty-five, he said. I was well pleased, but afterwards I thought, why, I've paid some old swindler to flatter me, that's all. But I think it was worth it... twenty-five! (*Pause*) Are you a reader?

Jimmy   Aye. I can read.

Alice   I like to read too. It makes a calming atmosphere. I'll take a halfpenny off if you'll read to me sometimes.

Jimmy   I have no books, except the Bible.

Alice   I have a book. I'll show you.

She gets a copy of some gothic pot boiler.

I'd like you to read me that. I find the Bible a wee bit tiresome. There was a navvy here who read to me. He had a nice voice... west country. He didn't drink a lot, not like him outside, but one pay day he started drinking. The whole encampment was delirious with drink. I hid under the bed, and I wasn't the only one. That was before the Midland Railway sent Mr Tiplady. They were shouting and carousing, like devils on the rampage. And fighting viciously, picking on each other and charging like bulls. My friend - Gentleman Sydney, he was called, because he was so polite and soft spoken, and he wore a nice hat - he was stumbling about with the rest of them and he must have passed out on the tramway. His head was cut off in the morning by the first engine. The driver said he felt a little jerk, so he stopped the locomotive and found Gentleman Sydney's body a distance from his head.

It was a big funeral. A sorry sight they were, heads bowed and sober. And he was right in the middle of the story. I'll show you the page... If you could carry on from there.

Jack The Lip   (*Struggling to his feet*) Leave the man alone, woman. That's a bad book - don't touch it!

Alice   Go back to sleep, Jack. This conversation has nothing to do with you.

Jack The Lip   Tell him about Yankee Tom and Starch 'em Stiff.

Alice   Keep your mouth shut.

Jack The Lip   Three men have read to her... All dead. One from a fall of clay, the other from a gunpowder blast. Don't touch it – death is on every page.

Jimmy   Perhaps I will read you the Bible, missus, but I have no interest in frivolous novelettes. Such words can lead the imagination into sinful habits.

Alice   Are you accusing me of sinfulness? Is a woman not allowed to have some pleasures on this bleak moor? You're a dull soul, and that's for certain.

Jack The Lip   Would you have any money for ale, now I've saved your life?

Jimmy   Does no one ever sleep in this wretched place?

Alice   I'll not have fighting in my lodgings.

Jack The Lip   Let the man sleep. He's got shadows under his eyes as black as the sky outside.

Jimmy staggers off to sleep. Alice picks up her book and exits. Jack becomes Mr Crossley, reporting to the Midland Railway.

Mr Crossley   (*As if speaking to a board*) You've heard the nuts and bolts of it. If it seems that some of my estimates were a little low, my answer is that if any of you here have seen the severeness of the weather conditions, you would surely have understood the nature of the task. At present, frost has stopped all masonry work on the viaduct, the two most southern contracts are entirely obscured by snow. Only in the bowels of Blea Moor is work continuing – relays of men are hacking and shovelling, working twelve-hour shifts for ten shillings a day. What can I say? Good weather and men are what is needed. At present I have neither. The labour force dwindles daily, due to men drifting off to easier work, and who can blame them?

He puts his papers in his bag.

To complete the work, gentlemen, by the required deadline I need another five thousand men and you're going to have to pay for it. For these men and their families we need accommodation and adequate supplies. At present, the living conditions are barely adequate. There are children running barefoot in the snow, illness is rife. Perhaps you should come and see for yourselves? I must say this room we sit in might just as well be heaven compared to what I have left. You have no idea.

He exits.

All the cast put on wigs or half masks. They represent respectable Victorian society at its various levels.

Society Lady   I have heard, Isabella, that the navvy is extraordinarily virile. Have you heard that? That he has haunches like a stallion and arms of iron muscle. He is of course, rough in the extreme. More of an animal than a human being.

Man With Eyeglass   I have not, in my travels, seen anything so ugly as that disorganic mass of labourers, sunk three-fold deeper in brutality by the three-fold wages they are getting. Incidentally, it seems the English are the worst and I am gladly surprised to hear that it is the Irish who are best in behaviour, sending wages home. The English, who eat twice as much beef and consume the residue in whisky, do not trouble the postman.

Missionary   Godless, diseased, reckless, proliferate, fornicating, violent, intimidating, foul-mouthed, sinful.

Society Lady   I mean, a navvy is no ordinary labourer, is he, Isabella? More like a pirate, or a smuggler. Woe befall any woman with the slightest share of modesty, whose ears and person they might assail. Imagine!

Man With Eyeglass   These ugly public works, slicing through the landscape. Who can blame the navigator? His task being to trample, tunnel and scar the natural beauties of hills, fields and dales. What does he care for beauty, or anything for that matter, except drinking and debauchery?

Missionary   Unmarried women, unchristian men, unchristened children, unmarked graves. For all this I still forgive. We must go among them, teach them to live in the light of the lord.

The cast sings a song.

SCENE FOUR

Rainbow Ratty (*Recites drunkenly*)

I'm a navvy, I'm a navvy, workin' on the line
Choppin' up the worms, makin' one worm fit into nine
Some jobs is rotten jobs, other jobs is fine
But I'm a navvy, I'm a navvy, workin' on the line

Sore   I saw a cat!

Blackbird What are you talking about, man?

Sore   A black, wild cat, its eyes gleaming out of the swamp.

Ratty   It's game we're looking for, not cats.

Blackbird I'm stuck in some mud. Give us a leg up.

Sore   There it is again!

Ratty   Sore, you'll end up in the asylum. I could eat a sheep.

Blackbird I could eat a cat.

Sore   You'll be out here all night if you don't get your leg out, it's up to your thigh. Puss, puss.

Blackbird Pull us out then, Sore.

Sore   You're a big man, Blackbird. I'll never do it on my own.

Ratty   Maybe it was a sheep?

Sore   Help us pull him out.

Ratty   Oh, leave him. I never liked him anyway.

Sore   Rainbow says to leave you.

Ratty   Tell him I'll break his legs.

Sore   He says he'll break your legs.

Ratty   What kind of place is Batty Green Hole?

Blackbird This is no time for melancholy. Ten shillings a day is no mean wage. I'm out. Where's that man? Leave me in a swamp, would you? I'll twist your neck until it cracks. Come here!

Ratty   (*As he exits*) Mind the hole!

Sore   Wait!

SCENE FIVE

Back in the Shanty Hut.

Jack   I know you.

Alice   Leave the man alone, Jack.

Jack   I know him. Where did you say you were from? Bradford? I was in Bradford, but that was years ago. Have you ever been in Cork?

Jimmy   Never.

Jack   Have you been tramping long?

Jimmy   Long enough.

Alice   Put some wood on the fire and stop your chatter.

Jack   I've seen his face. Look at his face. I know those eyes. The shape of your head. Was it in a bar? Were you ever in London?

Jimmy   No, friend.

Jack   Do you recognise me? Irish Jack. There's not a man would forget me. I tell a story, you must have heard it, about the little people and me old granny. Surely you remember that? I've told that enough times.

Jimmy   Friend, I've never seen you before in me life.

Jack   And you say you're not a drinking man. But I could swear I've seen you with a bottle in your hand. But you're not old, but then again, you're not young either. Were you married? To a girl named Patsy?

Jimmy   I've never been married.

Jack   I've a memory like an elephant and I know that face. What about the house of correction? Did you ever come up against hard times and end up there? I wouldn't hold it against you. Why, I've been in there a couple of times. Not for anything serious.

Alice   Thieving, no doubt.

Jack   More for enjoying myself, if you don't mind, madam.

Jimmy   I'm just an ordinary navigator.

Jack   No you're not. Alice, has he told us one word about himself? The man could have come from the moon for all we know. He could be the devil himself. What are you hiding? Well, Alice... we don't know do we? He won't tell us. Or will he tell us? (*Long pause*) Jesus, Mary and Joseph! What's the matter with you?

Jimmy   I don't like to fight, but I'll beg you to shut your mouth.

Alice   You brought it upon yourself.

Jimmy   Am I not entitled to any privacy?

Jack   I like to know who I am sleeping next to, that's all.

Alice   How about reading from the book, Jimmy?

Jack   Shut your book, there's enough story in this man's face!

Jimmy   What are you doing?

Jack   Looking in your sack. You've got me all suspicious.

Jimmy   Leave my things alone!

Jack   A leather bound bible, a white shirt...

Jimmy suddenly loses his temper and grabs Jack by the throat. Alice starts screaming and grabs a knife.

Alice   Out, both of you, out. I'll not have brawling in my house.

With extraordinary strength, she grabs the two of them and hurls them to front stage, exiting herself. Jack and Jimmy, dazed, sit up and look round.

Jack   I was only curious, that's all. I just wanted to know more about you. I didn't mean things to get quite so explosive.

Jimmy   Lord, forgive me. I am afraid of my own temper. I swore on the Bible not to fight, and here I am thrown out of my own lodgings for brawling. Alright, Jack. You asked me where I was from. Before I came here I tramped from London. I was working there, on the Enfield Line. I met up with some Christian folk and found the Lord.

Jack   You told a lie. Carry on, we've got all night.

Jimmy   Not a lie. As far as I'm concerned my life began with Jesus. Before that I was worthless. I only came here because there was no other place I could work. My father was a mason. He had a skill, but all I'm good at is hacking hard clay and tunneling in the dark. No one will remember us. The navigator, the one who went first, with his bare hands and pickaxe. They'll marvel at the engineers, at the businessmen. But not us. I used to be an angry man, before I found the Lord. It was an anger that I lived with every day, a bitter anger. I used to protest about conditions, about men left penniless because a sub-contractor wouldn't pay up at the end of the week. I lost many jobs that way, speaking up. But in the end I learnt that you could never change the lot of the navvy when the very government itself was made up of the same men who ran the railway companies.

Jack   So you've had some ups and downs then?

Jimmy   More down than up. I'm here to work and pray, Jack, and maybe save enough to stop working on the public works.

Jack   You could be a preacher.

Jimmy   Aye, I'm hoping Mr Tiplady will help me with my education.

Jack   You would know what it was like, which is more than I can say for some of the readers, with lily white hands and starched shirts. To be sure, you could move amongst us and influence us. Mind, the Irish would have none of it, they're already spoken for.

Jimmy   Will she let us back in?

Jack   To be sure she will, though she's as strong as any navvy. We'll creep in when she's asleep and lie under the table. But she'll be waiting behind the door with the carving knife for an hour or two, so if you don't mind I think I left a bottle of whisky by the sheds at the top. I think I did.

They get up and start clambering about

Jimmy   Do you believe in God?

Jack   I'm a Catholic. Catholics don't so much believe in God as put up with him. (*He crosses himself*) But you're a convert, it must be hard for you.

Jimmy   I was saved, thank God. We have met before.

Jack   Now, was it London?

Jimmy   Yes, London.

Jack   I'm never wrong. It was in the Three Crows, was it?

Jimmy   The Queens Arms.

Jack   It would have been busy then. There would have been a crowd, and fiddle music, and a poet perhaps.

Jimmy   I remember the story about your granny and the little people.

Jack   And I was just about to tell you the same story. (*Disappointed*) You remember it well, I suppose?

They are walking. There is some background fiddle music, very faint.

Jimmy   I was sitting in the corner. We didn't speak. I just saw you across the bar.

Jack   The Queens Arms is not a bar for quiet conversation, is it? Now, this is where I left my whiskey. And here it is, what's left of it.

Jimmy   It was before I worked on the Enfield Line.

Jack   You would have been a young man then?

Jimmy   That's right. I was barely sixteen. I used to drink as much as any man though, and use foul language. I knew no other way.

Jack   Then what happened?

Jimmy   Nothing. I was a poor man until I found the Lord.

Jack   Jesus, you're a poor storyteller.

Jack passes him the bottle.

Jimmy   No, I don't drink whisky.

Jack   What do you drink, milk?

Jimmy   I took the temperance pledge.

Jack   Missionaries, they cram everything down your throat but drink.

Jimmy   I feel a better man for it.

Jack   But you're not a happy man, are you, Jimmy the New

Man? I find that, with the English Christian. They don't like a joke, they don't see a joke coming. They're always thinkin' and thinkin'.

Jimmy   That's not true. I have found true happiness, Jack, not the drunken stupor that you call mirth.

Jack   And Christians have an answer for everything!

Pause.

Jimmy   You know, the London clay was bright blue when you first cut into it, then it changed to orange as the light touched it.

Jack   Are you a poet perhaps?

Jimmy   I write some verse, but I find the rhymes hard.

Jack   Did you stay till the end? On the Enfield Line?

Jimmy   No. I heard from a navvy on the tramp that the day it opened the gangs had a great celebration, running railtrucks under the tunnel as they left and letting off fog signals. The villagers thought it was an explosion, they thought the earth was going to crack beneath their feet. But it was just the navvies, saying goodbye.

Jack   They would be glad to see the back of them. Did you write a verse about that?

Jimmy   No, I nearly starved.

Jack   You were sick then? But that was nothing to here. They built that line in the sunshine. You'll not last in this climate.

Jimmy   I lost a friend. In an accident. I was sick after that. I didn't want to stay. But it was all part of God's plan, you understand.

Jack   So you've got it off your chest. Have a drink.

Jimmy   No, man.

Jack   Please yourself. Christ be Jesus, you're appalling company.

Jimmy   You shouldn't swear, Jack.

Jack   Does it offend the sheep?

Jimmy   God's creatures understand foul language.

Jack   It just comes out. I'll confess when the priest comes around.

Jimmy   Yet you should consider your words before you speak.

Jack   Recite one of your verses. I like a bit of poetry.

Jimmy   Will ever a one remember the times our voices rung
When you were limber and lissom, and I was lusty and young
Remember the jobs we've laboured, the beautiful songs we've sung?

Jack   Did you write that?

Jimmy   No, but I would like to have done.

Jack   That was sweet to me ears. Why for a moment, Jimmy, I thought I was in the Queens Head in London Town!

A song here.

Jimmy and Mr Tiplady sitting together. They are getting on very well.

Mr Tiplady   When I look over this construction, Jimmy – more tea? – it brings to mind a passage from the Bible. I quote, 'Which of you, intending to build a tower, sitteth not down first, and counteth the cost, whether he hath sufficient to finish it!'

Jimmy   A railway is an ugly enough construction, but an unfinished railway is far worse.

Mr Tiplady   How true. How do you find your lodgings?

Jimmy   Fair enough. It is what I am used to.

Mr Tiplady   Yet you are well read, an unusual quality in a navvy man.

Jimmy   I made it my business to read the scriptures. Sure, it was hard and I would still call myself an ignorant man. I hope to not spend the rest of my days working to put brass in the pockets of entrepreneurs. Manual labour may be good for the soul, but this work leads nowhere.

Mr Tiplady   Ask and it shall be given to you.

Jimmy   Excuse me speaking so frankly, but there are men who see the common labourer as little more than cattle, as mere figures in a book.

Mr Tiplady   They know not what they do.

Jimmy   Mr Tiplady, is it wrong for me to want to improve myself?

Mr Tiplady   Not at all, it is a rare quality, but if in improving yourself you also help others, why that can only be for the good.

Jimmy   Sometimes, sir, my faith is very faint, but other times, it is strong and certain.

Mr Tiplady   It is a struggle, the bleakness, but do you not feel that in the dark we see more clearly? When I was appointed scripture reader my feelings were very mixed. I had to leave comfortable accommodation in Bradford and my friends and family and to come here, where most of the population is, I will give you, civil in the presence of a scripture reader, but entirely disinterested in religion. Some days I feel as if I'm talking to the wind for all the reaction I get. But then, a man like yourself appears, just as I had run out of white paint, and was feeling very forsaken, and things improve. You have even brought a glimmer of sunlight!

Jimmy   I feel better when I talk to you of books and good things. When I am down in the tunnels, I'm afraid. I feel insignificant, like an ant amongst thousands of other ants, building a great anthill. Sometimes there's a terrible silence.

Mr Tiplady   Do you pray down there?

Jimmy   No, I just work.

Mr Tiplady   Prayer can dispel fear.

Jimmy   In the land of darkness and the shadow of death...

Mr Tiplady   There is light, Jimmy, there is always light.

SCENE SIX

Jack and Jimmy and other actor are tunnelling. They lie on their stomachs a distance away from each other. Their conversation is stilted, we see their faces.

Jack   Can you hear me?

Other   Aye.

Jimmy   I'm to your left.

Jack   I'm to your right.

Other   Stand back!

All cover their heads as there is some kind of blast.

Jack   Are we all present?

Other navvy   (*Coughing*) I'm up to me waist in water.

Jack   Jimmy?

Jimmy   I'm here.

Jack   Send the buckets back. Speed up, get some of this dirt shifted. Did you know, boys, there's ladies in London that pay good money to be lowered into tunnels like these? For the thrill. Can you believe it. Down into the inferno. (*Imitates*) Oh my! it's so... exhilarating!

Other navvy   I could tell you a story.

Jimmy   Speak up. I can't hear you.

Other navvy   A ghost story.

Jack   It will have to do.

Other navvy   At the public house, there was a man who told me.

Jack   Was his name Old Blackbird?

Other navvy   That's the one.

Jimmy   Watch out, Christ protect us.

Jack   What was that?

Jimmy   A fall of earth. I'm alright.

Jack   Carry on. He's out. I think I know the story, but it will pass the time.

Other navvy   There was a navvy at Chat Moss.

Jack   I heard it was Birmingham, but never mind.

Other navvy   Tunneling.

Jack   I heard he was blasting.

Other navvy   His name was Tiny.

Jimmy   What did he say his name was?

Jack   Tiny.

Jimmy   He was a small man then?

Jack   Not the way I heard it. He was six foot tall.

Other navvy   Tiny always wore gloves, thick leather gloves, and nobody knew why, but he would never take them off. Perhaps some of his fingers were missing? One day Tiny was undermining clay when it suddenly cracked away. He'd worked too far under if you get my meaning.

Jimmy   Pass down beams.

Other navvy   The poor devil was completely crushed. Only his glove could be seen, that's how they found him.

Jack   Did you hear that, Jimmy boy? Just his glove.

Jimmy   I heard.

Other navvy   Five years on they did repair work on the same patch of line and Old Blackbird was working on the face.

Jack   I suppose he swore on his mother's grave.

Other navvy   He said it was gospel.

Jack   It was night, wasn't it? You couldn't see his face.

Other navvy   Are you listening or not?

Jimmy   Aye.

Other navvy   Old Blackbird was working on the face when the same thing happened, a great mass of clay cracked away and started to fall and then a glove appeared, just as Old Blackbird was about to have the bowels crushed out of him, and pushed him to one side. Saved Old Blackbird's life.

Jimmy   It was a close thing then?

Other navvy   He was within an inch of his life. And there was no sign of the glove afterwards. It was Tiny's ghost. Stand Back!

They all cover their heads again. There is another blast.

Jack   Are we all here?

Jimmy   Aye. Thank God.

Jack   Are you there, friend?

Silence.

Jimmy   Is he alright? It was a fierce blast.

Jack   Are you there?

Silence.

Jimmy   Is he dead?

Other navvy   Give us a hand!

The man laughs, but Jack and Jimmy look queasy. Suddenly, there is another, even louder, blast.

Jimmy   Jack, I can't move.

Jack   Send someone down!

They slide backwards, retreating face forwards to audience.

Jimmy   Where's the other man?

Jack   Buried.

Jimmy   Have you got your whisky, Jack?

They find each other in the gloom.

Jack   Just a drop will do you good. You're shaking. Come on, lets dig him out. He might live yet.

Jimmy   Help, there's a man buried! Help us!

SCENE SEVEN

At the scripture reading. Mr Tiplady stands on a rostrum. Jimmy and Elizabeth stand with their hats in their hands, looking pious. All sing.

He who would valiant be
'gainst all disaster
one here will constant be
follow the Master

there's no discouragement
shall make him once relent
his first avowed intent
to be a pilgrim

Mr Tiplady   We are gathered here today to praise the Lord,
and to remind ourselves of all that is good and decent. Over the
last weeks there have been many incidents, due often as not to
that demon substance, alcohol, which many of you seem unable
to resist. Indeed, families are left destitute, thanks to that fateful
liquor that soaks up a man's wages and leaves him with nothing
but a bad head and no money in his pocket. Magistrates are
weary of the endless stream of men brought before them on
charges of drunkenness. I urge you to sign the pledge, either this
evening or privately, to renounce this foul habit.

I have written to the Midland Railway Company to tell them of
my disapproval of the placing of a public house next to the pay
office. A brewery too!

With these sober words in mind, let us sing and ask the Lord to
send us sober thoughts and good judgement.

Sung drearily.

The line to heaven by Christ was made
With heavenly truth the rails are laid
From earth to heaven the line extends
To life eternal, where it ends
Repentance is the station then
Where passengers are taken in
No fee for them is there to pay
For Jesus is himself the way
God's word is the first engineer
It points the way to heaven so clear
Through tunnels dark and dreary here
It does the way to glory steer
God loves the fire, his truth the steam
Which drives the engine and the train
All you who would to glory ride
Must come to Christ, in him abide
In first and second, and third class
Repentance, faith and holiness

You must the way to glory gain
Or you with Christ will not remain
Come then, poor sinners, now's the time
At any station on the line
If you'll repent and turn from sin
The train will stop and take you in.
Amen!

Mr Tiplady   Now, we have a visitor in our midst. Elizabeth
Garnett is the secretary of the Christian Excavators Union. She is
going to be staying among us for some weeks and visiting you
with her message of faith and hope. Step up, Elizabeth.

*Elizabeth comes to the rostrum and looks benevolently about her. Her speech is
completely sincere, not a caricature. She believes implicitly in the righteousness of
what she is doing.*

Elizabeth   Friends. I wish to tell you of an experience I had as
a young girl of barely ten years. My father, the Reverend Joshua
Hart, a Yorkshire man of great dignity, who dedicated his life
to the saving of poor souls, such as yours, was unveiling a
monument commemorating the deaths of twenty-three miners
and navvies who unfortunately lost their lives on the Bramhope
Tunnel Works. The sermon he preached to the poor families and
remaining workforce has stayed with me, word for word, ever
since and I have always known, friends, that my task was to move
amongst ordinary men, such as yourselves, and tell you of the
ways of the Lord. This is why I have single-handedly formed the
CEU, which is, I believe the salt for Christ on our public works.
One wing of our work is the Temperance Pledge, which you have
been invited to sign this very evening. I have brought with me
blue ribbons, which I would ask you to wear on your jackets to
show your fellow men that you have been brave enough to take
this step into the light of the Lord. And perhaps you will be killed
suddenly by a fall of earth, by the blasting of a rock, by the
crushing blow of an engine, by a bruise that may fester, and
mortify, and poison the life blood; by a fall, by the slow torture of
disease, or by the burning heat of fever, but however it may be, or
where it may happen, let me ask you, are you ready now? Shall
you be ready to meet death then? And friends, the wages of sin
are death, and no drunkard shall inherit the kingdom of heaven!

She looks like she wants to continue, at length, but Mr Tiplady steps in.

Mr Tiplady   We shall greatly enjoy your presence here, Elizabeth. Elizabeth will be handing out copies of her excellent sermons for your edification, which usefully include information on public works all over the country and the names of men killed or injured.

(*To Elizabeth*) My dear, the sheets are very popular with the men. There are some refreshments available at the back of the hall. I look forward to speaking with you over a cup of tea.

Mr Tiplady picks up a saucer. Jimmy looks out of place and is also holding a teacup. Mr Tiplady glides over to him.

Mr Tiplady   I was sorry to hear of the accident today, Jimmy. He was an unfortunate man. Not an attender. But some souls are lost forever.

Jimmy   It's very cruel down there, Mr Tiplady. We are working face to face with death.

Mr Tiplady   And are you afraid? You need not be, Jimmy. Many of the accidents that happen are unfortunately due to recklessness, and you are not a reckless man.

Jimmy   With due respect, sir, it is hard not to be reckless, when everything around us is so dangerous. I cannot blame men for drinking. It soothes the fear.

Mr Tiplady   Not in the long run, Jimmy. Not in the end. (*Pause*) It is the children that concern me. I have written many letters to the Midland Railway, telling them of small babies sitting on damp marshy land, which cannot be good for their health, and their education is ruined. It saddens me greatly. Why, I am hoping that Elizabeth might turn her energies a little from speechifying and help me to establish a Sunday School.

Jimmy   It's a pitiful sight, sir. I have thought the same thing.

Mr Tiplady   And now this latest tragedy.

Jimmy   Sir?

Mr Tiplady   Two cases of smallpox, down at the bottom huts.

It will spread like fire in these conditions. A hospital is to be built, to isolate the cases. That at least I have achieved.

Jimmy   Smallpox is a terrible condition. That is bad news, sir. How soon will the hospital be built?

Mr Tiplady   Very fast. It must be. There is to be a deadhouse where infected bodies must be laid. There is only one way to deal with the disease and that is forcefully and immediately.

Jimmy   You sound despondent, Mr Tiplady.

Mr Tiplady   Oh no. I am dedicated to my work, Jimmy. I know no other. I am just a little cold, and tired.

Elizabeth comes over.

Elizabeth   It is as I feared. Many of the men are unmarried. There is much work to be done persuading them to lawfully take vows. Are you living with a woman?

Jimmy   Me? No.

Elizabeth   Or have you left a woman to whom you were not married?

Jimmy   No!

Elizabeth   It is a common condition.

Mr Tiplady   This is Jimmy Armstrong, my dear, a Christian man who has come from the mission in Bradford, and is also pledged to temperance. Jimmy has been of great assistance to me and is of great moral value to the men, as he is working alongside them with this message of God.

Elizabeth   You must agree with me then, that proper marriages are vital if working men are to make their peace with the Lord.

Jimmy opens his mouth to answer, but Mr Tiplady jumps in on his behalf.

Mr Tiplady   I agree, of course, dear Elizabeth. But my dear, you must admit, it is very hard for a navvy, who is bound to roam the length and breadth of the country searching for work, to sustain a marriage. Why, we have problems with bigamists, who have married several times out of conscience.

Elizabeth The path to righteousness is hard country, my dear Mr Tiplady.

Mr Tiplady A navvy woman can at least take another's name if abandoned without formal ceremony, otherwise she would starve.

Elizabeth You seem to be defending this immoral state, sir.

Mr Tiplady Not at all, I am just stating the facts, which I must say, I have become accustomed to through contact with the men. Would you agree, Jimmy?

Jimmy (*Very controlled*) It is very hard for a man to behave in a proper manner when he must work or starve. A good woman's heart will break if she were to wait for one man, and she will be thrown from her accommodation the moment her navvy has gone if she does not take another man's name.

Elizabeth Oh, I understand the pressures. I understand them very well, but this does not make it proper for a man and a woman to live together without marriage.

Jimmy No, madam.

Elizabeth I'm glad we agree at last. You must spread the word to your fellow workers, Jimmy Armstrong, who are more likely to hear the words of a man such as yourself than I, a lady of higher rank.

Mr Tiplady sighs. They turn away from each other and leave the stage.

SCENE EIGHT

We return to Mr Crossley's report to the Midland Railway.

Mr Crossley I am glad to say, sirs, that with the slightly improved weather conditions, work has speeded up somewhat, and the workforce is at this moment expanding. Most of the workings on the south side of Blea Moor tunnel are well opened up, the gullets being well driven in advance. About 150,000 cubic yards have been taken out. Two locomotives are used to convey earth to the bank. Most of this work is let to Batty Moss gangs and the men divide their earnings equally amongst themselves, in proportion to the hours they work. The men, on account of this co-operation, earn good wages and might do very well for themselves, were it not for drink, which meets them at every step.

Batty Moss Viaduct will be an extraordinary achievement and by far the finest piece of masonry on this new line, with 24 arches. Only a cathedral is more audacious in concept!

More accommodation has been erected for men and their families and I can thankfully say that since last I reported to you, conditions are much improved. A hospital has also been placed on the site, for, sadly, it seems that smallpox has reared its ugly head amongst the navvy population. All efforts are being made to isolate cases, huts are being limewashed, but it is mainly children who succumb to the foul disease.

He exits.

Enter Jack The Lip, alone and exceedingly drunk. He sings a song.

Jack   Good evening to you, Mr Crossley! Is that a nurse or a sheep? Good evening to you too! Jesus, where am I? I'll tell you a story, you! Where are you? I was with some other boys in the public house, but not one of them would lend me any money and it's a whole week to payday and all I've got is credit slips in me pocket for rotten meat from the rotten butcher.

Anyways, this is the story. There was a sad navvy workin on some hole, who murdered six men. *Six men!* Can you believe it? He murdered them because they wouldn't buy him a beer, and he says to this woman, will you marry me now? And she spits in his face instead of kissing him, which was what he had hoped. It's a good story, if I could just remember it right. The man wore gloves right up to his elbows, because he'd lost a finger in the wars. Is that right? And on a lonely night you can still see his gloves waving at you in the dark.

He exits. Enter Jimmy, carrying his Bible.

Mr Tiplady   Is that Jimmy Armstrong? Will you wait a moment?

Jimmy sits, looking self conscious. He notices a letter addressed to Mr Tiplady and glances at it.

Jimmy   (*Reading*) You wrote to us of Jimmy Armstrong, who was here with us at the mission. You will find him a great asset, as he is a religious and reliable man. We are glad he arrived safely. Incidentally, we at the mission had some problems understanding his rather thick Geordie accent, but perhaps in the course of your excellent work with the navvies you have grown accustomed to such a guttural dialect. May you go with God.

Enter Mr Tiplady.

Mr Tiplady   So, Jimmy. How are you today?

Jimmy   I am well.

Mr Tiplady   There is a matter we must speak about, Jimmy.

Jimmy   Yes.

Mr Tiplady   (*Picking up the letter*) Some weeks ago I wrote to the mission in Bradford, praising your character and telling my friends there how much I enjoyed your company, and our Bible readings together. Why, it is a long time since I have met such an intelligent and diligent working man on railway works such as this.

Jimmy   Thank you, sir.

Mr Tiplady   Today, I received word from them. Apparently, Jimmy Armstrong harks from Newcastle and has a voice to match. Now, I want you to be honest with me. If there is something you are hiding, then make your peace with the Lord. I want the truth, Jimmy.

Jimmy   I cannot tell you, Mr Tiplady, much as I would like to.

Mr Tiplady   Have you been in trouble?

Jimmy   I don't know what to say.

Mr Tiplady   Have you committed a crime?

Jimmy   No, sir, but there are those who think I have.

Mr Tiplady   So you are wanted by the authorities. In what name?

Jimmy   No, that time is gone. I have put it behind me.

Mr Tiplady   Which is worse, Jimmy, if that is your name – to live a life of falsehood, or to come clean before the Lord, whatever the consequences?

Jimmy   My name is clear with the authorities. I have committed no crime. But I fear for my life, from other men.

Mr Tiplady   And your name is?

Jimmy   John.

Mr Tiplady   And the letter, where did you obtain the letter?

Jimmy   From the real Jimmy Armstrong, who is unfortunately passed on, having caught the smallpox. I was there with him when he died. It was he who gave me your name.

Mr Tiplady   Is this true?

Jimmy   You have my word. Sworn on the Bible.

Mr Tiplady   And, apart from telling lies, you have committed no crime?

Jimmy   No, sir.

Mr Tiplady   Then we will speak no more of the matter. Out of thine own mouth shall I judge thee. I will take you as you are and ask no further questions.

Jimmy   I thank you, sir. You are a good man.

Mr Tiplady   Yet I trust you shall try even harder to live in the shadow of the Lord. My confidence in you is a little shaken.

Jimmy   I promise you, Mr Tiplady, I shall do my utmost to live up to your expectations.

Mr Tiplady   Good. That is all then.

He watches him leave, warily

SCENE NINE

Enter Old Blackbird, Sore and Ratty. They are working with pickaxes, sleeves rolled up. Sore talks very loudly as his hearing has been impaired by a gunpowder blast.

Blackbird One...

Sore   And two...

Ratty   And three...

Blackbird How far have we come?

Sore   A few inches. The clay is hard as granite.

Ratty   How long have we been working?

Blackbird Some hours. Stop for a drink.

Sore   The foreman's over t'other side!

Ratty   Use your lip, you never know where he'll be – he creeps around like a reptile. (*Speaking loudly*) Now, Old Blackbird, I'm going to get a tiddly wink of a pig's ear, so keep your mince pies on Billy Gorman.

Sore   What?

Blackbird I'll have a fisherman's daughter!

Ratty   A fisherman's daughter? A jug of water.

Sore   A jug of water, aye, a fisherman's daughter.

Blackbird I'm ready for me Jimmy Skinner.

Ratty   Lay down your Lord Lovell.

Sore   Lord Lovell?

Blackbird Sore, you're not over quick are you. Me shovel - me Lord Lovell.

Sore   It's my ears, from the dynamite blast. Everything comes from so far away.

Blackbird Stop your moaning.

Sore   It was only yesterday. Before that my ears were like any other ears.

Ratty   Would you care for a drink?

Sore   Aye.

Ratty   You heard that alright! Get away with you.

They settle down, with bread and beer.

Sore   What?

Ratty   We didn't say anything!

Blackbird Up at Intake Bank, they've been tipping for a year without any advance. It's fools' work this. I'm going to get me kit and be off on the frog and toad soon.

Ratty   And I may blackbird and thrush me daisy roots too, for sure. It was worse in the Crimean War. Would you agree, Sore?

Sore   I lost me finger in the war.

Ratty   That's not all you lost.

Sore   What?

Blackbird Do you know the reason for the name Batty Green?

Ratty   I heard that Batty was a man of the moors, who wooed and married a poor girl from Ingleton, but he fell into evil ways and the poor wee girl threw herself into the deep hole. That's what I heard.

Blackbird I heard it's where Batty's wife did her washing!

Sore   Perhaps she fell in when she was washing? When you go on the tramp, I'll be coming with you.

Ratty   Two's company.

Blackbird If he'll carry the bags, perhaps he might.

Ratty   Blackbird says you can carry the kit...

Sore   (*Resigned*) Aye.

Blackbird And where will we walk?

Ratty   There's no work left in this godforsaken country. We should take the boat. To Australia or the east.

Blackbird Australia, Sore, they need men.

Sore   Shall we be taking the boat?

Ratty   We shan't be swimming.

Blackbird Pack up, Jimmy Gorman's on his way. Pick up your Lord Lovell. Now then, my china plate, out with your cherry ripe, off with your steam packet and set your Lord Lovell going!

They wander off.

Interval

ACT TWO

SCENE ONE

Mr Tiplady, very agitated, paces up and down. Hannah sits with him, a baby in her arms. She looks defiant.

Mr Tiplady   Are you sure we are talking about the same man?

Hannah   I know he is here. I've told you what he looks like. He is the father of this baby here. I have tramped hundreds of miles to find him. I have even advertised in the papers asking for his whereabouts. He abandoned me, with nothing except a child in my belly.

Mr Tiplady   My dear, some women – and this is not meant as a slight – will name a man as the father of their child in order to gain protection from him.

Hannah   I could have had any man, sir. I needn't have walked the length of the country. Why don't you fetch him and let him speak for himself? You say this John is of fine character and a good Christian man? Well, he has you all duped.

Mr Tiplady   I have sent for him.

Hannah   I warn you, the sight of him will make me even angrier than I am already.

Mr Tiplady   Please. Control yourself.

Enter John.

John   Hannah! How did you come to be here?

Mr Tiplady   So it's true, then? You abandoned this woman?

Hannah   Here I am, John. Look at his face, sir, the face of a snake!

John   Hannah... I was going to return.

Hannah   Seven long months you have been gone. Seven

months! I am half dead from searching for you.

John Sir, she is an acquaintance.

Hannah Hardly an acquaintance. Sir, this is the father of the child in my arms.

John That I am not.

Mr Tiplady John, I already know that you arrived here under a false name.

Hannah He is afraid, sir, that his past will catch up with him.

John No! I was not afraid. After I left the Enfield Works I found the Lord, Hannah.

Hannah So you are even mimicking a Christian man now, John Brown?

John I have educated myself in the scriptures. I have tried to live an honest life.

Hannah And this is your so-called honest life?

John I have been trying to save money and educate myself, with the help of Mr Tiplady. I was going to return, but the work is here and the pay is high.

Hannah You're just the same as any other navvy, picking up women in whatever place you happen to find yourself. I expect you have deceived some poor girl here.

John No.

Mr Tiplady I advise you, John Brown, to marry this woman, and I wish to hear no more about the matter.

John But sir... Very well. I have no option and no defence. We will be married.

Mr Tiplady When shall the day be?

John   Tomorrow, today... who cares? It shall not be a happy occasion.

Mr Tiplady   Very well. Tomorrow then. I suggest you find some food for your new wife.

John   Sir, one day you shall know the whole story. But forgive me now. May I still come and see you?

Mr Tiplady   (*Very coldly*) That I do not know. Good day.

He exits. Hannah goes up to John and hits him.

Hannah   So here is the man who loves me.

John   I have changed.

Hannah   The man who follows me like a dog, who writes poor verse about my beautiful hair and my sweet mouth!

John   Why did you come here?

Hannah   To find you. To see how great your love was.

John   You look very tired.

Hannah   Oh yes, I am tired. But I could be dead for all you cared.

John   I would have come looking for you in the end.

Hannah   You're a poor liar.

John   I feel confused. You always had the power to make me feel like this.

Hannah   So you thought you'd keep away and keep your sanity.

John   No.

Hannah   What then?

John   I found the Lord.

Hannah   You found the Lord! What has he got to do with it?

John   Is that why you came to find me? To punish me?

Hannah   I came to find you because I am your responsibility and as you know I am not a woman who endures bad treatment from any man. You left me, knowing I had a child. And what were your words? I promise, dear Hannah, to return. Perhaps you were drunk when you said it?!

John   It is not my child!

Hannah   Does it really matter whose child it is?

John   It matters to me.

Hannah   What is it, John? Has your new Christian friend forsaken you because rough, dirty Hannah appears and suddenly you're not as pure as he thought you were.

John   He has been a friend.

Hannah   All he is interested in is your soul. He'll have written all about you in his neat, educated hand. You're a number on the holy scoreboard, that's all.

John   You are very hard.

Hannah   I am hard. I have become hard and bitter. I tell you something – we can be married and you shall support me until the day you die, but I've had it with love. There is not one ounce of love in my heart. Love is a luxury that I can no longer afford. It has been driven out of me with iron and gunpowder.

The three actors become the three buffoons

Sore   Did you hear about the wild woman with a baby on her back who came striding into the settlement and beat a navvy black and blue?

Blackbird   I heard about the wedding.

Sore   A wedding when bride and groom were not speaking, and not a drop of drink to be had. The most dowdy affair you could ever imagine. What's the point of a wedding without liquor?

Ratty   None at all.

Blackbird By the sound of it she's not a woman to be crossed.

Ratty   I wouldn't let a woman treat me that way.

Sore   I would.

The other two look at him with disdain.

Blackbird She's the first visitor in a week.

Sore   Who?

Blackbird The woman with the baby.

Sore   It's not a place to visit on the whole, is it?

Ratty   Smallpox.

Blackbird Churchyard's chock full.

Sore   I know the funeral service off by heart. Sometimes I think I'm at my own funeral and I just don't know it. That I've died.

Ratty   We have a cuckoo in our midst.

Blackbird There's enough dying going on without discussing it day and night.

Ratty   There's very little else to talk about, but bad food and the bad railway companies, and the bad weather.

Blackbird Sing then.

Song.

Jimmy and Hannah sit back to back, occasionally exchanging glances. There is much tension between them. Enter Jack, sober, for once.

Jack   May I come in? And a very good day to you.
I thought I might visit for a little while, to see you settled.

Jimmy   Jack. Yes. Come in.

He sits between the two of them, oblivious to their problems.

Jack   It's a fine morning, if there can be such a thing in
these parts. Would you have something hot?

Jimmy   Hot beef tea.

He looks at Hannah, who doesn't budge, and gets it himself.

Jack   I'm very happy for you, Jimmy. A toast to the bride
and groom. I wanted to tell you, I shan't be staying much longer.
I have a wish to join my fellow countrymen working in another
part and to tell you the truth, I'm dog sick of myself being picked
on by lesser men than yourself. Tis a sport to torment the poor
Irishman and I've had enough of it. There's a fight brewing, I feel
it in me bones, so I think I'll be going. Would you have a drop of
brandy? I think I have a cold coming on.

Jimmy   You know this is a temperance house.

Jack   You never know though, do you? Do you mind if I
have a drop of my own? I've been to Mass, you understand, and
it is the custom to have a small drink before dinner.

Jimmy   Dinner?

Jack   Would you be having dinner on this fine Sunday?

Jimmy   Why, yes. Stay for dinner, Jack.

Hannah   There's not a great deal to be eaten.

Jack   That's alright, a little is better than none.

Hannah   The baby has colic. Will I never get any peace?

Jack   Why look at her. She's the image of you, Jimmy.

Hannah   That's right.

Jimmy   She's not... Ah, never mind. I'm tired of bickering.

Jack   You're a dark horse, you know that. You're the talk of the public house.

Jimmy   I have been publicly shamed.

Hannah   And about time.

Jimmy   Why are you doing this, woman?

Hannah   Revenge.

Jack   Now, now. God knows you're a miserable couple, but perhaps you'll learn to live peaceably in the end. I'm saying nothing. I've worked side by side with this man and I've found him to be a good mate, to be sure.

Hannah   Oh aye, the men always side with each other and the poor woman is left destitute. Navvies... you think you're the blood of England, but you're nowt to the women who feed you and stick with you. It's us who have built the railways as much as you.

Jack   She's got a tongue in her head.

Jimmy   We are all God's creatures, men and women.

Hannah   Stop your babble, it doesn't wash with me.

Jack   He's not one for a joke, is he? I wonder that you married him at all. There are plenty of men here looking for a woman.

Hannah   Better the devil you know.

Jimmy   Don't hate me so, Hannah.

Hannah   It is you who hates me, not the other way round.

Jimmy   I don't hate you. We have fought now for nearly a week. I'm exhausted.

Hannah   I'm glad. At last we have something in common.

Jack   Shush now. I'll tell you a story to pass the time, now I'm not too tongue-tied with the old John Barleycorn.

Jimmy   Not now, Jack.

Hannah   I would like to hear a tale, John Brown, if you don't mind.

Jack   Thank you. I thought as I was sharing your dinner, the least I could do was to amuse you. Perhaps you knew the navvy in question? The story is, there was a man working on the Enfield Line, where the clay turned from cobalt blue to orange in the light.

Hannah   That's right, it did.

Jack   I can't recall how I knew that! So, our navvy, whose name was Sad John, on account of his predilection for melancholy, was working on the line, when he saw a woman called Catherine, who was bound to another navvy, and fell in love with her.

Jimmy and Hannah recognise the story and become extremely interested.

Jack   He loved this Catherine so much he didn't know what to do with himself. He wrote her poems and slipped them under her door, and struggled to find ways to be near her, but she would have nothing to do with him. In the end, in his madness, he devised a scheme. He decided to murder her navvy, and then to offer her his name as protection, knowing the poor woman would have no choice but to take him.

Jimmy   Who told you this story?

Jack   Tis a popular story a man told me, in the public house. His name was Sore, and he knew the man personally.

Jimmy   You say it's true?

Jack   True as a story can ever be when it's travelled hundreds of miles and been told and retold by intoxicated men.

Hannah   Go on.

Jack   So one day, the opportunity arose. Our navvy was working high above the other man, lowering heavy buckets on ropes down to him, and he cut the rope.

Jimmy   Lies!

Jack   And that's not all – the big bucket hit our man square on the head and bless his soul he died instantly. But as he fell, he pulled down four other men with him, so five men died that day.

Jimmy   One other man.

Hannah   Just one other man.

Jack   So you know the tale? Then why am I sitting here telling you it?

Jimmy   Finish the story.

Jack   But our man was seen and the navvies turned against him for killing one of their own, so he ran to Catherine, who spat in his face.

Jimmy   It's a sorry tale, Jack.

Hannah   Tell him the truth, John.

Jimmy   I'll be finished here if I do.

Hannah   If you won't tell him, I will.

Jack   You know the story then? Jimmy, you must have done a terrible thing. Was it you? A murderer? And I've walked the moors all alone with you and worked beside you down in the tunnels, and beneath you, just like the poor man who lost his life.

Jimmy covers his head.

Hannah   He's not a murderer. Until not long ago I would have said he was a good man. Until he left me, out of cowardice, all alone to fend for myself.

Jack   It's true then.

Hannah   The man who died was John's brother, who went by the name of Jimmy Mackie. His half-brother anyway. The two men were very close, they had lived and worked next to each other since they were young men. And Jimmy Mackie was my navvy. I had fallen for the bold navvy man and I curse the day that I left my village.

Jack   There's not a woman would say otherwise.

Hannah   The three of us lived in the same accommodation, shared the same food, even the same bed when there was no other. We had two wages coming in and there was gossip. Why, I had the love of two men, for there is no denying, John, that you cared for me as much as Jimmy.

Jimmy   I was wrong.

Hannah   It seemed fine to me.

Jack   The navigator lives by different rules. The priest shakes his head, but it's true.

Hannah   One day, I remember, the gangs had laid down their tools and refused to work on account of the unsafe nature of some of the work. There had been an accident and the company had claimed it was due to carelessness and not the fault of their poor equipment.

Jack   No, that is foolish. When has a public works been safe? Why, danger is the nature of the work!

Hannah   That may be so, but John had spoken out against the company and was in danger of losing work because of it.

Jimmy   You tell the story well, Hannah, but I was not such a hero, not by any means.

Hannah   Then the accident happened, when John was working above Jimmy, and the bucket fell, because the pulleys were old and insufficient, and the ropes were thin, and Jimmy was killed and another man who was well loved by the navvies, called Happy Peter.

Jimmy   I couldn't believe what had happened. I ran to Hannah.

Hannah   And tis quite wrong to say I spat in his face. Why, we clung together like children, weeping and wailing. But the contractor was a bad man, who wanted no trouble with the company and it was him who invented the tale of love and jealousy, an easy story to fabricate, as it was already in people's minds. So the navvies turned against John and swore to kill him and there was no one to speak up for him but myself, and no one heard my voice. So John ran and never returned and that is why I came to find him, only to discover that he has been taken over by the missionaries and seems to have forgotten me.

Jack   So the baby is not his?

Hannah   I don't know.

Jimmy   I do not believe this child is mine, that is the honest truth.

Jack   But it could be. Jesus, you're a dark horse. You had us believing you were so righteous that you were as virgin as the day you were born. I tell you now, never believe a navvy – he'll lie his way to heaven!

Jimmy   I had not forgotten you. I believed you would have found some other man and been better off for it.

Jack   Well!

Jack pours a big drink for himself. Hannah and John watch him nervously, waiting for judgement.

Jimmy   And now we have related the whole sorry tale to Jack the Lip, who even talks in his sleep. We are at your mercy.

Jack   It's true I'm a talker, but Jimmy... John... whoever you are, I am not vicious. I tell you what, I'll tell the honest story when I get to the next place and let it filter through the public houses and shanty huts, and if you're guilty, then I would still say there are men in London far guiltier than you. If you think I would go round calling you a murderer, then I am quite offended. I am an Irishman. I know what it is to be victimised. It is a condition I am over familiar with.

Jimmy   I have behaved like a Judas.

Hannah   Leave the Bible out of it, John Brown. You are a coward and that is your shame. I'm no Virgin Mary, am I?

Jack   Be careful how you speak of the Virgin Mary. Don't look so gloomy, Sad John. There's hope for you yet. Your boats aren't burned, your milk isn't spilt.

Hannah   You'd think he'd be pleased to see me!

Jack   But you'll be needing to renew your acquaintance. There's a fellow I want to see, so I'll be leaving you to make amends. John, would you have a shilling for a poor navvy?

Hannah   Here you are, Irish Jack!

Jack   I remember where I saw your face, Sad John. Not in the Queens Arms, although you may have been a young face in that crowd. It was in the newspaper. It was this very story. But you were acquitted, but not proved innocent or guilty. Now I can see that was a very difficult thing to live with, suspicion and doubt.

Jimmy   So you knew all the time.

Jack   To tell you the truth, I've always worked above you, not below, to be on the safe side.

He leaves.

Hannah   So, Sad John. What do you say now?

Jimmy   Kiss me.

Jimmy and Hannah embrace.

SCENE TWO

Enter Mr Crossley. This time he looks worn out and he has a cough. The share-holders sit and yawn, while Crossley gives his report.

Crossley   We plead for another extension. There is still much work to be done on all contracts. As I said before, good weather and men are what is needed. Yes, sir, I am aware that expenditure has exceeded two and half million. We have been dogged by bad luck and delay. The men work hard but do not hurt themselves. The death toll on contract number one averages one death a week. What can you expect? Both churches of Settle and Chapel le Dale have been forced to expand their graveyards. The men have raised money amongst themselves to erect tablets commemorating their comrades. They thank you for your kind donation. Only the parapets are needed on the Ribblehead Viaduct. Two months of fine weather will make all the difference.

He slams his book shut.

That is the end of my February report. I thank you for your interest.

A song here.

SCENE THREE

Elizabeth   Mr Tiplady. I have the answer.

Mr Tiplady   Yes, Elizabeth.

Elizabeth   Divorce.

Mr Tiplady   I beg your pardon.

Elizabeth   We must encourage those who have married and then separated to divorce.

Mr Tiplady   Do you not think that a little impractical?

Elizabeth   Not at all. It is the only way.

Mr Tiplady   A divorce costs something in the region of thirty pounds, my dear.

Elizabeth It is a high price, but it will pay for freedom, a good conscience, and a happy home.

Mr Tiplady   You will have a hard task persuading a navvy woman to spend thirty pounds on her soul.

Elizabeth The deserted wife will have her furniture, a man his strong hands. If they strive not to spend one useless penny it is possible.

Mr Tiplady   Yes. Hmmm.

Elizabeth I will discuss the matter tonight at the scripture reading.

Mr Tiplady   Tell me, how do you find John and his wife Hannah?

Elizabeth Who?

Mr Tiplady   John has been a good attender, yet since that matter last year I have not taken him into my confidence. I wonder if I have been too hard on the man.

Elizabeth He is very quiet.

Mr Tiplady   I must speak to him again, when I return from Bradford.

Elizabeth Ask him his thoughts on divorce.

Mr Tiplady   He seems happily married. Although the marriage started off on a bad footing. Indeed, as he is not a drinking man, he now lives in a comfortable hut and eats well. He reads too. Yes, I may have been hard on him. We had a good relationship for some months.

Elizabeth It is our task to forgive, after all.

Mr Tiplady   Yet it is hard to forgive when a man will not take you into his confidence.

Elizabeth You do not trust him then.

Mr Tiplady   He has always behaved well here. Whatever he
has done, he has not repeated the crime. Will you have more tea?
I must prepare for my trip. I am very much looking forward to it.
Bradford will seem quite beautiful compared to this bare place!

*Old Blackbird, Sore and Ratty sit side by side with beer mugs. They are very
drunk, swaying from side to side as they speak.*

Sore   We've drank our pay, Blackbird. What do we do now?

Ratty   We'll drink our jackets.

He takes his jacket off.

Sore   But it's the only jacket I have.

Blackbird The landlady is a fierce woman. She might not like
your jacket.

Sore   Shall we ask her nicely for a drink?

Blackbird No. We'll have to steal.

Sore   But there's no one to steal from.

Ratty   Or beg.

Sore   Or beg from.

Blackbird Sore, do you have a silver watch?

Sore   Oh, that's a very dear thing to me, my watch. It's the
thing I value most in the world.

Ratty   Take it to the bar and say you'll exchange it for ale and
then you can come and collect it later, when you've been paid.

Sore   Aaah, I suppose there's no harm in it.

He totters off.

Ratty   He'd sell his own mother for drink.

Blackbird The man's a burden. He's run out of stories, he's deaf in one ear and he can hardly pick up a shovel.

Ratty   He can't pull his weight, that's true, Blackbird, and he's getting on, nearing forty.

Blackbird But he has the heart of a saint.

Ratty   Oh, he has a good heart. Why, he'd pawn his only bit of silver to buy a friend a drink.

Blackbird But he's holding back the gang. Work advances slowly enough without carrying men.

Ratty   Do you say we should drop him?

Blackbird The man's an old mate. He's pulled me out of swamps and seen to me wounds and carried me home.

Ratty   Sore's a good man. Yes, you're right there.

Blackbird He's very trying at times.

Ratty   Very trying.

Sore returns with three ales.

Sore   There's more on the way. She liked my silver watch.

Ratty   I bet she did.

Blackbird A toast... to Sore!

Sore   To me? Aye! When do we get the boat, Blackbird?

Blackbird When we've got enough to pay our passage.

Ratty   We've less than when we arrived. We've exchanged everything but our shirts for drink.

Sore   It's true. We're ruined men.

Blackbird We'll start a kitty.

Ratty   Put half our pay in.

Sore   It's a few weeks to payday.

Blackbird Two weeks.

Ratty   It's nearly all gone on credit already.

Blackbird Have a bit of heart! Believe old Blackbird, we'll be on the boat by Christmas.

Sore   Aye. To Christmas on the high seas.

Ratty   To Australia!

Blackbird To the sun shining in the sky!

They look despondently at the sky. Jimmy is calling up to a window. We don't see Elizabeth.

Jimmy   Mr Tiplady!

Elizabeth Who is that? Have you come to attend the prayer meeting?

Jimmy   It is John. Hannah is ill and so is the baby, with the smallpox, I think. She is very feverish!

Elizabeth Mr Tiplady is gone to Bradford for some weeks. He left this morning. I am here. You must take her to the hospital.

Jimmy   The hospital is full, and anyway I cannot move her!

Elizabeth Are there not strong men who will help you?

Jimmy   No one will come near for fear of the smallpox. She is very delirious and drenched with sweat.

Elizabeth When my prayer meeting has ended I shall walk to the hospital myself, John, and ask a nurse there to visit you. You say the baby is also sick?

Jimmy She lies beside her mother, they are in the same condition.

Elizabeth I will pray for them sincerely, as you must do, but I had better not visit. It is a virulent infection. Do not let anyone in your house.

Jimmy I must speak to Mr Tiplady.

Elizabeth I told you, he is gone.

Jimmy To a preacher then.

Elizabeth Go home. I will see what I can do.

Jimmy Mrs Garnett, I do not know what I shall do if she dies.

Elizabeth John, if that is the will of the Lord...

Jimmy If he takes her from me, I shall bury my Bible with her!

Elizabeth Now, that's no way to talk. Why, it is in our times of need that the Lord can most help us.

Jimmy So where is he now?

Elizabeth John, you are over-excited, perhaps delirious yourself. Go and nurse your wife and pray for her, as she would do for you.

Jimmy Very well. I can see there is no assistance to be had here.

He turns. Hannah lies behind him.

Hannah Who are you?

Jimmy It is your husband, John.

Hannah Where is my Jimmy Mackie? You aren't my husband.

There are black angels on the ceiling. Look, they flutter their dusty wings and the dust falls on me and burns me.

Jimmy   Sssh! Drink water so that you might get well.

Hannah   I am burning! Why are you putting these burning cloths on my head?

Jimmy   They are cool, it is you that burns.

Hannah   All the flesh is gone from me, I am just bones. That's what the navvy life has done to me. Navvy men, with their bragging and brawling. What did I think I would find, Jimmy Mackie, when I ran away with you?

Jimmy   I am John.

Hannah   No, not John. He is the one who looks at me sideways when he is in the house. John is gone from here. Did you know how John looked at me, Jimmy? He desired me. He would brush against me and whisper in my ear, but I didn't even look at him, Jimmy, I swear I didn't. I only love you.

Jimmy   I'm sorry, Hannah.

Hannah   But I was young then, with black eyes and shining hair. John wouldn't be looking at me now, would he?

Jimmy   You are still beautiful.

Hannah   What's that? Beauty? I haven't seen a thing that is beautiful since I took to the road with you, Jimmy, and signed up with the rotten railways.

Jimmy   Sssh, Hannah, it hasn't been so bad. Here we have lived well, we have saved money. Soon it will be over. We can leave this place and find some land.

Hannah   John? (*She recognises him again*) Land. We will grow potatoes and have an apple orchard, shall we?

Jimmy   And livestock.

Hannah   But no sheep.

Jimmy   No.

Hannah   Tell me again, John, about the land.

Jimmy   When we have saved enough we shall purchase a small plot of land somewhere in the south, where the climate is kind.

Hannah   The sun.

Jimmy   That's right, there will be sun, and though it will be hard, we'll farm that small patch, and grow our own produce, and the children shall grow strong and healthy from all the good food.

Hannah   Potatoes, but no sheep.

Jimmy   But we will have a cow, for the milk and cheese, and hens for eggs.

Hannah   And a feather bed. That is what I would like, a bed so soft you could sink into it, that smelt of clean sheets and fresh air. I can just feel it. Come and lie with me, John, in my beautiful, soft feather bed.

She closes her eyes.

Jimmy   Hannah! So you would even do this, would you? This is no divine will. Lord, the woman was near to loving me and you took her away.

SCENE FOUR

Enter Mr Crossley. This time he writes a letter aloud.

Crossley   Sirs, to coin a phrase, we can see the light at the end of the tunnel. After five years' hard work and the immense outlay of capital, this important new railway is nearly finished. Of course, owing to the somewhat rough state in which portions of the line still remain, it cannot yet be thrown open for ordinary traffic. However, a Pullman Carriage of saloon carriages has passed over the entire seventy-two miles from Carlisle to Settle, with Midland Railway directors sat proudly overlooking their achievements.

I must say, I too look forward to my retirement, although I am glad that my working life has given me just enough vitality to see the completion of this extraordinary feat of engineering.
Incidentally, the termination of all scripture readers' contracts has caused much hardship and although I write cheerful news today, understand that for our workforce, conditions are as difficult and arduous as ever. Scripture readers significantly helped to modify the habits of some of the men. I ask you to reconsider. That is all.

A song.

SCENE FIVE

Enter Jack, as if on the tramp.

Jack   I was walking one day, when I met a fellow countryman tramping, who gave me a shilling and we fell to talking. He had come down from Batty Green Moss and had been working on the Viaduct and the Blea Moor Tunnel. Oh I said, so you're still all in one piece, not blown to smithereens, or sick from the smallpox, or deaf from gunpowder lasts, or even venereal disease. Oh aye, he says, I've been lucky, for sure, though I hate the English even more than I did. And that reminded me of my friend Sad John, so I asked this Paddy for news of him and he told me the end of the story.

Enter John, carrying Hannah, who he lays on the ground.

Jack   Hannah dies from the smallpox and the next day the poor dear babby dies too and Sad John takes the bodies to Chapel Le Dale to meet the preacher and to bury Hannah and the child that bears his name. When he gets there, it seems the preacher has forgotten and John is all alone with his bible and his grief.

Jack sits on one side and plays the mouth organ. In silence, Jimmy rings the bell.

Jack   He rings the bell, but no one comes, so he buries poor Hannah and the babby all alone, and with her his holy Bible.

Jimmy   And I curse the God who looks over the building of this railway line, and who smooths the tongues of the railway managers, and the missionaries, and the religious men who move so daintily in our midst. I curse them, Hannah, as you would. And I curse the day I met you as much as this, the day I bury you, and I curse all men who knowingly send men to their deaths, and with them the poor families who follow wearily. And I curse the brass in their pockets and the port in their glasses after dinner, those who blah, blah, blah, blah with a handkerchief in one hand and a purse in the other. And this place, this cold, cold, grave-yard. Come back, all of you, and ghost the embankments and the tunnels and the viaducts. Rattle the wheels of progress as they tear on, heedless of those in their path.

Jack   But there was no one there to hear him. And Sad John went straight from there to the public house and drank himself silly on ale and stayed drunk for over three days, until he was thrown into a ditch. And Paddy tells me that in the public house he met an old navvy there called Blackbird. But before that, our Mr Tiplady comes to find him, carrying all his bags because the Railway Company has finished his contract.

Enter Blackbird, who sits beside Jimmy.

Jack   (*In the voice of Mr Tiplady*) John, how did you come to fall into the hands of the devil?

Jimmy   You're too late, Mr Tiplady, sir.

Mr Tiplady   John, come home with me and we'll sober you up. Surely you can see that the Lord has not, as you believe, forsaken you? Why he waits for you to come back into his arms.

Jimmy   He can wait some years then.

Mr Tiplady   I deeply regret my absence these last weeks. Why, if I had been here, I would have guided you through this misery.

Jimmy   It's alright, Mr Tiplady. You'd abandoned me long ago and you were right. I'm just a bad navvy man. There's blood on my hands, Mr Tiplady sir, as there is blood on the hands of every man who has come near the railway works, even you. Me, I murdered my own brother. At least I watched a rope fray and snap and didn't reach out to prevent the heavy bucket from falling, just because I wanted a woman. And I got her, for a while. Now who is the sinner, Mr Tiplady? Is it me, or the contractor, or the engineer, or the ones that never get their hands dirty at all?

Mr Tiplady   Now, John, you don't know what you are saying.

Jimmy   To tell you the truth, sir, I don't care anymore. Why, look at the great arches of the viaduct. Let that be the gravestone of the navvy men. It's finer than you'll ever get. Navvy men are like the earth we tunnel and blast – when we die you just throw us into it and let us rot.

Mr Tiplady   I'm disappointed in you, John.

Jimmy   You must be a disappointed man. Why, how many souls have you saved, Mr Tiplady? Tell me that. And Mrs Garnett, how good is her harvest? Who is the winner? You or that great monument over there?

He turns his back on Mr Tiplady.

Mr Tiplady   Your bitterness brings me great sorrow, John. If you should ever want to find me I shall be in Bradford. Perhaps you could visit me there when time has healed your unhappiness.

Jimmy   Goodbye, sir.

Mr Tiplady   You may not think so, John, but in my small way I believe I have improved the spiritual quality of shanty life. Many have told me so.

Jimmy   (*Sarcastic*) I'm sure you haven't done any harm, sir.

Mr Tiplady   Goodbye then.

He reaches out to shake Jimmy's hand, but Jimmy shakes his head and drinks from a bottle instead.

Blackbird   You're not a merry drunk, are you friend?

Jimmy   Merry enough, but what is there to be merry about?

Blackbird Nothing here. It's a railroad planned by devils.

Jimmy Who care nothing for the navvy. All they care about is his soul, and that was lost long ago.

Blackbird So you're not a church-going man?

Jimmy No.

Blackbird Tell me, have you ever considered travelling across the water?

Jimmy No.

Blackbird Because you seem to have plenty of silver to throw around, and you'd be better placed spending it on a ticket to a happier location.

Jimmy Is that your plan? To go to the other side of the world?

Blackbird A navvy is accustomed to being upside down, but you could go, friend. But me and my two mates, we have no funds, so we are bound to tramp and starve.

Jimmy I would like to get as far from here as I can. They say Australia is a hard country?

Blackbird No worse than here. What do you say?

Jimmy Why not?

Blackbird And the small matter of your fare... Perhaps you could see your way to lending three hard-working men their passage? Which we would repay you on securing work.

Jimmy Why should I believe you?

Blackbird You have Old Blackbird's word!

Jimmy Very well, tell your friends we will travel together and I will buy drinks to celebrate the decision!

He gets up, and falls over, then stumbles into the shadows.

SCENE SIX

Enter the three navvies in a great state of happiness.

Blackbird The man had clearly lost all his faculties, so I laid him gently down, and as he had promised me the money, I took the purse from around his neck. Why, in that state he could have been robbed! And anyway, before that I heard him admitting to a scripture reader that he'd murdered a navvy for the love of a woman.

Ratty   He deserves all he gets then. Is he still out cold?

Blackbird Hardly in this world at all, but I left a few pieces of silver in his pocket so the man shall not starve.

Ratty   You're a very fair man, Old Blackbird!

Sore   The thought of all this money makes me giddy. Remember my silver watch? Why, I'll be having that back.

Blackbird Sore, we must make tracks. When he realises his money is gone he will report us! We'll be buying new kit for the journey in Liverpool. You must forget your silver watch – it is nothing to the treasures you will reap in Australia.

Sore   It is hard to forget my fine watch, but very well, if I must.

Ratty   Shall we divide the money now?

Sore   Tis alright, I have it here in my hand.

Blackbird I should keep it round my neck, being the most honest man among you.

Ratty   What if you spend it behind our backs?

Sore   You wouldn't do that to your own mates.

Blackbird Give me the money, Sore.

Sore   Will it be hard in Australia?

Ratty   I've heard it's a quiet place. Much like here, but warmer and more relaxing.

Blackbird The money.

Sore   I like the feel of the leather, the jangle of the coins inside. You can have it in a minute.

Ratty   Shall we count it again?

Blackbird We should set on our way before the demented man awakes. He could change his mind any minute.

Sore   Which way do we go? I'm ready.

Ratty   This is the way to Liverpool.

Blackbird No, this way, but there's a ravine in between.

Sore   A what?

Blackbird Look, fool, a ravine. We'll have to walk around.

Ratty   I could jump that.

Sore   It's wide.

Blackbird It's a good start to the journey. I dare you all to jump. (*To Ratty*) Sore will never make it, his poor legs are too stiff.

Ratty   (*To Blackbird*) But he holds the pouch and won't let go.

Blackbird Throw the money to the other side, Sore. It will act as enticement and make us jump all the higher.

Sore   Aye!

He throws the money to the other side.

Sore   Who will be first?

Ratty   Here is a long piece of grass. The shorter is first, the longer is last.

Sore   And the middling in the middle.

Blackbird And I'm the first.

Sore and Ratty A one two three! Jump!

Blackbird runs and jumps.

Sore   Blackbird's fallen.

They look down into a seemingly bottomless pit

Ratty   God bless the man! It's me next. Count us over, Sore.

Sore   A one. Two. Three. JUMP!

Ratty jumps and falls. Sore looks dolefully down into the black hole.

Sore   Wait for me, boys. Sore is coming! And ONE. TWO. THREE. JUMP!

He too falls.

Enter Jack, who picks up the pouch of money and puts it in his pocket.

Jack   I said I'd bring home money and Jack is always true to his word. The work is nearly all done anyway. Good evening to you. If you're travelling from Settle to Carlisle, remember Jack the Lip, and Sad John, Jimmy Armstrong, Sore, Ratty, Old Blackbird, Alice and Hannah, Shadow and Bones, and all the others. Why, the work's all dried up. They'll be using machines next, and lets hope no other railway will be like this one again. Bad luck from start to finish.

EPILOGUE

James Allport I am pleased to announce that the Settle-Carlisle Railway Line is open for traffic. This announcement is mixed with some sadness, for our Mr Crossley, an engineer who drove himself untiringly through the building of the line, and who has reported to us dutifully over the last seven years, has died, just four days after the opening of this extraordinary railway. Why, just four days ago, Mr Crossley rode the length of the line in an open truck and was heard to remark, Finis Coronat Opus. And so be it: Finis Coronat Opus.

Song.

The End

The Women Who Painted Ships

This play was written as part of Live Theatre's *Twelve Tales of Tyneside*, a contemporary mystery play cycle project dreamt up by Peter Flannery, which involved many writers from the North East. It was subsequently commissioned by Kate Rowland at BBC Radio 4 for a live broadcast which took place on a very exciting, nerve-wracking evening at Live Theatre.

It was one of the first things I wrote for Live and I remember feeling terribly stuck. The brief was to take some aspect of North Eastern history and write a short play for a small cast. My friend, the actor Charlie Hardwick, told me about her Auntie Ursula who had painted ships during the war at Swan Hunter's Shipyard in Wallsend. I was interested in stories like this, of forgotten histories, but I didn't really have a dramatic angle or way of exploring the story, and I didn't want to write a documentary. Auntie Ursula was now one hundred and one, but still very alert and living in a terraced house in Wallsend. Charlie and I went to visit her. She was tiny, with a silvery laugh like a bird, and a great sense of humour. Ursula was very amused by our interest in her. She had hurt her leg and I remember our conversation was quite surreal, as we chatted about her visits to doctors in between her extraordinary memories of the shipyards, her husband, and her friends. There was this air of magic about her and of otherness. Perhaps it was the ethereal quality of the very old. She was so alive, yet almost angelic, and as excitable as a small child.

After our meeting I wrote the play. It was the first time that I had used such poetic language and sensibility in a piece of drama, and though the play is very short, it marks a changing point in my work. For some reason, it always makes me cry. I am not sure why.

Julia Darling

The Women Who Painted Ships was first performed at Live Theatre, Newcastle upon Tyne as part of *The Twelve Tales of Tyneside* production of short plays on 16 May 1997. It was directed by Max Roberts with associate direction by Wils Wilson and designed by Perry John Hudson.

CHARACTERS

Edith A very solid, definite person in her nineties who speaks very clearly and surely.
Edna A bit more flighty and excitable, but also very old.

CAST

Edith   Charlie Hardwick
Edna   Phillippa Wilson

They speak to an invisible young interviewer who is sitting, imaginary microphone poised, opposite them. They are both a bit bemused.

Edith   You want to know about the shipyards?

Edna   Look. They're over there. Just outside the window.

Edith   What did you want to know exactly?

Edna   It used to be very noisy and dark, didn't it, Edith? Cake?

Edith   Are you from the pensions fund?

Edna   Thump Thump Thump.

Edith   What did she say she was, Edna?

Edna   A writer! Like Carla Lane. Or Lynda La Plante. You know. What do you write?

They hear the answer.

Both (*Disappointed*) Oh.

Edith (*Speaking as if interviewer is deaf or daft*) Me and her, we worked at Swan Hunter's shipyards in Wallsend during the Second World War.

Edna   Bombs and everything.

Edith   They kept us on afterwards. In my case until 1962, but Edna left in '58.

Edith   I was a riveter's assistant. A holder-on, and a tacker, but mostly we both painted ships, and mostly we painted them red. They called us slap dashers.

Edna   One lump or two?

Pause for question.

Edith   The first day?

Edna   You got a little disc, remember, Edith.

Edith   That's right. When I left I threw mine out there in the flowerbed.

Edna   Three six three. That was my number. I use it for the lottery now.

Edith   We do the lottery every week.

Edna   We threw them in a basket at the end of every working day. The timekeepers sorted them out. Heh, we were always trying to trick the timekeepers.

Edith   I remember my first day. It was primitive. I was quite shocked. Stank of diesel and rusty iron, red lead and urine. The men just went to the toilet in an open trough. We had to go miles, didn't we? Used up half an hour at least, going to the toilet!

Edna   Place was crawling. We were like little ants. Everything made bit by bit. We used to say, "How on earth did that ship get built?" when it was launched.

Edith   Aye, we did.

Both   What?

Edna   We didn't think about being women. Money was good.

Edith   It was better than the rope factory. I'd seen a woman get her hair caught up in the machine, nearly pulled her head off, that's what sent me to the yards. Can I have one of them gingery biscuits, Edna? I was glad to go there, not that it was much safer.

Edna   Foremen were gods, weren't they? Managers wore little hats. Like Hovis flour men. One of the foremen was called green bus, because he came along every ten minutes.

Edith   We liked to dodge the foremen, didn't we, Edna? To brew up a cup of tea, have a game of cards.

Edna   But it wasn't safe at the yards. The air was full of that stuff.

Edith White asbestos. We had no helmets. No earplugs.

Edna Thumping and clanging all the time.

Edith And there were so many ships to paint.

Edna Red ones, grey ones, and forget-me-not blue ones. Eau de nil, they called them. Half of Wallsend was painted with eau de nil.

Edith It's a nice colour in a bathroom.

Edna Tell her about your leg.

Edith Oh, yes. When I left the yard I had some vouchers to spend. Everyone got a gold watch, or vouchers, and because I'd stayed there so long I got quite a few vouchers. We went on holiday, didn't we, Edna? To Bruges. Nearly choked on an open sandwich.

Edna But she had some money left over. She kept it in an account.

Edith Look. Outside the window. See my little garden. It's only a square of earth, but I decided to take up a hobby, gardening, so I bought this rose bush. It looked wonderful in the picture. Bright red.

Edna A bright red rose.

Edith It was just a little stalk at first, but I watered it, and cared for it, and blow me, it grew fast!

Edna But it didn't grow roses. Oh no.

Edith It was the thorniest-looking thing you've ever seen.

Edna Do you want filling up? Do you know she's over ninety? The Queen will be launching her soon. Me? I'm only eighty-seven.

Edith (*Warming to her story*) Then, one morning, I went out and it had one rose blooming, and I swear it was the same colour we'd painted the ships all those years.

Edna   Red lead.

Edith   So I went up to it, to smell it. Well, I'm not lying to you, it smelt of the yards, of rust, and ships.

Edna   That's right.

Edith   Then, just as I was leaning over it, it went and scratched me.

Edna   On her leg. Look!

Edith   I stuck a plaster on it. Dab of Dettol, like you do. Didn't make a fuss.

Edna   But...

Edith   It didn't end there. Oh no. After a few days it was throbbing really badly, so I peeled off the plaster to have a look. I showed it to you, didn't I, Edna?

Edna   Get yourself to the doctor straight away, I said!

Edith   What did you say? How many women worked at the shipyards? Oh, I don't know. It varied.

Edna   Two, three hundred at the height of it.

Edith   Well, I went to the doctor and she slapped this blue stuff all over it. I came home after and I remember that was the day that Swan Hunter's went to the receivers because I watched it on the television with my leg up on the poofee.

Edna   That band Dire Straits were on at the City Hall.

Edith   I was in dire straits! Soon I couldn't walk.

Edna   And the doctor had to come to her!

Edith   Mrs Armstrong, he said.

Edna That's her married name. Before she was Lamb.

Edith We'd better have you in the hospital.

Edna Can you believe it?

Edith Next thing I know, I'm having a general anaesthetic.

Edna They were whispering amputation in the corridors.

Edith When I come round it's all bandaged up. Huge and white like a balloon. We thought that was the end of it.

Edna Oh no.

Edith When they take off the bandage it's turned the most awful colour. Green and yellow and purple. Have you got to go already? Have another cup. Go on!

Pause.

Edith You see, the doctors didn't know what was going on.

Edna So they radiated her. They nuked her leg with radiation, and that, thank God, seemed to be that! Meanwhile, as her best friend, I felt duty bound to act. I got an axe and set about the rose bush with a passion. When the blade struck it, there were sparks. I burnt it, in a big fire in the yard, and it stank of solder. In its place, while Edith was still in hospital, I planted forget-me-nots.

Edith When I got home, I just sat by that window, watching the forget-me-nots growing. They grew so fiercely. Then I realised what the colour was.

Edna Eau de nil! The Waters of the Nile.

Edith My little patch was a blaze of blue.

Edna The problems at the yard were getting very bleak. It was so quiet. Nothing moving. No ships, nothing.

Edith Until the last employee turned out the lights. Did you see his picture in the *Sunday Sun*?

Pause

Edith   One night we went outside to watch the sunset.

Edna   Sky was as pink as a prawn.

Edith   And a flock of seagulls flew down and ate the forget-me-nots, stalks and all, leaving just the bare earth, and me stuck in the chair, waving a dishcloth at them, screeching. They didn't take any heed, they flew right over Swan Hunters.

Edna   They flew down there, to where the cranes are. We just stood there with our mouths open.

Edith   And as the birds disappeared into the horizon, just for a moment we heard it again. We did. The shadows of the great ships.

Edna   The tarry, sweaty smell of work.

Edith   That was our lives you see, dear. Our best years.

Edna   Painting ships.

The End

Venetia Love Goes Netting

I was on chemotherapy when I wrote this play, and feeling very vague. Max Roberts, Artistic Director at Live Theatre, wanted me to take part in a two-part evening of monologues written by writers with a connection to the North East, and the playwright and screenwriter Lee Hall was facilitating the project.

At the time I was also working on a project with the Alzheimer's Society with the photographer Sharon Bailey. We would spend time in day clubs or just talking to carers or people with dementia. It was peaceful, interesting work, and it suited my state of mind, as I was a bit blurred at the edges myself.

I was interested, as I always have been, in the voice of older women; the person that no one sees, and her view on the world. I also felt very moved by the plight of those whose partners suffered from Alzheimer's, often completely changing the personality of the sufferer. This was the beginning of my pre-occupation with the plight of the longhand letter. Venetia was a Post Mistress and symbolises the whole feeling of the British Post Office, which is, I believe, a cultural institution, not a business.

Anyway, I cobbled a few pages together in between sleeps and visits to the world of dementia (We even went to look at brain scans at the local hospital. They look like sliced cauliflowers.) Max and Lee liked the play, and Jeremy Herrin, who directed it, introduced me to Madeleine Moffat, an actor who I have worked with many times since, and who managed to convey the essence of Venetia Love with great skill.

Julia Darling

Venetia Love Goes Netting was first produced at Live Theatre, Newcastle upon Tyne, as part of *NE1* on 30 November 2000. It was later presented as part of *NE1* at Newcastle Theatre Royal from 7-9 June 2001. It was directed by Paul James (Live Theatre production) and Jeremy Herrin (Theatre Royal production) and designed by Perry John Hudson.

CAST

Venetia Love   Madeleine Moffat

The monologue takes place in a sitting room. There is a computer set up on one side, looking out of place, and a more old-fashioned desk on the other. There are photos of a smiling husband and son and ornamental snowstorms on a shelf. Venetia Love is rather prim, and buttoned-up. She's in her sixties. The monologue begins with her reading a letter, glancing irritably at the computer as if she is trying to ignore it.

Venetia reads aloud as she writes:

Dear True Bloom Magazine,

Thank you for your ridiculous communication, which I received this morning, and your magnanimous invitation to attend the champagne evening in Birtley. Unfortunately, I will not be attending this function as I am otherwise engaged. Just because I have recently retired does not mean I have all the time in the world to waste. I shall not be subscribing to your magazine for older ladies as I am far too busy reading more substantial literature to read badly written articles about bladders, or wrinkle creams. Not all older women are obsessed with their families either. Some of us have brains. Please stop sending me junk mail and entering me for your prize draw. I do not want a million pounds. My job at the Post Office has left me with a perfectly good pension. Actually, I find your letters insulting. Maybe it's hard for you to comprehend, but I DON'T WANT ANYTHING!

I enclose my form with the word NO underlined in black ink in the appropriate box.

Yours Truly, Venetia Love

She folds up the letter and puts it into an envelope in a post-mistressy way. Then looks viciously at the computer.

I was sitting at the table eating a Marks and Spencer teacake when a white van pulled up outside and a woman got out, with a furrowed expression and a map. She stared at my front door enthusiastically. I made no effort to get up. I don't believe in moving whilst eating. She opened the back of the van and pulled out a box and staggered to my front door with it. I was just chewing the last bit of toasted teacake when the doorbell rang and I slowly went to answer it, my heart sinking.

'Hello,' she says. 'I've got a surprise for you, Mrs Love.'

'I'm sorry,' I said. I hate surprises.

'It's a present from your son in Australia,' she says.

'Who, Ewan? It's not my birthday.'

'It's a computer. So you can keep in touch. He thought you'd appreciate it. If you don't mind, this box is heavy.'

Then she bustles past me, her face rather red, and plonks it down in the middle of the floor.

'Where do you want it?' she says.

'Hang on a minute!'

She swings round and holds out her hand. 'Eliza Perks, Computers for Older Women. He's paid for some training too. I'll just set it up today, then we'll work out when I can come and teach you how to use it.'

I'm quite flabbergasted. Before I can protest this, Ms Perks is on her hands and knees with plugs and polystyrene all over the floor.

'I wouldn't mind a cup of tea,' she says, 'If you're offering. Milk, two sugars.'

Then I'm boiling the kettle, and it's nearly five o clock, and I've got things to do.

'Excuse me,' I say. 'I'm going out. I've got to go and see someone.'

'Nearly finished,' she says, and takes the mug from me and sips away, looking at the computer with a pleased expression on her face.

'What if I don't want it?' I say.

'It's the latest model,' she says, 'You'd be daft, Mrs Love. Look, I'll give you a phone on Monday about the sessions.' Then she has one last gulp and she's off.

When I get back, it's still there, squatting in the front room, smelling of offices. What on earth was Ewan thinking of? Why didn't he ask me first? It's just typical, I'm thinking, just typical of his lazy attitude to things. Keep Mother happy, buy her a computer, then maybe she'll stop writing me boring letters. Poor old Mum, nothing to do. Let's buy her something.

She's furious now and picks up her pen.

Dear Ms Perks of Computers For Older Women,

I am writing to ask you to take away the computer which you delivered yesterday. I have thought carefully about the uses of the internet and so on, and please don't imagine that I am incapable of using a computer as I was well acquainted with information technology as part of my work at the Post Office. In fact, I attended several training courses, although I must admit that I found them immensely boring, mostly run by people with small eyes wearing cheap suits who had no grammatical skills at all. I shall be writing to my son to thank him for this unwanted gift and to tell him that I would far rather receive a letter than a casually written email.

She puts down her pen.

But he wants everything done quickly. He won't write anything down. I think that's why he lives in Australia where they are always running towards the sea, always active. And of course he wanted to get away from us. It was all too much for him.

She writes again.

I really don't want this computer at all. It's cluttering up my front room, and causing me unnecessary stress.
   I believe in the longhand letter, Ms Perks, and do not wish to engage with cyberspace. I prefer to keep my feet well on the ground, thank you very much !

Yours, Venetia Love

PS Don't you think COW is an unfortunate abbreviation for your organisation?

She throws a blanket over the computer. She begins to look through a box of letters.

I keep all my letters. I just like to know that they exist, that they are in a box at the back of my wardrobe. I wouldn't say that I read them often, but I like to touch them. They feel exquisitely private. My life is in that box. There are letters from people who died long ago, tender letters, angry letters, letters filled with feelings.

She closes the box and puts it away.

Don't misunderstand me. I am not addled by nostalgia, although lately the past comes over me like a net. I try not to indulge myself in it too often. I think it's a side effect of retirement. I am post-everything now. Post-Post Office, post-menopausal, post-millennium, and there are no more posts to pass. Just one straight track to the finishing post. Gallop, gallop, gallop. Or perhaps hobbledee, hobbledee, as I'm in no hurry. No, on the whole I try to ration looking backwards. It's probably unhealthy.

I got an invitation a couple of days ago, asking me if I would like to go on a coach trip to Scarborough with a crowd of elderly ex-postal workers. Perhaps I would have said yes if my friend from High Heaton was going, but she's moved away, and without her it would just be a trip for old people. No, I couldn't go. I have realised that there are very few people I really like. I am sure that some of them would drink too much and become saucy, with slipped lipstick and blurred eyes and whoops, where's that banana? kind of talk. Old women can be very lewd.

My God, it's five already? I have to go. Let's hope it's better today.

The next day. She picks up a letter from the mat.

Hand-written, black ink, Newcastle postmark. Hmmmm.

She opens it.

Dear Mrs Love,

Thank you for your letter. I am sorry that you don't like your son's gift. As I said, he had arranged a series of training days for you, and I seriously think that you would enjoy the computer once you got going. Perhaps if I ran through a few things with you then you might be persuaded. But of course there is no problem if you want to return it.

You say you are a great letter writer, and I am sure that you have boxes of old letters that you keep under the bed and at the back of your wardrobe. I wonder what will happen to them after you die? Have you thought about that? Maybe your son will have to sort them out ? It's not much fun, sorting out someone else's memories.

By the way, I didn't mention it when I was at your house, but I collect snowstorms too. I have two hundred and thirty. How many have you got?

Let me know when we can come and collect the computer, or perhaps you might let me show you some of its wonderful corridors first.

All the best, Eliza Perks

PS I thought COW was rather funny. Obviously not your kind of humour.

She laughs and sits down at her letter-writing desk.

Dear Eliza,

Any day will do, although I am out every day between five and seven. I enjoyed your letter very much, and appreciate you replying to me so quickly. I find very few people reply to long-hand letters these days. They seem to find it too much of an ordeal. I see what you mean about keeping letters. The past does clutter up our lives. But then, what is the point of collecting snowstorms? Or keeping anything for that matter? Frankly, I don't care about what happens when I die. They can throw the whole lot in the bin.

By the way I have two hundred and sixty snow storms. I've been collecting since 1958. I never tire of watching the flakes swirling, then falling. My favourite one is from China, a little couple sitting together on a bench beneath a tree. A dear friend gave it to me and it always brings a lump to my throat.

Back to the letters. It is perhaps rather arrogant to think that one's history is important, but I like to reflect upon my life's correspondence in much the same way as I like to shake snowstorms.

Yours, Venetia Love

She puts the pen down, licks the envelope and puts a stamp on it.

There is something decent about a letter, its firmness, its privacy, the sound it makes when it falls from the letterbox to the mat, the assertiveness of a stamp, the postmark, the stiff oblong of the envelope. Something English about the sealing, the licking, and the sticking down.

And it's not just letters with their firm words forever scratched on paper, it's the Post Office itself, which is, I would say, a country of its own. With red post boxes that don't change, that stand like decent men on street corners, decent, reliable men who won't be late or stand you up. Rodney was like that. You knew exactly where you were with him. He always looked as if he'd just been painted.

And the postmen, trudging the dirty streets with sacks over their shoulders, carrying the post to every single person's door, and patient post mistresses who watch on while old ladies fumble with their pension books and giros. The Post Office, if I might be overwhelmingly sentimental, and why not as I'm alone here and can say exactly what I like now I have retired, with no hobbies to speak of, the Post Office is the TRUE England. You meet decent people in the Post Office, even if I don't want to go on coach trips with them. It is neat and careful, with valiant mail trains that thunder through the night, and very few corrupt postmen if you compare it to the police force.

I am mad. I sound mad. I am a batty old post mistress, High Heaton branch. Never once closed for sickness. Awarded most efficient post office counter in the North East 1996.

Ewan. I must write to Ewan.

Dear Ewan,

Thank you very much for the computer which arrived last week. Of course I appreciate the thought, but I'm afraid I shall be returning it. It's just not my kind of thing. You should have consulted me first.

   I haven't heard from you personally for over six weeks now. Are you dead? If not, do you have any plans to visit England? Your father is much the same as ever, but perhaps seeing you might help.

   As for me, I have just finished reading Pat Barker's trilogy. We did it in my book club. I thoroughly enjoyed it. Could you please send me some Australian stamps, I would be interested. Give the children my love. How are they getting on at school? A photograph would be nice.

From YOUR MOTHER

From your displeased, ignored, martyred MOTHER.

She wakes up in the middle of the night, from a nightmare.

I was dreaming. The sky was all black and heavy and I looked up and it was all full of words, waiting to be pulled down onto someone's screen. It was so heavy with all those unused words, waiting to be sentenced. Then I looked around me and I was in a crowd and everyone around me was empty and vacant, with their mouths open, and their eyes glazed and stupid, as if they had no words at all. Nothing.

(*To the computer*) You want me don't you? You want all the old people. We're useless without you. Ga ga, holding up the queues, getting in the way of progress. That's what you think. I want Ewan, not an ugly grey machine. I want my son, do you hear me?

She cries.

The next day. She's putting on a hat.

Five o'clock is Roddy time. Unfortunately, my husband has lost his mind. I've seen the scans. I still look for flickers in his eyes. Anyone would. I search for him in the swirl of flakes. He says I LOVE YOU, again and again, but he says it to everyone, even the cleaner.

In the back of my wardrobe there are letters from my husband. Letters that state in black and white that he loved me and only me. LOVE IN BLACK INK. I like to read them to him sometimes, those early tender love letters. I like to read them to myself.

But before you get your hankies all wet, those are not the only love letters that I keep. There was my friend Helen from the Post Office, who has moved away. She wrote a delightful letter, in a beautiful hand. The relationship ended when Roddy began to ebb away. That's what happens. You look around one day and everyone has gone. Ewan, Helen, Roddy, and all you've got is a box of letters.

So every day at five o'clock I catch the 42 bus to Longbenton, where Roddy sits. As I walk into the room, they are usually playing war songs. There is a circle of floral armchairs, and a trolley with cups and saucers and fairy cakes. Look, Roddy, says the care assistant, it's your wife, Venetia. Hello, Venetia! How are you today? Roddy stares into space, a plate resting on his knees. I take his hand, which is warm and dry, and I squeeze it. How has he been today? I ask. Not bad, they tell me. He ate his lunch. He went for a little walk with Alfie, and then we watched a film.

The people that look after him are genuine, caring people. I don't know how they manage that kind of patience. I couldn't. He's been there for over a year. I couldn't cope at home. Not after Ewan went to Australia. Rodney didn't know who I was. He thought I was a burglar sometimes. He even hit me. Then he would run away with no clothes on. Things like that. If you had known him before... he would hate himself if he knew.

The next day.

I was waiting for Eliza to come round. I had put all my best snowstorms on display. Dare I say it, I was excited. I had even got some wine in the fridge, just in case Eliza liked a tipple in the afternoon.

The doorbell rings, and I go to answer it, and standing there is a man with overalls on, and a big face. Who on earth are you? Alf, he says. I've come to collect the computer. But where is Eliza? I ask. She hurt her back, he says, carrying things. Is she alright? Oh yes, she just didn't want to hump things about. She sent a note. He pulls an envelope from his pocket and watches me as I read it.

Dear Venetia, it says. Sorry, I had to send Alf. I am available for snowstorm comparisons, discussions, computer training and afternoon tea, but not lifting heavy boxes. Yours, Eliza.

I stare at Alf. I am disappointed.
Shall I come in? he says.
No, I say. I've changed my mind. I want to be trained.
You could have phoned, missus, he says. I've come all the way from Killingworth.
I only just changed my mind, I mumble. It would be stupid to look a gift horse in the mouth, wouldn't it?
If you say so, says Alf, who looks rather like a horse. And off he hobbles.

She goes to the computer, starting to take off its blanket.

So you and I are going to get to have to get to know each other. Are you happy now?

The next day. Eliza is in the kitchen.

Have some cake, Eliza. It's on the side!

Eliza lives on her own, she tells me, with her snowstorms. She never married. Actually, she's a lesbian. Strange, I have never said that word before... LESBIAN. Together, we have nearly five hundred snowstorms.

I let her turn on the computer. I just sit and nod while she fiddles with the mouse, and tells me about icons, windows, cursors and all the rest of it. I like the way she gets on with things. She has no time for the past, for regretting. I told her about Rodney while we created a letterhead. That's a pain, says Eliza, you must run out of things to say to him. I do, I said. It's not my husband sitting there. It's just someone that looks like him.

We type the word 'snowstorm' and start to surf. There are snowstorm enthusiasts all over the world. They have conventions. Go on, she says, get your fingers going. Let's go. Let's do a bit of flirting in a chat room. Really, I said. I don't think...

Venetia, she said, you're just a silly sausage.

No one has ever said that to me in my life before. A silly sausage. You can find out anything you want from this computer. See it like a door, she says.

And she laughs, a big, generous, hot laugh, and I laugh too. And then I said it. Eliza, I said, it's not information I want. It's love.

I can't believe I said that.

You can find that too, she said. Then she kissed me. She tasted delicious. Of cake crumbs.

How long is the training? I said. Unlimited, says Eliza.

That's when I opened the champagne left over from my silver wedding anniversary. That's when I really started to surf.

She is sitting in the care home.

You see, love, Ewan sent me a computer. I was going to send it

back, but then I started thinking about all the stuff we've got.
You can get rid of a lot of stuff once you get going on the
computer, Rodney. I mean, you don't dwell in the past, do you,
Roddy. All you've got is this place, the bed and the chair, and the
table. A fairy cake sometimes, a cup of tea. And breathing. We've
all got that. In and out, our hearts pumping. I was getting tired of
hanging onto everything. I just want to let it go, all those words
and memories, to let it float up into the sky and stay there. I don't
love you any less.

I'm still here. If you feel a sudden absence, or you wonder where
I am, I'm not far away, just free falling for a bit. Just pulling in
the net to see what's there. There's no harm in letting go.

She leaves.

The End

The Last Post

The Last Post was commissioned by Live Theatre in collaboration with Elements, a project from Durham County Council which aimed to tour new plays to rural venues. I had been involved in an Arts Council-funded Year of the Artist residency with the Post Office, and had spent some time talking to Post Office workers and sorting offices, and thinking about the role of the long-hand letter versus emails and other forms of communication.

It was an interesting project, that started with the short play *Venetia Love Goes Netting*, then expanded into the touring play, *The Last Post*, then was used in part to create episodes of *Posties* for BBC Radio 4. The stage play was well received, and the set by Imogen Cloet was particularly beautiful and ingenious. The play explores the lives of characters involved with letters: an elderly postman who is mugged and whose wife starts writing letters to God, an asylum seeker who is befriended by an elderly woman when a lovesick postman starts chucking all her letters through the asylum seeker's door and a young girl who never writes letters.

I have always loved letters, even the smell of them! I am sad that we are losing this contemplative way of communicating, in favour of faster methods. I think many people feel the same, and the play seemed to touch people who saw it.

Julia Darling

The Last Post was produced by Live Theatre and was first performed at Bishop Auckland Town Hall on 22 March 2002 and then toured to sixteen venues in North Yorkshire, County Durham, Tyneside and Cumbria. It was directed by Jeremy Herrin and designed by Imogen Cloet.

CAST

James	Donald McBride
Milosh	Gez Casey
Merrill	Madeleine Moffat
Winifred	Judi Earl
Tilly	Sharon Percy
Kenny	Joe Caffrey

PROLOGUE

James is delivering letters. He trudges around methodically. Lights down.

As he walks around he recites a poem, based on WH Auden's poem Night Mail.

I am a postman at the end of a round
Consigned to Consignia, cyber bound,
I'm a museum, I'm an antique,
Carrying letters to the old and weak.
Pulling up to the West, a steady climb
I've got Postman's Knee, but I get there on time.
Trudging past progress, from door to door
Delivering post to the rich and poor.
Got blocked sinuses, but I don't stop.
Taking the mail to each office and shop.
Old women watch me, they smile and they wave,
I'm a piece of the past, keeping them safe.
Dogs growl and bark, but I plod on
Bringing the post to everyone.

The sack lightens, the round is done
Down to the depot I descend
Through the muddle of the city, droning
with progress, the apparatus
of English days. Where communication
is a cloud of words, scattering like birds
Alighting on the lines, then flown again, gone.

(The other actors join in)
There are letters of thanks, letters from banks,
Complaining letters, chain letters from cranks,
Hospital appointments, the results of tests,
Letters from North and South and West.

Love letters, junk mail, invitations,
Letters from strangers and lost relations,
Photographs, postal orders, magazines, cards,
Soft pink letters, some white and hard,
Or crumpled brown, re-directed,
Letters that tell you 'You have been selected'
Old lady letters with curly 'l's,
Letters that tempt you, letters that sell.

Broadsheets, circulars, statements, notes,
Postcards of beaches, blue skies and boats.
The letters that daughters write to their mothers
Bookclubs, catalogues, plastic covered,

CDs, free gifts, questionnaires,
A personal letter from Tony Blair,
The clever, the stupid, the short and the long
The typed, the franked, the spelt all wrong.

(James by himself)
Treasure me in my orange coat,
For when I'm gone, they'll be nothing of note
To brighten the morning, to fall on the mat,
My life has been letters, but enough of that.
We are all asleep, in the steam of our days
The letters are fading. Consignia says
We must move with the times, speed on, think quick,
Send our thoughts out like arrows and hope they stick.

But we may wake soon and hope for letters,
And none will hear the postman's knock
Without a quivering of the heart.
For who can bear to feel themselves forgotten?

ACT ONE

SCENE ONE

Enter Milosh, holding a letter. He looks confused and worried. He has a bag with him.

Milosh   Number 31.

He shows her the letter.

Merrill   Mmmm.

Milosh   Endless Street.

Merrill   Sorry?

Milosh   Sorry.

Merrill   What's that you've got? A letter? This says 31 Endless Street.

Milosh   Yes.

Merrill   So!

Milosh   So.

Merrill   You must be new to the area?

Milosh shrugs. He doesn't know what she's on about.

Merrill   That's the river down here.

Milosh   River.

Merrill   The town centre's that way, Woolworths and so on. Over there: allotments, vegetables, old men. See that dog, it's called Baby, it's vicious, should be put down. That's our corner shop, best bajis in the West. And there's the postie, she'll be going by number 31. I didn't think anyone lived there to be honest with you. Manky curtains! Where are you from?

Milosh shrugs again, bewildered.

Merrill   You could have made an effort to learn English before you arrived. And what are you doing here anyway? I hope you're not a terrorist or something.

Milosh smiles, then breaks out of the conversation.

Milosh   Dear Anna,
Let me write to you of this dark town. They put me on a coach in London after the time in the detainment centre. They said we must all be dispersed. So I have been dispersed to the North and given accommodation. Picture me, if you can, with my old blue holdall, standing at the bottom of a long hill, with redbrick houses stacked either side of it. A woman in her seventies approaches me. I would say she had a thyroid problem. She is certainly arthritic. She takes the notification of my accommodation and starts waving it about, talking all the while. Her words sound like barks. It starts to rain. In the distance I can hear a siren. She points with her stick up the hill, and on I go, hearing her voice behind me. I think she is telling me to go back to where I came from. But maybe not. Perhaps she is telling me she is delighted to see me, and she hopes I enjoy myself here in...

He looks at the envelope.

Both   Endless Street.

Merrill   That way, up there on the right! Could you do something about the wheelie bin?

Milosh is marching on.

Merrill   The bin on wheels. It's fallen over. In the back lane! It's unhygienic. And you could do with a wash and all. Bloody scrounger.

SCENE TWO

Winifred and James are at home. He is getting ready for work, putting on his postie's jacket. Winifred is busy doing something worthy.

Winifred I've done you some salmon paste, love.

James What? It's Thursday. I have corned beef on Thursdays.

Winifred But you like salmon paste.

James Aye, on Fridays I like salmon paste. On Thursdays I like corned beef.

Winifred How can you like something on one day and not on another? I haven't got time to make any more.

James kneels down to polish his boots.

James Think me boots are going to need seeing to, Winnie. The tongue's coming undone.

Winifred Wear your brown boots.

James What? On the other hand it might last...

Winifred You've only got another month before you retire. It doesn't matter, does it?

James I don't want to throw away a good pair of boots.

Winifred Well, don't then. Keep them.

James But the tongue's coming undone.

Winifred I don't know. You decide.

James Do you think I might get lazy feet, when I retire?

Winifred Is that a medical term, like? Lazy feet?

James You know what I mean. Your feet spread out. I've got good feet. Firm instep. Thanks to the boots, like.

Winifred It's not as if you're going to stop walking about when you retire. Are you?

James   No, no, course not. (*Looks worried*) Bye, love.

He kisses her, as he must have done a million times before, and leaves. Winifred sits down with a pad of writing paper. We get the feeling this is part of her routine.

Winifred (*Aloud*) Dear God, Today, as I am sure you know, I am making jam for the Save the Roof Fund.

I find with jam that it can go either way. I mean, it's a matter of seconds before it gets too thick, and there's nothing worse than hard jam. So, God, I'm writing to see if you could oversee things and help me get the right consistency. Also, help me to not have competing feelings about Mrs Clodhorn's marmalade. Thanks.

Look after James at work and keep an eye on the church roof while we're raising funds. That's all for today. Your true Winifred

SCENE THREE

Sorting at the Post Office. James is walking up and down putting letters into boxes and sacks. The radio is on playing brass band music. Tilly comes in and changes it to Radio One.

James   Who changed that?

Tilly   It's only me.

James   That was Billie Hays and his big band sound.

Tilly   It does my head in, it's like wallpaper paste or something. Thick and squidgy.

James   I always have that programme on. But if it does your head in...

Tilly   Alright, alright. I'm new. I didn't know.

James   You're late anyway.

Tilly   It's not my fault, had a telling off with Squires this morning, outlining the areas I need to improve. Everything, really. Where am I supposed to be?

James   You're over there (*Points to where she's supposed to be working*) on the mail sort. What did you do?

Tilly   I was delivering a parcel, see, and they weren't in. But the window was open, so I chucked it through.

James   That's not what you're supposed to do, is it?

Tilly   Yeah, right. Well I did. Anyway, I knocked over the fish bowl, didn't I, and the little fish fell onto the carpet and was wriggling about on the floor.

James   It wouldn't have been able to...

Tilly   Yeah, right, breathe. Then I had a brainwave. There was this ginger tom in the garden, so I chucked the cat in the window too and the cat ate the goldfish.

James   Dear oh dear, that's not the right procedure, is it?

Tilly   But it's quite funny though.

James   What happened then?

Tilly   I ran off. People came back, found a wet packet, a pile of goldfish bones and a strange cat. How was I supposed to know it was unspayed? They hate cats apparently, allergic. It was next door's.

James   There are ways of doing things, see. What's your name
again?

Tilly   Tilly.

James   Aye, Tilly, procedures you're supposed to follow.

Tilly   Oh yeah, la la, I said I was sorry.

James   It's not right.

Pause.

Tilly   Where's that other bloke? The young one?

James   Who? Kenny? He's due in.

Tilly   He's dead quiet, isn't he?

James   Nice and quiet, yes.

Tilly   He's got a picture of Frankie Curtis in his locker.

James   Who's Frankie Curtis when he's at home?

Tilly   SHE. A singer from Glasgow.

James   Never heard of her.

Tilly   Well, Kenny has. She's coming to the City Hall.

James   What kind of music? Hippy hoppy?

Tilly   No, she writes really good lyrics and she wears a balaclava. She's like a cult.

James   I beg your pardon!

Tilly   A cult. C-u-l-t.

James   You should listen to Billie Hays. That's proper music. Big music.

Tilly doesn't seem to be doing much. She starts reading The Courier, *a Post Office newspaper.*

Tilly   Here, look at this. You write poems, don't you?

James   Sometimes I do. Who told you that?

Tilly   They were talking about you in the canteen.

James   Oh, talking about me, were they?

Tilly   Don't look so worried. It's a poetry competition. Look.

James   A poetry competition?

Tilly   You win money. It gets displayed in post offices all over the country. You only have to write about the post, letters or stamps or anything. That's right up your street, that is.

James   I'm just an amateur.

Tilly   Well, I don't know anything about poetry but there's the address.

James   Well, maybe I will.

Enter Kenny, stamping and frozen.

James   There's Kenny!

Kenny   Christ, I'm knackered. Got blisters the size of stamps all over me heel.

James   Look at your footwear! Trainers! D'you want a plaster? I always carry plasters. Here, give us your foot.

Kenny   You wouldn't want to see my foot.

James   You should get better shoes.

Tilly   Hiya. I'm Tilly.

Kenny   Hiya. I'm Kenny.

Tilly   Hey, Frankie Curtis!

Kenny   Aaah, Frankie Curtis.

Tilly   Have you got *Blistered Womb*?

Kenny   Yeah, I just bought the live CD. *Cross Wired and...*

Tilly   *Velvet.* I want that CD so bad.

Kenny   I'll make you a copy, if you like.

James picks a bunch of letters that he's sorting.

James   Who's doing Endless Street?

Tilly   Don't talk about Endless Street.

Kenny   I'm the regular on Endless Street.

James   Got one here for Merrill, Endless Street. Been in dead mail, waiting for weeks. Is that one of yours?

Kenny   Rings a bell. Let's have a look at it.

James   It's airmail. Indian.

Kenny   I think it's Fisher. Number 12 Endless Street. She gets a lot of airmail. I'll take it round.

James   What about this one? To GOD?

Kenny   Chuck it in with the Santas!

James   Frankly, I don't think Santa and God are the same at all.

Kenny   Don't worry about it, James. Put it in the file anyway.

James   (*Pause*) I don't know, I'll have to think about it carefully. I've, er, volunteered to be Santa this year, it being my last year. So it's me who's going to have to face this question. I mean, there's Jack Frost and the Tooth Fairy, you could say they were Santa equivalents. But God, that's quite another matter.

Tilly and Kenny exchange glances.

Well, I suppose it can go in there for the time being. Look at these letters. No surnames, no postcodes. What are people thinking? A lost letter, you know, like a vague, it keeps me awake at night, just thinking about it, lying there in the dark.

Kenny   Don't think about it.

Tilly   What's a vague anyway?

Kenny   A letter without a postcode.

James   They go in this docket. And dead mail waiting, those are the letters that have no hope. They keep on coming back, can't find a home for them.

Tilly   Oh, I see. Can I open them?

James   No! Course you can't! Those are Her Majesty's.

Tilly   Nobody wants them though. I don't see why you're getting so up a height about it all.

James   Because it's my duty, that's why! I mean, no one really cares any more, do they? It's just a job to you lot.

Tilly   Er, yeah.

Pause. Kenny and Tilly want to change the subject, and cheer James up.

Kenny   Written any poems lately, James?

James   I suppose you're going to scoff at that and all.

Kenny   No, James. You've been here much longer than we have. You've got a different attitude, that's all.

James   I certainly have.

Kenny   Sorry, James.

James   Tilly here just showed me this competition in *The Courier*.

Kenny   Looks good, right up your street. Poems about any aspect of the Post Office! You should definitely go in for that.

James   How about this one?

James starts getting out a notebook. We get the feeling that he is always performing his slightly strange poems. Kenny looks alarmed and nudges Tilly.

Tilly   Look at that, it's lunchtime already!

Kenny   Put it into the competition, James.

SCENE FOUR

Tilly and Kenny are comparing phones in a pub.

Kenny   What I really want is a Motorola V666e tri-band for use in five continents.

Tilly   Five continents?

Kenny   You can phone people all over the world, send them messages. What have you got?

Tilly   Nokia 330. But how do you meet them? The people you send the messages to.

Kenny   Chat rooms. This one's got games on, look.

Tilly   Pretend people.

Kenny   They're not.

Tilly   Yeah they are, with made-up names. Old blokes pretending to be sixteen-year-olds.

Kenny   Doesn't matter. It's a laugh.

Tilly   How fast are you?

Kenny   What do you mean?

Tilly   Texting. How quick?

Kenny   Quite quick.

Tilly   You want to have a race?

Kenny   No.

Tilly   You're scared I'll beat you.

Kenny   No I'm not.

Tilly   What's your number?

They fiddle on, telling each other their numbers.

Tilly   Right, God Save the Queen. GO!

It's like a Western, with both of them trying to draw phones and write messages. Tilly's phone makes a 'message received' tone. She's the winner.

Tilly   Told you I was fast.

Kenny   I wasn't ready.

Tilly   That's what they all say. Frankie Curtis is coming to the City Hall.

Kenny   I know. Are you going?

Tilly   Am I going!

Kenny   I'll see you there, then.

Tilly   Excellent! Are you going on your own?

Kenny   Yeah.

Tilly   I'll go with you, if you like. Meet you outside.

Kenny   Yeah, alright. You get out much?

Tilly   Not much at the minute. I split up with me girlfriend.

Kenny   Oh, your girlfriend, right.

Tilly   She won't speak to us and none of her mates will either. She reckons I've been going behind her back, but I hadn't. Wish I had now.

Kenny   I hate that.

Tilly   You got a girlfriend?

Kenny   No, not at the minute.

Tilly   We're a right pair, you and me.

Kenny   Couple of Billy No Mates.

Her phone bleeps, so does Kenny's. It's like a gun draw again, but then they laugh.

Tilly   What's this? Go blo tut quoi?

They laugh.

Kenny   I've been looking for a new girlfriend, on the internet.

Tilly   What do you mean?

Kenny   Surfing about, looking for a girlfriend.

Tilly   Have you found one?

Kenny   I had a few email romances, that's all. You ever done that?

Tilly   I'm not that sad.

Kenny   It's just a bit of fun.

Tilly   But you don't touch anyone, do you? You just write about how you'd like to touch them. Stupid. I don't like writing things down, feelings and that. I had a crush on a teacher once. Really liked her. It was like carrying round this brick in my chest. They called her Mrs Caroo, Angela Caroo. She taught French. I thought I'd send her a postcard. It took ages writing this thing. I said something like, you are so sexy, Mrs Caroo, I think of you, blah blah.

Kenny   That's different, sending proper letters. Email's just a laugh.

Tilly   They didn't send emails all the time then. I was only fourteen, seven years ago.

Kenny   People keep letters, don't they?

Tilly   Yeah, well I started writing loads of them, just with little messages on and stuff. A few little presents. I didn't put my address on. I mean, it was harmless really. Then one day I got the whole lot back, in a jiffy bag with a really snooty letter from the police. Bloody cheek, like I was a pervert. She'd recognised my handwriting like, in French.

Kenny   Well, that couldn't happen with email. No one sees your handwriting.

Tilly   When you looked at them all together, hundreds and hundreds of them, they looked really stupid. I burnt them all in the garden. They smelt awful. Bloody Angela Caroo. So I left school, so that's why I haven't got any GCSEs. Bloody love letters. And they weren't even letters, just postcards of rabbits and cats and stuff.

Kenny   See, with email, she would have just deleted you or blocked you. You shouldn't have left the school just because of that.

Tilly   Well, I felt self-conscious, didn't I? Like everyone knew.

Kenny   But they didn't.

Tilly   Yeah they did. I told them. I've never been any good at keeping things to meself. And Angela Caroo left the school anyway. She married the PE teacher.

Kenny   They always marry the PE teacher.

Tilly   What about you?

Kenny   What about me?

Tilly   Your last girlfriend.

Kenny   I went out with this girl, Sally. She worked in a call centre. She talked on the phone all day, and then when she saw me, she'd say she didn't want to talk because it was like work. So we didn't.

Tilly   What?

Kenny   Didn't talk. We just sat in bars, drinking our drinks. Humming.

Tilly   Humming?

Kenny   You know, humming tunes. She never used to phone because she didn't like talking, so she used to text me. Said things like U R sweet, luv Sally.

Tilly   She liked you, then?

Kenny   But then the text messages got less and less, and the last one I got just said SAL, so I erased it. And then she was gone. I still don't know why really. I mean I erased her and everything. We just, ran out.

Tilly   Oh. Well, it's no good if you can't talk, is it?

Kenny   No, look at us, a couple of lonely posties.

Tilly   Carrying other people's letters around.

SCENE FIVE

A doorbell rings.

Kenny   Excuse me? Is there someone called Merrill here? It's the post.

Merrill   Is it the one with the good complexion? It's Kenny, isn't it? Come in, dear. What's that? A letter? Special delivery, is it?

Kenny   It was improperly addressed, missus, but I knew it was you. Not many Merrills up Endless Street.

Merrill   That's from my friend in India. Fancy writing that.

Doesn't make much sense. Merrill, Endless Street. No number, no postcode! He's not that good at writing is Mr Sujata.

Kenny   I recognised the airmail too. You get a lot of airmail.

Merrill   It's the Penpal Club. Look! Letters from all over the world.

She shows him a pile of letters on her desk.

Kenny   That's a hell of a lot of letters...

Merrill   It's nice when your postie knows who you are. Who's that other one? The small lass.

Kenny   Tilly. She's new.

Merrill   Poor girl. You can see her mind's not on the job.

Kenny   Would you mind signing this please, madam?

Merrill   You'll be going home now, I expect, to your family. It's late for a postman.

Kenny   I live on me own, in those flats round Cathedral Street.

Merrill   Housing Association?

Kenny   Yeah, single flats. Bit noisy like, town centre. You've got your letter then.

Merrill   I write back straight away, you know. Do you get letters?

Kenny   Yes, sometimes. Not often. I don't write them much.

Merrill   Not many people do these days.

Kenny   I send text messages. On the moby. CU @ 4 (*He signs it in the air*).

Merrill   Yes. Well it's not what I call a meaningful way of communicating. I like news, me.

Kenny   What kind of news?

Merrill   About other people's lives. Not round robins. Hate them, they go round too many people. I like the personal touch. I like someone who speaks to me, you know what I mean?

Kenny   I used to have a penpal once. From Germany. He wrote to me in English. It was a school thing. Wrote for years, and I wrote back. We were both growing up, about feelings and girls and stuff. Then the letters stopped. Just like that. I was about fifteen. Young for my age. Never found out what happened to him. Hans he was called. I didn't really know him in one way, though in another way I knew him better than anyone.

Merrill   Even better than your mother? Your brothers and sisters?

Kenny   I grew up in care, actually. Nice place.

Merrill   I see. And now you're a postman. I hate that, me, when the letters stop. It's like a death, even if they aren't dead. Makes me mad.

Kenny   I expect he just, lost interest, Hans. Perhaps he'd said everything.

Merrill   It leaves you guessing, doesn't it? I can give you some penpal addresses if you like. I've got a lovely young man in the Philippines.

Kenny   No thanks. I haven't got time. But thanks all the same.

He leaves.

Merrill   Oh (*Shouting down the stairs*) if you've got any old envelopes and stationery at all, I'm always grateful. Thanks for botherin'.

She sighs, resuming her writing.

SCENE SIX

James and Winifred's house. James is sitting at the table. Winifred is saying grace, but it's going on too long and James's food is getting cold.

Winifred And please may Mrs Barkforth next door get over her piles, and may Horace's medication start working.

James Winifred, love.

Winifred May the Lord deliver us...

James Have we got any ketchup?

Winifred From evil, for thine is the kingdom, the power and the glory...

James Isn't that enough now, Winifred? The food... Please, Winifred.

She stops and glares at him.

Winifred Amen!

James It's just a month now, Winifred. I'll be home all the time then. I was thinking about, er, changes, love. I've been writing off to places.

Winifred What kind of places?

James I thought we could live somewhere different. I thought, love, we could maybe go to the Isle of Wight.

Winifred Isle of Wight? What for?

James There's a lot of older people there, lovely gardens, change of scenery. We haven't got any grandchildren. We could retire there, to a bungalow.

Winifred A bungalow?

James No stairs, see. It would be easier for when we get much older. Soil's good in the Isle of Wight. What do you think?

Winifred I'm quite happy here, James. I've got my friends. The church.

James   There's other churches, other friends.

Winifred I was born here.

James   So was I, but I was thinking, when I retire, it would be good to explore somewhere different. You could write to your friends.

Winifred How ridiculous.

James   Look at the pictures, Winifred. A bungalow in Shanklin. We could sell this place.

Winifred You've been planning this for ages.

James   Not actually planning anything, love, just researching.

Winifred I wouldn't be able to visit Clara.

James   Clara wouldn't mind. She would come and see us. You could write.

Winifred No, James. I won't move. I don't like distance.

James   Distance? But I'd be there, Winifred. We'd be together, you and me. Near. Very near.

Winifred I'll ask for guidance.

James   But he's everywhere, isn't he, God? You can ask him for guidance from the Isle of Wight.

Winifred He might not like the Isle of Wight.

James   I'm sure he'll like the Isle of Wight as much as he likes the North East, my love.

Winifred I don't like islands.

James   But this is an island. England is an island. This house is an island. We are an island, you and me!

Winifred There's no need to shout.

James   It's just you don't hear what I'm saying, my love!

Winifred I hear you alright. It's what you say that's the problem. Moving's not going to help that, is it?

James   But it might.

Winifred You could come to church with me.

James   I don't like church.

Winifred And I don't like the Isle of Wight. And another thing, you may be retiring, but I'm NOT.

SCENE SEVEN

Kenny and Tilly have just been to see Frankie Curtis. They are excited by the concert, sitting in a bar somewhere.

Tilly   She looked at me, right in the middle of that song, straight into my eyes. Do you think I could get her phone number?

Kenny   Be ex-directory. She looked at me too. She's bisexual, you know.

Tilly   They always say that. I didn't see her looking at you.

Kenny   Well she did.

Tilly   She had dark glasses on.

Kenny   Well, how do you know she was looking at you?

Tilly   I just did. We should have gone backstage.

Kenny   I'm not a groupie.

Tilly   Yeah you are. I bet you've got pictures of her stuck up on your bedroom wall.

Kenny   One poster! I'm a fan, not a groupie.

Tilly   Yeah, yeah.

Kenny   It's her music I like.

Tilly   Oh yeah. What's wrong with being a groupie?

Kenny   I've got other fish to fry.

Tilly   Oooh Kenny! What do you mean?

Kenny   If I tell you, will you keep it a secret?

Tilly   Why?

Kenny   I like things to be private. I mean, I trust you.

Tilly   I won't say a word.

Kenny   I met someone.

Tilly   Who?

Kenny   A woman. A real woman. Not a virtual woman.

Tilly   Where?

Kenny   Tesco's.

Tilly   Tesco's. D'you pick someone up?

Kenny   She picked me up. She's called Shona.

Tilly   You're kidding.

Kenny   She just came up to me. I was by the tropical fruit.

Tilly   What were you doing there?

Kenny   Looking at a pomegranate.

Tilly   When was this?

Kenny   Couple of nights ago. I went up there late. It was after midnight, late-night shopping.

Tilly   To buy a pomegranate?

Kenny   I couldn't sleep. I'm in this pattern. I get up at four, do my round, get home at two, then I sleep until about eight-ish, then I don't know what to do. I don't want to get drunk because of getting up so early.

Tilly   So you go up to Tesco's at midnight. I see.

Kenny   It's quite good, actually. It's got music equipment and all sorts. I didn't go especially to buy a pomegranate, I was just looking at them. I'd just picked one up and I was holding it in my hand, and I sensed this woman standing next to me. She smells all scented, and I turn to look at her.

Tilly   What does she look like?

Kenny   She's quite tall, and she's got shiny hair, and... she looks like a model actually, and she's got a mango in her hand. She says, 'Aren't mangos strange?' and I says, 'Not half as strange as pomegranates.'

Tilly   That was very good, Kenny. Witty!

Kenny   And, get this, our trolleys are touching! Hers hasn't got much in it. Just some kiwi fruit and a bottle of Chardonnay. I says something like, 'Cost a fortune, does fruit!'

Tilly   Not so good.

Kenny   She says, 'What's a man like you doing on his own buying pomegranates at midnight?' 'I'm a postie,' I say. 'I work odd hours. There's not much time for shopping.'

Tilly   Oh dear.

Kenny   No, no, wait for it! She says, 'I come here because I'm lonely.'

Tilly   Are you making this up?

Kenny   No! And then I say, I say, get this, Tilly, I kind of lower my eyes and I say, 'I'm lonely too.'

Tilly   Do that again!

Kenny   I'm lonely too.

Tilly   Aaah. Then what?

Kenny   She says, 'It must be hard being a postie, carrying those heavy bags around. I bet you're dead strong.' 'Oh yes,' I say. 'I have to eat a lot, keep me strength up.' 'Do you drive,' she says? 'No,' I tell her, 'I've got an official Post Office bike.'

Tilly   That must have impressed her. Have you still got the pomegranate in your hand?

Kenny   Yeah, and it's getting quite hot!

Tilly   Sweaty?

Kenny   Yeah, with the excitement. And then she says, 'Do you want to go for a drive?' And I say 'yeah', and we go out to her car. Well, we pay for the shopping first. I got a bit red then, getting my wallet out and everything. My chocolate milk wouldn't scan.

Tilly   Oh Christ.

Kenny   And then I dropped my change. It was OK. She helped me pick it up. It was alright. We went to her car, it was a silver Rover, and we got in, and she drove us up to the coast, with the music on.

Tilly   What music?

Kenny   Barry White.

Tilly   Was she on the game?

Kenny   Course she isn't! We sat in her car looking out to sea, and I kissed her, Tilly. I kissed her for ages, with the music on. Then she took me home.

Tilly   To her house?

Kenny   No, to my house. Then she said goodnight. I'm meeting her at Tesco's again tonight.

Tilly   How romantic. Where will you start tonight? The cheese section? What do you know about her?

Kenny   She likes watersports and she plays the guitar.

Tilly   I didn't mean that. Is she married?

Kenny   No, course not. She wants me to write to her.

Tilly   What's her address?

Kenny   It's her work. An office somewhere.

Tilly   Oh, I get it.

Kenny   She's lovely, Tilly. I talked and talked. You should have heard me.

Tilly   You're not making it up?

Kenny   Honest, I'm not. I can't stop thinking about her. All the hairs on me head kept on standing up. Who knows what will happen tonight! Do you think I should wear after-shave, or not?

Tilly   Don't get carried away.

Kenny   It's the best thing that's ever happened to me. She fancies me, Tilly. I didn't have to say anything.

Tilly   But what's she doing driving up to Tesco's in her silver Rover at midnight, buying kiwi fruit? Don't you think it's a bit odd?

Kenny   No, it's no odder than me going up there. It's a shop, people go shopping.

Tilly   That's one way of describing it.

SCENE EIGHT

Winifred's house. She is writing a letter.

Winifred Dear God,
It's me. I thought you wouldn't mind if I dropped you another note. It's about James again. Tell you the truth, I'm not looking forward to him retiring either. He's not a bundle of laughs. What is he going to do all day? And what will I do? He keeps going on about the Isle of Wight, but I've always lived in the North East, and I don't like the idea of those needles and what have you.

We haven't actually had a conversation about a topic, like fishing, or homosexual priests, something like that, for years. He thinks I'm stupid. But I'm not stupid. You know I'm not.

I feel a bit down in the dumps, God. Please get back to me a.s.a.p.

Your Winifred

SCENE NINE

The Post Office canteen. Tilly sits in the canteen, trying to write a letter enquiring about a dog management course. Kenny is looking restless and lovesick. James reads the newspaper.

James   Seen this, Kenny? More lay-offs.

Tilly   (*To James*) James, how do you spell 'enquiring'?

James   E-N-Q-U-I-R-I-N-G. Is it a job application then, Tilly?

Tilly   Yes, I've had enough. Squire's told me off again. For fucking swearing! How do you spell 'management'?

James   Shall I have a look at it, Tilly?

She passes him the letter.

You've spelt 'dog' right.

Tilly   Alright then. I can't bloody do it!

Kenny   Urgh.

Tilly   What's up with you, Kenny?

Kenny   I'm not feeling too good. I haven't been sleeping.

Tilly   Been up at Tesco's again? Want an Aspirin or something?

Kenny   (*Annoyed*) No, no, I've had some.

James   Tilly, I think you should write it with a pen. It looks a bit rough in pencil. Shall I type it up for you?

Tilly   Oh yeah, would you, James?

James   I think it's a bit rash, dog management.

Tilly   Don't start! It's only an enquiry, that's all. What's wrong with it anyway? You lot think you're married to the Royal Mail.

Kenny   Consignia.

Tilly   Whatever. You think it's your bloody family or something. The thing is, boys, the letter is dead. It's an outmoded form of communication. You don't need to clart on with envelopes any more, and stamps. It's medieval, that's what it is. Do you know what I think?

Kenny   No.

Tilly   Soon we'll just have to speak. We'll all have little gadgets that recognise your voice and writing things down will be unnecessary, that's what I think. Bloody letters. Waste of trees, if you ask me, all that dear so-and-so, and yours sincerely business, fucking stupid. Postcodes, it's all about selling stuff and surveillance.

James   Why not be a nurse, love?

Tilly   Why would I want to be a buggering nurse?

Kenny   Steady now. Language in the workplace! He's only trying to help.

Tilly   You're one to talk.

Kenny   There's other people listening. Squires is next door.

Tilly   Fuck it.

James   Can I just say, about what you said, about letters, it's all part of having a regular life. The letters come in the morning, you read them, think about them, reply slowly. Some people get hundreds of emails a day. And they're all about nothing, most of them. It's not healthy.

Kenny   You can't stop things changing though, can you?

James   That's a philosophical point you're making there. It might be better if things didn't change.

Tilly   Well, something's got to change. I'm so bored with this job. Look at you with your socks and your thermal vests and your push-bikes. You sit around here moaning about standards and wages, and then when Squires comes in you're all... servile. That's what you are, servile, like you're England's servants.

James   What's wrong with that?

Kenny   So what are you then? If we're England's servants?

Tilly   I'm a free spirit, that's what I am.

Kenny   Free spirit!

James   Calm down everyone.

Kenny   Freeloader, more like.

Tilly   It's no wonder he's tired.

James   Why's he tired?

Tilly   He's been flirting up at late night Tesco's, with his lady of the night.

James   Is that an expression, flirtin' at Tesco's?

Kenny   Shut up, Tilly.

Tilly   What's the big secret?

Kenny   It's my business, not anyone else's. I told you that in confidence.

James   Do supermarkets stay open late these days? That's not good for you. You should do your shopping on a Saturday morning.

Tilly   They stay open all night, that's where Kenny goes. Canoodling by the luxury fruit. That's why he's tired. He's got a fancy girl he meets up there.

Kenny   Leave me alone, right!

Tilly   Alright, keep your socks on.

Kenny   Look, I don't talk about your personal life at work, do I?

Tilly   That's because I haven't got one. My life is everywhere, Kenny. Oooh, Kenny, you're so compart... compi...whatever it is. You've got everything in little boxes, haven't you? All neat. Christ, this place is driving me nuts!

She runs out.

James   I was going to say to her... dogs, they're too narrow. You know what I mean? She could do with some GCSEs first. English or something.

Kenny   She could do with some manners.

James   Aye, you're right there. Manners would help. It's like most of the new recruits, they look like American tourists, not postmen. We used to get sent home if we hadn't polished our shoes when I was a telegram boy.

Kenny   Yeah, yeah, yeah. I've heard all about it, James.

He gets up rudely and leaves. James looks abandoned.

SCENE TEN

Endless Street. Milosh is trying to make a phone call from a payphone. He is anxious and keeps on dropping stuff. He is holding a phrase book.

Milosh   Hello, hello, I want to speak to my solicitor, Mr Collet. Help me please. I can't understand what you are saying. It is my appeal. Please, is this Mr Collet? He is where? Do you please have a number for him? My name is...

Milosh is beside himself with frustration. As his money runs out Merrill appears. She is posting letters and notices Milosh. She peeps at him through the glass, giving him an awful shock.

Merrill   It's only me!

Milosh   Who?

Merrill   Merrill.

Milosh   Oh my God, it's that woman with the goggly eyes.

Merrill   How are you getting on at number 31? I haven't seen any lights on. Have the Sisters of Divine Intervention been keeping you awake?

Milosh   I'll just nod and pretend I can understand what she's on about.

Merrill   You look a bit pasty. Are you having trouble with the phone? The PHONE! Is it broken again? Do you want me to try?

Milosh   You are wanting the phone?

Merrill   No, I don't want the phone. I'm offering to help, but you don't know what I'm talking about, do you?

Milosh   Smile. Perhaps she'll go away.

Merrill   You look like you could do with a meal. I'm just having some soup myself, would you like some? I mean, you look quite harmless. I know it's not normal for old women to invite men into their houses, but what the hell. It's been a long day, and no letters came this morning. Soup?

Milosh   Soup?

Merrill   Yes, soup. Yum yum.

Milosh   I think she is begging me for food. She doesn't look particularly hungry. Still, I will nod. Then make a run for it.

Merrill   Come on then. You're not a murderer are you, or anything like that?

Milosh   Now what? Follow her?

She hooks him with her stick.

Merrill   It's just here.

She leads him into her house and sits him down.

Milosh   Soup?

Merrill   Yes, Heinz tomato. Won it in a raffle, in fact. That's my desk. Where I write letters.

Milosh   The place is full of paper. Terrible fire risk. Smells a bit. Musty. I wonder if she's seen anyone about her thyroid problem. Carry on smiling and spooning.

Merrill   WHERE ARE YOU FROM?

Milosh   Yugoslavia.

Milosh looks upset again.

Milosh   It's the word. Saying the name of my country. SORRY.

Merrill   Are you one of those... what are they called again? Did you run through the tunnel? Or come in a truck?

Milosh   I am sorry... my English...

Merrill   I expect you get free English lessons, free everything?

Milosh   What's she saying about lessons? Smile, nod.

Merrill   It's all laid on, is it? That's my taxes paying for you.

Milosh   Yes.

Merrill   Where's your FAMILY?

Milosh   Family?

Merrill   Wife, mama, children, daddy.

Milosh nods ponderously.

Merrill   Well?

Milosh   Dead.

Pause. Milosh bursts into tears.

Merrill   I'm so sorry, er, look, have some more soup. I'll open another can. My daughter is also dead. Lots of dead people. Dying, happens all the time. Doesn't make it any better though, does it?

Milosh   I'll show her my papers, my vouchers. Then she'll understand that I'm not illegal. Otherwise she might call the police.

Merrill   Are those all your documents? Is that your wife? And children? The council must have put you in a flat or something.

Milosh   Finish the soup. I must get out of here. I mean, it was nice of her to offer the soup. For all she knew I could have been a thief. Stand up, Smile more.

If I were you I would go to the doctor, madam.

Merrill   I don't know what you're talking about. Tell you what, I'll get a dictionary tomorrow. He probably doesn't understand how anything works. Poor man. He's a bit of a mess really. Looks like a gypsy. Probably is a gypsy. Shouldn't think he knows what's going on.

Milosh   Bye bye. And that's about all I can say really. Hello, bye bye. And I was such a talkative man, a chatty doctor, jokes and songs. I had a nice life. It was nicer than your life, old woman.

Merrill   Have a packet of biscuits.

Milosh   Oh, thank you, lady, thank you. Sorry. Byee byeee. Thank you, sorry.

Milosh backs out of the room.

SCENE ELEVEN

Endless Street. Kenny stands under a spotlight with his postbag. Milosh is on the other side of the stage, learning English from a phrasebook.

Kenny   Hello, is Shona there? It's Kenneth. Where? She's been in a meeting for hours. Tell her to phone me, tell her it's urgent.

Milosh   How do you do? Here is a house. Come into the sitting room. Ah, would you like a cup of tea? Do you take milk?

Kenny   Sorry, it's Kenneth again. Could I leave a message please? Tell her I'll meet her after work. She's got my number.

Milosh   This is the kitchen. Here is the knife, here is the fork, here is my kettle which I will... boil... and with which I shall make you a pot of tea.

Kenny   Number one, Endless Street. Rubbish blowing about in the garden. What have I got for you? A catalogue, smiling family in pale blue jumpers and slacks, shining hair.

Milosh   This is my mother and this is my father. This is my grandmother and here is my cat. And the floor and the ceiling. Do you take milk?

Kenny   Number three. Students. An Indian bedspread for a curtain. A letter from mummy, from where? Surrey, blue envelope.

Milosh   The weather is very mild for the time of year.

Kenny   Five. Greasy door, oil around the doorknob. A motor-bike magazine in plastic. My legs start to ache.

Milosh   Shall we have CAKE? Yes, thank you. Here is your cake on a plate. Here is your cup on a saucer. How is your health?

Kenny   Seven. A letter from the hospital, official, stamped. Net curtains, a ramp instead of steps. Phone me, Shona, phone me.

Milosh   I have a cold. This is my handkerchief. BLESS YOU.

Kenny   Nine. The door is open. A doorway full of stuff. An ancient one-eyed cat arches its back. Post is six brown envelopes with the word URGENT stamped on the front.

Milosh   Let me show you the bathroom where you might go to the toilet!

Kenny   A postcard from Spain, then a book wrapped in cardboard, then a long thin letter, YOU HAVE BEEN SELECTED.

Milosh   There are the taps, hot and cold, and here is the BASIN.

Kenny   Number seventeen. A quite blue door with a Neighbourhood Watch sticker. Flowery curtains, a dog with a squeaking bark. Number nineteen, a shopping questionnaire.

Milosh   Now let us go and sit on the sofa and watch the news on television. Here is a cushion.

Kenny   It doesn't get any lighter, it just goes on and on. Number 21 a giro, number 23 a letter from your MP.

Milosh   These are the walls, the table, the chairs. I am Milosh.

Kenny   Twenty-five. A letter in neat black ink, to Deirdre Belize. Twenty-seven a pack of bibles, Divinity House, for the sister superior. Twenty-nine, a girl in a sari staring at me with hollow eyes, a crumpled airmail letter.

His phone beeps.

Kenny   Shona! Shona! Oh, it's Tilly. (*He erases the message*) Please God, help me, help me.

Milosh   This is where I live. This is my address. This is my HOME. My HOME. HOME.

Kenny   Number 31. No one lives here. The place has been empty for months. Curtains like grey cobwebs. FUCK IT. FUCK THIS HILL. I'm not doing it, I can't do it any more.

He chucks all the letters into the letterbox of Number 31. We see Milosh on the other side of a door as the letters cascade in.

Milosh   Dear Anna,
The letters poured through the letterbox. There were so many. There are many beautiful letters with lovely stamps. How interesting they are, those stamps. Sometimes there are parcels, and things inside them. Every letter is a work of art, even the circulars and the trash, a work of art that someone has thought about, written, bought a stamp for, this thing which has travelled maybe thousands of miles, and here it is. On the doormat of Number 31 Endless Street.

I do not open them. I stack them neatly in piles. Why is this happening with the letters? I fear that it might be to do with me. I wonder if someone will come looking for them, that I shall be caught, or accused of stealing them. I wish you were here. I wish you could advise me. If only, my love, there would be a letter from you.

SCENE TWELVE

The sorting office. Tilly and Kenny are working.

Tilly   I sent you a text.

Kenny   Did you?

Tilly   Are you still not speaking to me?

Kenny   Course I'm speaking.

Tilly   Go on then.

Kenny   What?

Tilly   Speak!

Kenny   (*Hesitates for a moment*) Alright then. What do you want to know?

Tilly   How's it going?

Kenny   What?

Tilly   How's it going? With Shona?

Kenny   Great, it's going great.

Tilly   You've moved on from Tesco's then?

Kenny   Tesco's? Yeah. She's practically living with us now.

Tilly   It's serious then?

Kenny   Yeah. It's serious.

Tilly   What's it like?

Kenny   What do you mean?

Tilly   Being serious. What's it like?

Kenny Good. Time-consuming.

Tilly Not like Sally then?

Kenny Nothing like Sally. Look, Tilly, I've just been wrapped up with it all. It's a big thing for me. I didn't mean...

Tilly Don't worry about me!

Kenny We'll have a drink or something. The three of us.

Tilly Does she like Frankie Curtis?

Kenny It's not her thing, balaclavas and that.

Tilly Oh. What does she like?

Kenny Me, she likes me. She thinks I'm... Hello, James.

James stands at the door, looking dazed.

James Baseball bat. Some kids... came up behind...

Tilly Call an ambulance, Kenny. I'll get first aid.

James On my round. Just walking along.

Tilly Didn't anyone help you?

James No, I walked here, from Forth Banks.

Tilly And the police, Kenny. Quick, sit down, James. Get him some tea. Someone took a swing at you? What for?

James Back of me head. They took me sack.

Tilly Christ, what were they after?

James It was a special delivery, to a factory. They broke me specs.

Tilly Sssh, shhh... You should have called an ambulance straight away. Where did it happen?

James   Not far, the back lane. I never saw them coming.

Kenny   They're on their way. You're going to need stitches there, James.

James   I didn't see anything. They just hit out. Two of them. It was a baseball bat, I think.

Tilly   We'd better phone up your wife. Tell her to get over here!

James   No, it's nothing. Don't phone Winifred. Just let me get cleaned up. I'll be alright.

Tilly   Don't be dumb. You need to go to hospital.

James   I don't want any... fuss.

He passes out.

Interval

ACT TWO

SCENE ONE

Milosh's flat. Merrill appears with a pile of blankets, a thermos flask etc. Milosh is reading an English phrasebook.

Milosh   Who is it?

Merrill   It's me, Merrill. I've got supplies.

Milosh   Hello, Mrs Soup.

Merrill   It's a bit bare, isn't it? Haven't you got any things? No radio? No TV?

Milosh   No TV. How are you? My name is Milosh.

Merrill   Yes, I know that. My name's Merrill, not Mrs Soup.

Milosh   Yes.

Merrill   Where shall I put these?

Milosh   Yes.

Merrill   Alright, I'll put them down here.

She gets out a phrasebook.

Merrill   Where shall we start? (*She sits down with the book open*) So, how are you today? Oh, I've got you a city map.

Milosh   Map! (*He grabs it hungrily*) We are here. Endless Street. Tell me, where is Brag End?

Merrill   Brag End? Why would you want to go up there?

Milosh   Vouchers (*He searches about in his pockets*) Here. I must go to Brag End Post Office. Would you have tea?

Merrill   Would you LIKE tea? Milk, two sugars. Don't forget to warm the pot. Oh never mind. Give us a look at those. Brag

End? But you're in the West End. You should be going to Endless Street Post Office. It's only two minutes away.

Milosh   Brag End Post Office Counters.

Merrill   It must be a mistake.

Milosh   (*To himself*) Yes, a mistake, the whole thing is a mistake. I spend most of my allowance travelling about trying to find things. She looks confused.

Milosh   Yes. A mistake.

Merrill   I said two sugars. You'll have to take it back from where you got it.

Milosh   How?

Merrill   Well, you get on the number eighteen bus into town. Where is this place? River Street. You'll have to walk down there. He doesn't know what I'm talking about.

Milosh   Nod and smile. Smile and nod.

Merrill   I'll go. You and me go.

Milosh   Now what? She's taken my vouchers.

Merrill   You and me go to River Street to get the vouchers sent to the nearest post office.

Milosh   Yes, please, you and me, River Street, to get vouchers.

Merrill   I don't know how you're supposed to find your way around. Who's in charge here? This is England, Freddie!

Milosh   England, yes. God save the Queen.

Merrill   Steady! We'll go when the rain stops, shall we?

They sip their tea.

Milosh starts searching through the phrasebook.

Milosh   A funny thing happened to me today.

Merrill   A joke! Go on.

Milosh   A joke?

Merrill   Go on, tell me a joke.

Milosh   Oh, OK. A man walks his donkey (*He has to keep looking up words and doing actions*) on the street. Like Endless Street.

Merrill   A donkey on Endless Street?

Milosh   The police come, they think to tease the man. So they say, ha ha (*Laughing to himself*) they say you need a belt, like this, to be riding a donkey.

Merrill   A safety belt?

Milosh   Yes. You will pay a... fine. We send a letter to you, the man, for ten pounds, or to the donkey for five pounds. Which will you have, they say to the man?

Merrill   What does he say, this man?

Milosh   Man says, to me, not the donkey.

Merrill   Not the donkey, even though the fine is only five pounds? Why is that?

Milosh   Because... because, the man he says, my donkey, he is to become a policeman and he must not have a...

Merrill   Beard?

Milosh   Crime history, ha ha, ha ha.

Merrill stares at him.

Merrill   Oh I get it.

Pause.

You would say clean record, Milosh, not crime history.

Milosh   It is not a funny joke here in England. (*He sighs*)
Another funny thing happened to me today.

Merrill   Oh dear.

Milosh   Letters (*he looks through the phrasebook*) vomiting through
the door, and yesterday too. I have them.

Merrill   What's that?

Milosh   I show you.

He shows her the pile of letters.

Merrill   Christ almighty! The postman's gone rotten, she's been
flamming. It won't be that nice Kenneth. It will be the girl with
the acne.

Milosh   Acne? (*He leafs through the book again*)

Merrill   What must you think? The postal service in England
is one of the best in the world. It's highly irregular, Milosh.
Things like this might happen in Yugoslavia, but not here.
I am embarrassed.

Milosh   Is she saying that it's because I'm from...? Perhaps she
thinks I did it?

Merrill   You've sorted them out. It's quite interesting really,
who gets what. Pile of bills for number ten, eighteen gets a lot of
postcards. Mmmm.

Milosh   Many, many posts.

Merrill   This is my post here.

Milosh   You?

Merrill   Me, my penpals. See, that's from Renate.

Milosh   What to do?

Where on earth is my link support person? At least they might know what was going on.

Merrill   We'd better deliver them.

Milosh   She wants to take THEM away now. What shall I do?

Merrill   Do your coat up, Millie. We'll do it on the way to River Street. It may be raining but the post has to get through.

Milosh   She gives me a plastic rainhood and a carrier bag full of letters.

Merrill   We'll do it together.

Milosh   Will I ever get rid of this woman?

They set off, with Milosh looking bewildered.

SCENE TWO

Winifred is in hospital visiting James, who now has a bandage round his head. He is listless and vacant, and hardly speaks.

Winifred There's a card from all of them at work, James. I'll put it there, look, with your fruit. How are you feeling now?

James   Alright.

Winifred You'll be getting compensation, I'm sure.

James   Mmm.

Winifred It's shock, isn't it, love?

James   Shock. Telling me...

Winifred You'll get over it. Bad luck after all those years and right at the end of it too. Leaves you with a sour taste. You have to forget it, remember the happy times.

James   Two of them. I couldn't do anything, see, Win.

Winifred I brought in your poem books, here, and I got you a pen. The doctor, he thinks you might need to be careful in case you got post-trauma stress syndrome. POST TRAUMA ha ha.

James is not at all amused.

Winifred Or something anyway. How's your memory?

James   What's to remember?

Winifred Well, everything.

James   It's like fog, Winifred. Bits here and there, disappearing.

Winifred The doctor will know what to do. Do you want a chocolate?

James   No. Take them away.

Winifred Have you seen the doctor lately?

James   I don't know any Doctor Lately.

Winifred Not Doctor Lately. Oh, never mind. Let's fill in the lunch card, shall we? Sponge and custard, or an orange?

James   Nothing

Winifred Nothing? You like sponge, James.

James shrugs.

Winifred You'll feel better in a bit. As we said, it's just the shock.

James   I always thought... Tilly, at work, always breaking the rules, and I said, if you don't do the correct procedures then things go wrong. But I did the right thing. I was just doing my job.

Winifred I expect we'll be hearing from the powers that be. The police will have got them by now. I'd better pray for them too, I suppose.

James   There wasn't a reason. It was just badness.

Winifred It's only a little thing, James. You'll be better soon.
They didn't really hurt you, as far as we know.

James   You'd think Squires might have sent a card. They
would have done in the old days. They would have come in,
straight off.

Winifred Tilly brought you a card in. Here, it says, thinking of
you, all the best from all your friends at work. And look at all the
signatures.

James   They'll be glad to see the back of me. I'm too slow for
them.

Winifred That's not true. You know that's not true.

James   I've had it.

Winifred Don't be silly. Still, there's no point going back to work
now. You were due to retire anyway.

James   That's it then.

Winifred You'll be having your retirement do still. The decanter
and four glasses.

James   I'm not well.

Winifred I know you're not, love. But you'll feel better in a
couple of days.

James   What if they come after me in here?

Winifred No, James. It's just the shock talking. You know what,
love, I was looking at those details about the bungalows in the
Isle of Wight. I brought in the brochures, love.

James   I don't want to look at those. We can't go anywhere.
There'll be investigations.

Winifred I think the police will do that. We could go down there and have a holiday. See what we think, of The Needles and whatnot.

James   I can't think...

Winifred Do you know what was in the packet?

James   It must have been money.

Winifred Staff training manuals. 'Procedures in the Event of a Robbery'.

James   Procedures? But they robbed me.

Winifred Is that what irony is? I don't know. Come on, James, don't look so worried. Let's have a little pray together, shall we.

James   No! Leave me alone, woman.

He starts climbing out of bed, thrashing about.

James   Let us get out of this place.

Winifred Nurse! Could someone help? Please.

SCENE THREE

Tilly and Kenny are in the sorting office.

Tilly   It's funny without James. I miss him plodding about. Do you, Kenny?

Kenny   Yeah. How is he?

Tilly   You're his friend, you should go and see him in the hozzie.

Kenny   Don't like hospitals.

Tilly   Well, write him a letter or something.

Kenny   Alright, I will.

Tilly   He's missed his party. He was meant to get his decanter set.

Kenny   He was looking forward to that. Christ, I've been that busy.

Tilly   Busy doing what?

Kenny   Work, Shona, been checking out package holidays, Tenerife and that.

Tilly   For you and her?

Kenny   Yeah. Somewhere hot, swimming pool, deckchair, window open at night, me and her. Just for a week, you know.

Tilly   You'll be getting a mortgage next.

Kenny   Maybe, maybe. Early days.

Tilly   Nice little family, get yourself a little car. Oooh super dooper. One of those smart little modern houses. I can just see it, wardrobes, the lot.

Kenny   Wardrobes? What are you on about?

Tilly   Couples, wardrobes and cutlery sets, bloody duvet covers.

Kenny   You're just jealous, man.

Tilly   No I'm not.

Kenny   Yes you are.

Tilly   I'm not. What would I want a wardrobe for?

Kenny   I don't want a wardrobe either. I just want... her.

Tilly   Yeah, yeah, I know.

They continue working.

Tilly   Listen, Kenny. I think we should organise a little party for James.

Kenny   He's in hospital! Leave him alone!

Tilly   When he comes out. Just a little thing. In here, with sausage rolls and stuff. Casual.

Kenny   He's not a casual sort of person, Tilly.

Tilly   It's better than nothing. Better than silence, after forty-five years, Kenny. Think about it. We could get him a present.

Kenny   I'm no good at organising parties.

Tilly   I'll do it. Can't say I've ever organised a retirement party, but you gotta start somewhere!

Kenny   I dunno. He's not well.

Tilly   When he's better. Go on, Kenny. How long have you known James?

Kenny   Ten years. He took me under his wing, like. But I don't know. He might be embarrassed.

Tilly   No he wouldn't. He'd be pleased. He loves it here. Go on, Kenny. Do it for James.

Kenny   I suppose so. What do you have to do?

Tilly   You just buy beer, stick a few balloons up, and sit around for a bit. Easy.

Kenny   Right. You'd better tell him then.

Tilly   I'll go round and see him when he gets home, shall I?

Kenny   To his house?

Tilly   Yeah, why not?

Kenny   He might not like it.

Tilly   He'll be alright! That's settled then.

Kenny   OK. I'll get Shona to drive us to Tesco's. In the Rover.

SCENE FOUR

Winifred is back home. We can see James, angry, glowering, as she writes.

Winifred Dear God,
You know how it is in marriage, the long deserts, locking up at night, the day to dayness of bedlamps and electricity bills, and have you done this or that, and the silence of it, the tick-tock of it, just you and him, each other's smells mingling, your whites whirring about in the washer, arms together. The not touching, the way you always do things, the comfort, the aching loneliness and boredom, the rooms that need painting, the weeds growing in the back of the garden. I mean, you can leave a marriage unattended for years, and it will carry on.

I think he might have gone mental. And you don't seem to be in, God. I keep on writing and there's no reply. All I can do under the circumstances is leave a message for you, to help him get over his worrying thoughts and give me the fortitude to not kill him meanwhile.

Yours, Winifred

PS If you are away, please send an angel. Is that A-N-G-L-E, or A-N-G-E-L?

She folds up the letter and puts it in an envelope.

SCENE FIVE

Winifred's house. Tilly appears, carrying the Santa file.

Tilly   Excuse me.

Winifred Eeh, God!

Tilly   Is James there?

Winifred You made me jump.

Tilly   It's Tilly, from the post office. I brought him this.

Winifred What's that?

Tilly   It's the letters to Santa. I thought they might cheer him up. He could answer them. He was going to be Santa this year.

Winifred He won't want those, dear.

Tilly   I could leave them here, just in case.

Winifred If you like. You're the first one to visit, no one else has showed up. There's no sign of Kenny or Squires, and no sign from the higher-ups neither.

Tilly   It's about the retirement too, about him missing his party. We thought we'd organise a little get-together for him.

Winifred That's nice, but I don't think...

Tilly   What's up with him?

Winifred You'd better come in.

Tilly   Is that a photo of James?

Winifred That's his first day at the post office. He was a telegram boy, you know.

Tilly   Look at him, with his brass buttons and his hat!

Winifred Yes, sweet, isn't he? I don't know if he'll see you. He's in a funny mood, you might set him off.

Tilly   Set him off where?

Winifred Hallucinating.

Tilly   Eh?

Winifred Seeing things, at night mainly. Men coming into the room. I says you ought to see a doctor, but he won't go.

Tilly   Oh. You wouldn't have a biscuit, would you? I'm starved. I just finished my round. Haven't had any lunch.

Winifred Help yourself. He used to be so... manageable, you know. He was no trouble for years. Very regular. Now he's not. Now he's irregular.

Tilly   What are these?

Winifred Garibaldis. Would you rather have a chocolate? He still hasn't touched the box you sent in from work. You might as well eat those.

Tilly   Great. D'you want one?

Winifred No thanks. It's shaken him, see. He can't sleep. He walks about. So I can't sleep either. Talks to himself.

Tilly   He'll probably pick up. Perhaps he's having a nervous breakdown?

Winifred Do you think?

Tilly   Probably. His routine's all gone to pot. You see it in dogs, when the routine goes.

Winifred He's very snappy.

Tilly   Does he still write the poems?

Winifred Just scribbles, funny drawings. Loads of them, all stuck round his room.

Tilly   Men fall apart so easily. One knock and they fall to bits!

Winifred Exactly. I've had a baby, I've had the menopause, and a hysterectomy and I've had to deal with the Women's Institute, and I don't fall apart!

Tilly   Me too! The things I've put up with... like Kenny's huffs! I mean, people are always offending me, but I don't harbour it.

Winifred Yes, the harbouring. You feel like you can't do a thing, right. As for affection, he's more loving to the toaster than he is to me.

Tilly   Bloody cheek. You're much better looking than a toaster.

Winifred I should think so! Are you married?

Tilly   I'm gay. Doesn't make it any easier. No one's touched me toaster for months.

Winifred Oh. Ha ha.

Tilly   Ha ha ha.

Winifred And as for the Post Office... Con-bloomin-signia. They should be ashamed.

Tilly   Yeah, Conbloodysignia.

Winifred Con bloody signia.

Tilly   Con fuckin signia. (*Awkwardly*) Why don't you phone them up?

Winifred James doesn't want me to.

Tilly   Tie him up or something.

Winifred I would if I could! He listens to all my phone calls. He won't even let me call a doctor. They might give him Prozac or something like that.

Tilly   Imagine James on Prozac!

Pause.

Winifred What about my life? I've got things to do. I've got to knit forty four-inch squares for Bolivian orphans, and I can't get on. I'm at my wits' end. Trapped. Vicar's been round, but James isn't interested. Says he doesn't like him in the house, and he's a lovely man. He's gay too, you should meet him. Does gay weddings sometimes.

Tilly   Oh yeah. Look, do you want to go out? To see your daughter or something? I'll sit with him for an hour.

Winifred What if he goes off it?

Tilly   I'll just cope with it. You got a cellar or anything? Rope?

Winifred I don't know...

Tilly   I'm joking. Go to the park or something. Go to the flicks if you like. It's nice here. You should see where I live. It will cheer him up seeing me. He can tell me off, like in the old days. I drove him mad, I did. Oh it's alright, not that mad.

Winifred Shall I tell him that I'm going out?

Tilly   I wouldn't. Just get out while you can.

SCENE SIX

Merrill and Milosh stand outside with a carrier bag, looking down on the city.

Milosh   Look!

Merrill Hang on... Is that the end of it?

Milosh   How slowly she walks, her old legs creaking. I tried to tell her I would go alone to deliver the letters, but she won't trust me. She comes every night. It takes hours to reach the summit.

Merrill What are we looking at?

Milosh   The lights of England.

Merrill Yes, there it is, all stretched out. All the little houses and streets and families and worries, all those hungry letterboxes.

Milosh Many letterboxes.

Merrill Telling me!

Milosh My friend. I am happy.

Merrill What's that? What's there to be happy about? Me legs are killing...

Milosh I have use.

Merrill You mean you are useFUL.

Milosh UseFUL. I give to England their lost letters.

Merrill With my help.

Milosh With you. How... how... good it is.

Merrill What?

Milosh This. All the houses in their lines. All...

Merrill Neat and square? Is that what you mean? All organised? Apart from the PO, seems like that's falling to bits.

Milosh Not like home. No lines.

Merrill You mean where you came from?

Milosh Yes, where I come from.

Merrill Now, now, Millie. That's all passed, you're alright now.

Milosh How is my English?

Merrill A bit better. Let's have a test. What's that?

Milosh Lamp post.

Merrill There?

Milosh   Grass. Dog mess.

Merrill   Very good. What do we say about that?

Milosh   A disgrace!

Merrill   And up there?

Milosh   Sky. Big sky. Stars. Moon.

Merrill   What about this?

Milosh   Leg. Bad leg. Varicose.

Merrill   Very good. Varicose vein!

Milosh   Varicose vein! See, I have learnt.

Merrill   At least you're making an effort.

Milosh   I must take exam.

Merrill   What for?

Milosh   To be a doctor. To be useFUL.

Merrill   What kind of doctor?

Milosh   Hospital doctor.

Merrill   It takes a long time to be a doctor, dear. I would content yourself with being a postman for the time being.

Milosh   I am a doctor.

Merrill   Not a proper doctor.

Milosh   I train for many years. I am a doctor!

Merrill   And they let you take an exam here in England?

Milosh   Yes.

Merrill   The state of the NHS! They'll take anyone these days.

Milosh   What is that?

Merrill   Never mind. Shall we catch the bus back? Have you got your fare? Watch me, Milosh. You stand at the stop and when the bus comes you wave your stick about like this, or the sodding bastards ignore you. What's the name of our stop?

Milosh   Queen Street, on the corner of Endless Street.

Merrill   That's the one. Come on, dear, let's get some soup.

Milosh   More soup. Yes, lovely soup. I am coming.

SCENE SEVEN

James and Winifred's house. Winifred is on the telephone.

Winifred Hello, Mr Squires, this is Mrs Stanley, James Stanley's wife. I expect you know that he's been poorly, after he was attacked, like. With the baseball bat. No. He's still not quite himself. Not ready to come back or anything. He missed his retirement, unfortunately. What we're wondering, Mr Squires, we were expecting a letter about the incident, about what happened, and also he was due to get his decanter and glass set. Yes, he got a sick note. Yes, he's been with the service for nearly fifty years. Oh, I see, you're not sure about procedure under new management. Yes. What shall I tell James, sir? Yes, I will. I see. We'll be hearing from you then? In due course?

She puts the phone down.

It's all the procedure or something. They're looking into it, but it has to be... processed, I think he said.

James   Like cheese.

Winifred Not like cheese. He was nice. He said it was all in the system anyway.

James   Forget it.

Winifred He'll be phoning back, I'm sure.

James Don't answer the phone. I'm not having it. I don't want anything from them.

Winifred It's just the new management. The changes.

James Changes, yes. A lot is changing around here, Winifred.

Winifred And what am I supposed to do?

James I don't know, do I? Please yourself!

Winifred It's not very nice, is it? Being stuck in here with paper on the windows. I'm only trying to make things better.

James Not now, Winifred.

Winifred When? What if someone phones me up? I've got a life out there, James.

James Go out there then. Don't worry about me.

Winifred Where's it going to end?

James It's already ended.

Winifred That's where you're wrong. It may have ended for you, but not for me. (*She pauses*) I'm going to Clara's.

James Go on then.

Winifred And I'm not coming back.

James What do you mean?

Winifred I'm not coming back. There's food in the freezer and when that runs out you'll have to go to the shops.

James Don't be stupid. I can't go to the shops. I can't manage.

Winifred I'm sick of all this gloom. It's like living in hell.

James   I can't cope on me own.

Winifred Neither can I, James, and that's what it's like. I'm on me own, you don't listen to anything I say. You treat me like a fool and I'm not a fool, James.

James   I didn't say that.

Winifred And by the way, I got your black boots fixed. Why not try wearing them?

SCENE EIGHT

Kenny is shoving more letters through the letterbox of Number 31. Tilly appears.

Tilly   Hey, Kenny! Do you want to come down the Empress? I've got some stuff for James's party. What are you doing?

Kenny   What do you think I'm doing? I'm delivering letters.

Tilly   No you're not.

Kenny   Yes I am.

Tilly   You're stuffing all the letters into that letterbox.

Kenny   Am I?

Tilly   Who lives there?

Kenny   I don't know, do I?

Tilly   You're wilfully delaying the mail.

Kenny   I couldn't face the hill. You know how it is.

Tilly   Be off sick then.

Kenny   I'm not sick. It's just a bad day.

Tilly   How could you do that?

Kenny   What?

Tilly   Flamming. How could you chuck people's letters away like that? They could be important. There could be all kinds of letters in that lot, test results, job offers, and you're just trashing them.

Kenny   Most of it's rubbish. You know it is. Look at this street. The only news these people are going to get is bad news. I'm doing them a favour.

Tilly   But it's their rubbish, not yours. That's the point of the mail.

Kenny   As I said, it's a bad day. Leave it, Tilly.

Tilly   It's a crime.

Kenny   I've seen you reading other people's postcards. That's a crime.

Tilly   I don't steal.

Kenny   Yeah, but you do daft things. You throw dog biscuits into people's hallways. I never said anything about that.

Tilly   Who says I'm going to report you?

Kenny   What are you going to do then?

Tilly   Stop you being a stupid arse.

Kenny   It's too late. I'm going home.

Tilly   I can't believe you can just walk away.

Kenny   Watch me.

Tilly   It's that bloody Shona, isn't it?

Kenny   You don't know her. You don't know what it's like.

Tilly   I can guess.

Kenny   What are you doing?

Tilly   Knocking on the door. You may not have any morals, but I do.

Kenny   It's empty. No one lives there.

Tilly   Are you sure about that?

She looks through the letterbox.

We'll have to break the door down.

Kenny   That's breaking and entering.

Tilly   You've got to get those letters out and deliver them properly.

She kicks at the door.

Milosh   (*Speaking through the letterbox*) Leave me alone! Go away. I am innocent.

Tilly   Someone's there. I'm sorry, sir. There's been a mistake. We need to collect the letters.

Milosh   Who is it? What do you want?

Tilly   The Post Office. We've made a mistake.

Milosh   No thank you. Please, sorry, goodbye.

Tilly   It's alright, sir.

Milosh opens the door a crack.

Milosh   Who are you?

Tilly   My friend here, he made a mistake. He put the letters through the wrong door and we need to deliver them.

Milosh   What the hell is this? Two people gabbing at me. One looks surly and the other looks apologetic. Are they going to arrest me?

Tilly   Look, I'm sorry, sir. I'll just take this lot, shall I?

Milosh   They might arrest me. But I've done nothing wrong.

I am a doctor! I am here seeking asylum. I was a prisoner in my own country.

Tilly   What's he on about? Thanks. I'll just take these then.

Milosh   Now they begin to argue. People stare from across the street. What else can I do but smile. Smile and nod. Nod and smile.

Milosh closes the door.

Kenny   Now what?

Tilly   You deliver them.

Kenny   I'm not doing it.

Tilly   D'you expect me to do it? I've done my round. It's your job.

Kenny   You should have thought of that before you started banging on people's doors. You could get in trouble.

Tilly   (*Angry*) You could get in trouble. You're like a bloody rottweiler. Once it's bitten someone, it's crossed over. You've crossed the boundary, Kenny.

Kenny   I AM NOT A DOG!

Tilly   Not you're not, unfortunately.

Kenny   Oh piss off!

Tilly   Don't tell me to piss off. Kenny! Kenny! Come back NOW. What am I supposed to do with all your bloody LETTERS? Bugger it.

Merrill appears and sees her.

Tilly   What are you staring at? It's not my fault, you know!

Tilly runs off. Merrill picks up the letters, shakes her head and goes to the phone box.

Merrill   I want to report a postal worker. She hasn't been doing her job properly. It's been going on for some time.

SCENE NINE

James is on the phone.

James   Clara, can I speak to your mother? Just tell her to come to the phone. What do you mean, she won't come? Tell her to get to the phone this minute. I won't shout. I know, I know. It's just a mess here, Clara. I can't undo the packet. The packet from Marks and Spencers. I can't work it out, love. It says about removing the inner sleeve. What sleeve? Can YOU come over then? Tomorrow! Another thing, they've sent me a card about a bloody party. It's the posties, they've got together and organised a do next Monday lunchtime, one o'clock. I want her to come with me, Clara. I can't go by meself. I don't know what she wants. Ask her, Clara, go to her and say, what do you want? What do you mean she won't say? How am I supposed to know then? I can't be doing with this, love. What am I going to eat? No it's not just about food. Shall I send over some flowers or something? They're not cheap, you know, Interflora! She's doing my head in, Clara. Tell her, tell her to phone me. I'll be sitting here, waiting for her, yes.

He puts the phone down, pauses and looks at his watch. He sees the Santa file, picks it up and then puts it down. He picks up the old photo of himself as a telegram boy, stares at it, puts it back, and then picks up the Santa file.

Wonder how long this is going to last under the new management? There'll be a charge soon, buy your letter from Santa. It's all wrong. I mean, look at this, Dear Santa, I want a frog. I've got lookimer. What's that? Lookimer, oh, leukaemia. And a frog would cheer me up as there's no animas in hoppital. She'd laugh at that, Winnie would. Frogs in hospital. You know what she'd do? She'd knit a bloody frog and send it in.

He looks at the next letter.

Dr Mr Claus,
I want my dad back for Xmas please. He didn't mean to be a robber.

Breaks your heart.

Dear God,
Today, as I am sure you know, I am making jam for the Save the Roof Fund. I find with jam that it can go either way. I mean, it's a mater of seconds before it gets too thick, and there's nothing worse than hard jam...

James sits down and reads.

SCENE TEN

Merrill and Milosh are at Merrill's house.

Merrill   You look happy.

Milosh   Something has happened. Look.

Merrill   What is it? A letter?

Milosh   I have passed the medical exam. I can practise as a doctor at the hospital. A man came to see me, a Yugoslavian doctor who already practises here. We talk for over two hours!

He holds up two fingers.

Merrill   Don't do that, dear, it's rude.

Milosh   Oh. I can't tell you how good it was to speak again in my own language. To truly be understood. How I talked!

Merrill   He might like to come round here and tell you how to make a proper cup of tea.

Milosh   What? I tell him about the funny thing.

Merrill   You told him jokes?

Milosh   No, with the letters. The funny thing. The postman who vomited, posted, the letters through the door, and you and I...

Merrill   It was the girl did it.

Milosh   No, my friend, it was the girl STOPPED it. It was the boy postie.

Merrill   I saw the girl.

Milosh   You saw wrong. I tried to tell you. They fight and fight. He is cross. She tries to make him deliver.

Merrill   Kenny? I reported her. She'll lose her job.

Milosh   Lose her job?

Merrill   We'll have to go down there. Why didn't you say this before, Millie?

Milosh   I did tell you, but you didn't hear.

Merrill   Oh. What else haven't you told me then?

Milosh   My asylum case my fail... of this I talked to my friend. He warns me to be prepared. These are not good times.

Merrill   When will you know?

Milosh   Soon. But at least I can work.

Merrill   And what happens if you go back?

Milosh shrugs. They are silent.

Merrill   Nothing we can do now. Put your hat on. We're going down the GPO to sort this out.

SCENE ELEVEN

We see James getting ready, polishing his shoes, putting on his postman's cap, making himself look like the boy in the photograph. He picks up his file. Accompanied by big band music, he gets on his bike. At the same time, Tilly is alone, reading an official letter.

Tilly   Dear Matilda Formley,
We have received a complaint from a member of the public that you were seen wilfully delaying Her Majesty's mail. As I'm sure you realise, this is an extremely serious offence, and one which we will investigate thoroughly. In view of this complaint we are suspending you from delivery duties immediately, pending an enquiry. You will be asked to give a statement in the near future to Mr Squires, your line manager.

SCENE TWELVE

The party. First we see Kenny finishing work, looking as if he wants to leave. Tilly comes in with a tray of sausage rolls.

Tilly   Put out the doilies, Kenny. What's the matter with your face?

Kenny   I'm not stayin', Tilly.

Tilly   What do you mean, you're not staying?

Kenny   I've got things...

Tilly   It's James's party!

Kenny   He probably won't turn up anyway.

Tilly   He will. Where is everyone?

Kenny   I don't know.

Tilly   Make an effort, Kenny. He'll be looking forward to seeing you.

Kenny   I know, I know.

Tilly   It means a lot to him.

Kenny   I KNOW. Where do you want these friggin' doilies?

Tilly   On the soddin' plates. And even if you're too selfish to do it for James then you should do it for me. I've been blamed for not delivering your letters.

Kenny   What do you mean?

Tilly   I'm probably going to get sacked because of you. Oh Christ, here's James.

Enter James, in all his regalia.

Tilly   Here he is. Are you alright?

James   First class! Kenny!

Kenny   James.

Tilly   Sit down, James. Get him a beer, Kenny.

James   Is Winifred coming, Tilly?

Tilly   I told her. I told everyone. There's this virus going around, isn't there, Kenny?

Tilly goes out to get Winifred. James goes up close to Kenny.

James   How have you been, lad?

Kenny   Oh, working and that.

James   Have you survived without me?

Kenny   Aye. Same old round, up Endless Street.

James   Endlessly. You look a bit pale, lad.

Kenny   I'm alright. How's the...

James   Me head? Better. I thought I might have seen you.

Kenny   It's been that busy.

James   Busier than usual?

Kenny   Weather's been bad.

James   Has it?

Kenny   A lot of sickness.

James   But you're still getting those letters though, aren't you, boy?

Kenny   Oh aye, like clockwork.

James   And I thought the place would fall to bits without me.

Kenny laughs. Enter Tilly.

Tilly   Look who I've found!

Enter Winifred. James jumps up.

James   Winnie, you're here.

He doesn't know whether to kiss her or shake her hand.

Winifred Just for the party, James. (*Pause*) You look nice, James. Shiny buttons!

James   I used that Brasso. Ironed me collar, see. Ooh, shall I get you a chair, love?

Tilly   White wine, Winnie?

James   Where would you like to sit?

Winifred Don't fuss!

There is an awkward silence.

Tilly   Kenny! Give him the present.

Kenny   What, now? It's a bit early, isn't it?

Tilly   Go on. We've got something for you, James.

Kenny gives him something tacky.

Kenny   This is from all of us.

Tilly   From all your workmates. (*Loud*) Not the BASTARD MANAGEMENT. We wanted to say how sorry we were, didn't we, Kenny? About the accident and everything, and we know it's only little.

James   I don't know what to say. Look at this, Winnie. Useful, eh?

Winifred Very nice.

Tilly   Speech!

Merrill   (*From offstage*) Excuse me!

James   Who? Me?

Winifred Go on, James! Say your bit.

James   Er, erm... I would just like to say that in all my years as a postman...

Enter Merrill and Milosh.

Merrill   Excuse me!

Tilly   It's Merrill Fisher.

James   Oh aye, it's Merrill, Endless Street, Indian airmail.

Merrill   We have come to make a complaint! That lad's been chucking all the letters away.

James   I beg your pardon!

Merrill   All the mail for Endless Street, he's been chucking it away!

Tilly   No he hasn't. It was me. I did it!

Milosh   NO, I see him with my own eyes.

James   What are they saying? I don't understand.

Merrill   He's been wilfully delaying the mail.

James   STOP! Who? Kenny? I don't think so, madam. Kenny's been working here for ten years. He's one of the best postmen you're likely to meet.

Tilly   It wasn't Kenny, it was me, James. You know me, I don't give a shit.

Milosh   No, every day that boy postie throw the letters through my door. He thinks there is no one there or that I cannot complain. But we have come to tell you that the post is arriving just the same, for me and my friend have been posties!

Merrill   But we cannot keep on with it. It's not our job, is it, Millie?

Milosh   She has varicose veins. Me, I like the letters!

Winifred Kenny?

Merrill   It's cruel. An old lady like me, in the penpal club, waiting for me letters.

Winifred Wicked!

Merrill   It's right up there with the cardinals. He should be sent to prison.

Tilly   Oh come on, no one's dead.

Merrill   People can die because the post doesn't get through.

Winifred That's right.

James   I'm not angry, Kenny. I used to think this job was everything. It's all I cared about, duty and being of service. It's not, is it, Winnie? How much do we know about each other, eh, Kenny? We've seen each other every working day for ten years and we don't speak to each other. Come on, lad, what's been going on?

Kenny   She picked me out, James. She found me in a shop. Selected me. ME!

Tilly   She picked him up at Tesco's.

Milosh   Picked him up? How?

James   Sssh. Let him talk.

Kenny   See James, for a bit I wasn't just some lonely postie in a uniform, plodding up Endless Street, going home to my single flat, writing emails to people who weren't there. I never had that, James, never had that feeling that someone just wanted you. I thought it was forever. I really did. I thought that once you had that feeling, that was it.

James   I see.

Winifred   Do you, James?

Tilly   He could have told me. I was here all along.

Kenny   I told you it was going great. I made it all up. The holidays, the nights out. Sometimes I could make myself believe it too. I followed her, James. I went and watched her house. I saw her coming out of her neat front door, with the burglar alarm and the rose bushes, and there was her husband with his briefcase, a respectable address, you know, and she had a little boy, standing there looking up at her. It was all so tidy, you know.

Tilly   I knew she was married right from the start.

James   Sit down, Kenny. It's alright.

Kenny   But it's not, is it? I says to her, I've seen you, Shona, I know who you are, and she says to me, I'm sorry, I'll leave my husband. What, and leave your little boy? I say. And I know she's lying. She's just one long lie. She sends me a letter, it must have come through this place, short, neat handwriting, smelling of scent, saying to leave her alone. I'm easy to throw away, see, like a bit of junk mail, just something trashy she picked up.

Tilly   Bitch! She doesn't deserve you, Kenny!

Merrill   I'm sorry, but that's no excuse for not delivering the letters, is it?

James   I don't agree with you. I mean, no one's been harmed. Mrs Fisher, Kenny has delivered your letters for the last ten years. He's even gone out of his way to bring you mail that's gone astray. I think we should all say nothing about this.

Milosh   Merrill, you must see, the boy is sick.

Merrill   I suppose. I'd better tell the PO that I made a mistake.

Tilly   Yeah, do that.

Merrill   What about those letters then?

Milosh   I have very much enjoyed meeting you and being at your party with these sausages in pastry and the many beers. And now I must go to the toilet for gentlemen!

Milosh strides off. For a moment we have Merrill, Winifred and James together.

Winifred Is he a relative?

Merrill   Millie? No, he's my friend. He can't manage without me. I look after him. He's foreign, you see.

James   I realised that.

Winifred Nice of you both to come down especially.

Merrill   Well, it was my duty, see. You know what I mean. (*Pause*) You know what we are? Us three?

Winifred Over sixty?

Merrill   Yes, old. We're the last ones.

James   The last whats?

Merrill   The last of the letter writers. It's not the same to them in there.

Winifred No, it isn't.

Merrill   Letters mean a lot to us. They don't to them.

Winifred Don't say that.

Merrill   But it's true. It's not the same.

James   She's right. Something's disappearing, right in front of our eyes.

Milosh re-enters.

Milosh   Merrill, you must come now. The bastard bus driver will soon be arriving on his number eighteen and we must wave the stick.

Merrill   Yes, yes, goodbye.

Winifred Goodbye, love. I'll be off too. Where's my coat?

Winifred and James are alone.

James   So.

Winifred Quite a party.

James   By the way, I found a letter addressed to you, Winifred. It has been in Dead Mail Waiting for weeks. Where is it now? Here we are.

Winifred A letter for me?

James   Seemingly. It's got your address on the front.

Winifred I wonder who it's from?

James   Open it then.

Winifred opens the letter and reads the poem.

Winifred Dear Mrs Stanley,

At last your letters came, your haunting notes,
floating like glass bottles lost at sea
searching for a harbour, or a port,
needing care, rapport, some sympathy.

James has been an idler in the land
Where those who lose the will to live are brought
They stick their dumb heads firmly in the sand.
But then your letters came, your haunting notes.

He didn't think of you. He looked away.
No matter how you called, or what you said
He let you drift through endless foggy days
While he lay in his tangled singled bed.

There's no excuse for him. He's very weak
His prospects (and his looks) add up to nought
Driftwood in the mud up some lost creek
Wishing for a harbour or a port.

And Mrs Stanley, all that can be said
About this useless shell of misery
Is that he sees that his wise Winnie is
The only woman who can pull him in

And he'll do anything, he'll sing your songs
Like psalms, and he'll stop being a sod
Pull him in with rope that's true and strong!

Please Mrs Stanley, please. From God.

Winifred Oh, James.

James   I just want you to come home, love. That's all I want.

SCENE THIRTEEN

Milosh is in a white coat. Merrill sits crossly in his room at the hospital.

Milosh   You have a thyroid problem, Merrill.

Merrill   No I don't.

Milosh   Yes you do.

Merrill   I'm not coming into hospital.

Milosh   You simply must take some medication. You must see one of my colleagues.

Merrill   What is a thyroid problem anyway?

Milosh   It's the reason why you feel so tired, so weary. You should have done something about it years ago.

Merrill   Don't get shirty with me, Mr Know All.

Milosh   I'm not. I'm just telling you.

Merrill   I'm old. People get things the matter with them.

Milosh   That's true.

Merrill   You're meant to say, you're very young for your age.

Milosh   I'm telling you this because you're my friend, and Merrill...

Merrill   Now what? Diabetes?

Milosh   I am going home.

Merrill   But you've only just arrived.

Milosh   My asylum claim has been turned down by the Home Office. I must go home.

Merrill   But you can't.

Milosh   Next week.

Merrill   (*She is very shocked*) So soon!

Milosh   So you must listen to what I say about your health, old woman.

Merrill   I'm... shocked.

Milosh   There is nothing I can do.

Merrill   I'll write to my MP.

Milosh   There is no point. It is too late for letters, for campaigns. You must be my penpal.

Merrill   Your penpal?

Milosh   We will write to each other.

Merrill   Yes, I suppose so. Give me that prescription then. I'll take whatever it is. Throxy woxy icing...

Milosh   Don't look like that, my friend.

He steps away into the darkness.

Spotlight on Merrill. She starts to compose a letter.

Merrill   Dear Milosh,

It's late. The sun is setting on Endless Street. It's a warm summer night and the door is propped open, so I can hear the children playing in the street.

It's been so long since I heard from you. Did you get the birthday card I sent you last week? Can you send me a photograph of where you live, as I find it hard to imagine it. I hope you are safe.

I still go down to River Street and help with the volunteers. That place needs management. To be frank, I don't know what they'll do without me.

Well, my friend, no more news, so I'll post this off.

Write soon

Your Friend Merrill

She starts to write it, mouthing the words. The lights fade to black.

The End

Personal Belongings

I wrote this one-woman play for the actor Zoe Lambert, who is a wonderful mimic and singer. It was a project that arose from a friendship, from laughing about characters that we had seen on trains, from the phrase, 'Please don't forget to take your personal belongings with you when you leave the train', which a muddled guard once said as 'personal problems' instead of belongings.

Live Theatre took the play under their wing, and we developed a series of country and western-style songs, with my lyrics set to Dave Scott's tunes. The play went on to the Edinburgh Festival and had a happy few weeks there.

Julia Darling

Personal Belongings was first performed at Live Theatre, Newcastle upon Tyne on 2 November 2001 and restaged as part of the Edinburgh Festival Fringe from 2-26 August 2002 at the Gilded Balloon Teviot, with the same cast and production.

It was directed by Jeremy Herrin with original music by Dave Scott. The play was performed by Zoe Lambert.

CAST

All of the characters are played by the same actor.

Mellie Spangle (a singing ticket collector)
Mummy (a middle-aged woman with a child)
Prof (a very large female academic)
Finola (an actor, on her way to an audition)
Jimmy McPhee (a psychic chess player from Motherwell)
Kirk (an Australian with a mobile phone)
Charlene (a glowering teenager)

Mellie Spangle (*Over Tannoy*) Helloo... testing, testing, one, two, one, two, one, two, three, four.

Finola appears on stage with suitcases. She sings:

SONG: Northbound Train

We're on the northbound train,
Hear her cry out loud
We're gonna ride, people, ride
Hear her shudder and spit
Gonna leave in a bit
We're gonna ride, people, ride
Ride, ride, children, ride

We're gonna leave this city
On the A track, brother
We're gonna ride, people, ride
On the Metal Horse,
We're gonna leave King's Cross
We're gonna ride, people, ride
We're gonna ride, people, ride
Ride, ride, children, ride

On the northbound train
On the northbound train
There'll be no stoppin'
Once the train starts rocking
We're gonna ride, people, ride

Cos a train's a collective
With the Get There objective
We're gonna ride, people, ride
We're gonna ride, people, ride
Ride, ride, children, ride
Ride, ride, children, ride

Tannoy   That seems to be working. Could all passengers who are not travelling with us, please depart. This is the eleven fourteen to Edinburgh, calling at Doncaster, York, Newcastle. Berwick upon Tweed, and errr, Edinburgh. The train will leave... in a bit.

Finola and others are clambering onto a train. Finola plays all characters.

Mummy Here we are, Natalie. Mind the lady. Excuse me, I have a child! Here's the table, we need a table for our games and colouring pencils. Perhaps some other people would like to play our games? Show the lady your new frog pencil case.

Prof   Sorry, can I just get on this damn thing? Fuck, fuck, my shoe's fallen off. Sorry, can you pass it over? I have got a fucking reservation. Is this coach D? Oh, a pencil case, how nice. With pencils in... bloody Nora!

Finola   This is my reservation... But that one's free. I need to be near the window so I can learn my script. It's very important. You see, I'm going for an audition. I'm an actor. Yeah, I used to be a policewoman, but it was a bit boring. They didn't let me arrest anyone ever and the uniform didn't fit properly. It looked stupid actually, didn't have a waist, like a tree trunk shape, so now I'm an actor and I've got to learn my script. It's a very important play, and anyway, that's my reservation you're sitting on, yours is there. That little girl wants to show you her pencil case!

Kirk speaks into his mobile phone from the table opposite.

Kirk   It's a bit busy, Ramona. Big train. I'm in coach D, I think. Here I go. What are you doing, eating toast? Let me have a nibble. Yum yum, jam on it. Call you in a bit. Love you, love you ever so ever so. I know you love me too, Ramona, I know. Kiss kiss, lubba dubbaa.

Teenager Charlene walks in huffing and puffing. She's got a Walkman on and is singing much more loudly than she realises.

Charlene (*Shouting*) God, is this like, Coach D? What? Thank you. WHAT?

Kirk   (*To Charlene*) There's someone out there, she's trying to say something to you.

Charlene I don't know her, it's just someone who's been following me.

Kirk   She's saying she's your mother.

Charlene Oh God, go away!

A phone rings.

Kirk   It's my phone. Ramona! I'm gonna eat my sandwich, brie and watercress with Californian currants.

Finola   Excuse me, this is the quiet coach. See the phone sign with the red cross over it? No, not the medical Red Cross, the DON'T DO IT red cross. That's why I'm sitting here, because I have to learn my script.

Kirk   Oo-er. I'm ever so sorry. (*Into phone*) Ramona, I'll have to go, you'll have to call me back. I'm sitting in the quiet coach.

Jimmy Mcphee shouts at the top of his voice.

Jimmy McPhee I'm not playin, Mr Strang! (*To characters on train*) I'll have you know I'm Junior Scottish chess Champion, 1995. Supposed to be playin Audrey Damart tomorra, he's got a face like cheese! He's got eyes like slugs, he moves his pieces like he's picking chocolates out offa box, makes me queasy. Then, I had this horrible vision... Audrey winnin. I'm a psychic chess player, see. (*To Mr Strang*) Stick it up yer bishop, Mr Strang! I'm going home to me mammy. Will ye mind me personal belongings, young lady? Where's the buffet?

Charlene appears to be suddenly fast asleep with her Walkman on. She looks up grumpily and shrugs, then slowly takes out a mirror and starts sucking in her cheeks, trying to be cool.

Charlene Eh? I dunno. The buffet? It probably doesn't even exist.

She writes maniacally in a notebook, whispering to herself.

I don't belong in this world. I am a changeling. I am in a no smoking carriage. Life is shit. I am going for a fag.

Finola   (*To Prof*) The play? It's called *Blood and Sex*, by Kevin Barks. I'm going for an audition in Edinburgh. Kevin thought I might be interested in playing the part of The Slag.

The Prof asks about the play.

It's fantastic, I love it. (*Whispering her lines*) Blood, blood
everywhere... I can't see anything. I am drowning. Pass me the
knife, you bastard. You think you know who I am, but you know
nothing about who I am! I am the knife at your... That's my bag
actually, sorry. Thanks very much. Bit chilly, isn't it? Go FUCK
yourself, you're scum, your mother was a WHORE. It's very
good. So passionate, and vair vair vehement.

Mellie Spangle (*Over crackly Tannoy*) Hello, helloo, testing, testing,
helloooo... welcome aboard, and let's hope you had a swinging
time in old London town. There is smoking accommodation
towards the rear portion of the train, and a buffet selling...
Tea, coffee, minerals...

(*Becomes a song*)

Basil and tomato soup, with croutons, emmenthal
Sandwiches, salmon with dill, and mustard seeds
Embossed in pork

There's cappuccino, foccaccia, haloumi,
Moussaka, tahini, barracuda and salami,

Hummous and tzatsiki, pecan pie, chocolate soufflé,
Nuts, crisps, smarties

And Jolene will be serving you, so let's
go say hello, stand by your flan, Jolene
or should I say, I'm begging of you
please don't take my flan
Ha ha, lovely

Natalie is making a racket.

Prof   Would you keep that child under control. What's she
called, GNAT? Do you spell that with a 'g'? Natalie, will you just
SHUT UP? Have some paper, for God's sake...

Yes go on, it's only my marking. That's right, rip it up. I don't
need it where I'm going. And here, why don't you scribble on
yourself with my red marker pen? Lovely!

Mother   Aaaaah, say thank you to the nice big fat lady, Natalie, for letting you tear up her boring papers. Thanks ever so much.

Finola makes another face, then returns to her avid script-learning, talking to herself.

Finola   Fucking take me, no one cares about me, I'm just a fucking slag.

Jimmy   Well, everyone, can I just say that I have been all the way down to the buffet and Jolene says she's only got crisps. It's going to be a long journey with nee sustenance. Wait a second, I'm seein somethin'. It's a vision. A cow! I'm seein' a cow!

Prof   Leave me alone! Nat, Nat. She's eating my fucking shoe.

Mother   We're going all the way to Durham, I think. Where are you going?

Prof   Fucking Alnmouth.

Jimmy   I beg your pardon, missus, there are wee kiddies present. Watch your tongue if ye don't mind, ye dirty beestie.

Prof   Sorry. I live in adult land normally. Fucking great. Yes, Cakes 'n' Things in Alnmouth.

Smoochy music plays.

Prof   To meet Finlay bustARD, as it might be my last hope and I have to bond with someone soon, or I'm going to be fucking past it. I mean, I looked up one day from a pile of tomes, and I saw myself outside myself. I stepped out of my huge chair-shaped body and there I was, sitting there like a vast bit of brainy fudge, and I thought, Hilary, it's time you got yourself into bloody bed with someone and got your shaggy equipment working. So I tried salsa dancing in a frock from Evans. I met a few men, but they were all so slight, like wafers. So I put an advert in *The Guardian*. Huge clever woman seeks big-hearted mate. Big is the quality I seek in every respect. I want a big personality. Could be either sex, I'm not bothered. Could be an animal, actually, with a vast den, or someone with a cavernous garage and a flaming cooker, and one of those immense barbecues and a sofa that is a planet unto itself. We would buy a continent and live on it.

Mummy You see, Natalie, this lonely lady wants to find a special friend, so she is going to meet a stranger in a café. Some people do that when they're really desperate.

Prof (*Gives mummy a look*) I'll get to Alnmouth and find Cakes 'n' Things and it will be one of those damp pine places with jam jars with cut out serated material lids and little china fucking hedgehogs, and I'll plump myself down, and in will come Finlay, who I have travelled over four hundred miles to meet, and he will have a neck like a rubber ring, and he'll plonk himself down, and we will be sweaty and he'll tell me there was a traffic jam on the A69. He'll fiddle with his teaspoon and then he'll reach across the swirly tablecloth, perhaps knocking over the ornamental salt and pepper pots, and he'll say, Hilary, will you be mine?

Pause.

Finola Then what?

Prof That's as far as I can fucking get.

Finola What if he's a murderer? Couldn't you look around a bit more first?

Prof But I'm terribly fucking busy, you see. I haven't got time to look around. I just want to get him installed. I mean, how do other people do it? (*Pause*) I'm not talking about it right, am I? Oh fuck off.

Kirk Hey, it must be really difficult, especially when you're so clever and all. I bet you cry yourself to sleep. I take off my hat to you. Not many ladies would be as brave as you are!

Prof looks very surprised and rather uncomfortable.

Prof Thank you very much, I think.

Mummy How about a game of I SPY?

Jimmy What's that?

Mummy One person spies something and they say, I spy with my little eye something beginning with, or the colour of... Stop kissing that lady, Natalie.

Jimmy Can I start?

Mummy Yes, go on then. Listen, Natalie. Don't give her that gum, please. It glues up her insides.

Prof Does it? Oh good!

Jimmy (*Through a mouthful of crisps*) I spy with my little eye... a buffet.

Looks from the other characters.

Mummy No, that's not right, is it? You don't say what you're spying, you tell us what letter it begins with.

Jimmy I spy with my little eye, something beginning with B. Pha! Let's play wink murder! I'll be the murderer. I wink at yoos.

Mummy But we're not supposed to know who the murderer is!

Jimmy I like being the murderer! (*To Finola*) I know you, I've seen you before. Perhaps in a dream, perhaps in another dimension.

Finola Probably the carpet advert. Yeah, I was the one smiling amongst the pillars of nylon underlay. Mmmm, I say. So soft it tickles. Don't be floored when it comes to carpets. Tum te tum.

Jimmy Here, everyone, we have a celebrity in our carriage!

Finola No, that was just a little part. This part I'm going for, it's much bigger. It's theatre, you know. It's really challenging work.

(*To herself, with music backing*) I wonder if Kevin Barks knows how much it would mean to me to get the part of The Slag? I would give a kidney, actually. The part is made for me. Acting! It's just a meat market. I've been rejected so many times I cry before I get there. I need someone to look me in the eye and say, God, Finola, you're fantastic!

I shall arrive in Newcastle feeling a bit sick. I'll stop in a pub and try to calm my nerves. In the pub I'll buy a small sandwich. I don't notice that the ham is a little bit green around the edges. I gobble it up. Feel rather queasy, and go to the toilet. Look at the toilet bowl for ages. Armitage Shanks. It's getting late so I get out of there and start making my way to the theatre. On the way there I start to see black dots. I will be sick in an alley, then sick again in a gutter. As I arrive at the hall I am sick again, only this time it's a weird green colour. Fall over. Wake up in hospital. Missed the audition. Lying there on a drip I am convulsed, literally crippled with loneliness and failure. I cry out, like this, oh boo hoo hoo, and the doctor comes running. I can't go on, I tell him. I'm no one. I am just a sick actor, lying here. I haven't even got a return ticket to London. Don't take on so, he says in a laminated voice. I think you're wonderful, Finola, at acting. He says, did you ever think of medical acting? Medical acting? I say. Yes, he says, you pretend to be a patient for foreign doctors when they sit their exams. You have to pretend to have different illnesses. It's very challenging work, he says. Okay, I say, why not! I will sit in little rooms in the medical school, doubling up with pain, and one by one, they'll come in and diagnose me. What's this?

(Doubles up in a spasm) (In foreign accent) It's rickets. Then one day, they say, we've got a very interesting disease that we would like you to portray. They take me into see this patient, and guess what? It's Kevin Barks, who has suddenly developed a nervous twitch, which I immediately emulate brilliantly! That's fantastic, says Kevin. I know you, don't I? You're the actress who never showed up. But it's not too late - *Blood and Sex* is going to the West End. Of course you must play The Slag. But I'm a medical actor, I'll say, as all the doctors plead with me to stay. Here, says Kevin, let me pay for a new cancer scanner.

She is abruptly disturbed from this fantasy by Kirk.

Kirk   It's amazing how things turn out, isn't it? Oh hell! Train's stopped.

Everyone reacts.

Charlene Oh no! I said to my mother, what's the point of going up north? It's been like that all my life, you know. Her making decisions for me that lead into an abyss.

Kirk   I met an Abbess once. She was really nice. Religious and everything. She wore this long frocky thing.

Charlene I said AN ABYSS. A dark and endless hole of nothingness.

Kirk   Oh right. Well, it is a bit of a hole, nothing much there. Wait a minute, there's a sign. It says, Doncaster.

Charlene Doncaster!

Mellie Spangle Sooo everybody, I am deeply saddened to have to tell you that we are suffering from an unavoidable delay. There's a cow asleep on the track!

Jimmy   I told you I seen a cow. It's meant!

Mellie Spangle Hmmph hrrrp. As we have a bit of time I'd like to entertain you during this short delay with a little number some of you may know, about that place just down the line.

SONG: Free Parking

Tell you a little somethin you travellin' folks need to know
If you're down at heel, got nowhere special to go
Like you been all night driving, that crazy A1M
You can stop in Donny any hour that heaven sends

Because there's free parking everywhere you go
Get your hand out of your pocket,
You don't need no dough
Some people come here drifting,
Don't know what they'll find
Well, it's one great parking paradise. The best of its kind.

Donny, oh Donny,
Not a meter in sight
Traffic wardens on the dole
You can park any time you like

You can park your trolley,
Why not get off the train?

Lay down your hat in Donny
You'll never pay to park again!

You can park outside the Rovers
Or by the old golf course,
Anywhere in the town centre
You can park a cart and horse.

You can park in the middle,
You can park on the side,
You can park a double decker bus
You can even park and ride....

Charlene But I don't want to go to Doncaster. We might as well give up. Might as well sit here and die.

Kirk   Yeah! What's your name? Mine's Kirk.

Charlene Charlene. And my best friend's called Marlene. Marlene and Charlene.

Kirk   Where are you going, Charlene?

Charlene My grandmother's. Newcastle. Thanks to some whim of my mother's. I couldn't possibly buy some of your lager off you, could I, Kirk? My nana, grandmother, will give you the money at Newcastle, but there isn't anything in the buffet, according to that man over there.

Kirk   Yeah, course you can, Charlene. Don't you worry about the money, I got loads of lager. Have a sandwich too.

Charlene Euh, thanks. What's in this sandwich? It's all chewy.

Kirk   It's Caribbean. From Marks and Spencers.

Charlene Marks and Spencers! Yuck.

Kirk   Oh, sorry about that. My girlfriend bought them. Here's a photo of her.

Charlene Eugh, lovely. She likes cuddly toys, does she?

Kirk   Oh yeah. I wonder how long we'll be sitting here? Still, I wouldn't want to be anywhere else. It's really great, isn't it? Just sitting here, not a care in the world, drinking Stella Artois!

Charlene I don't want to be anywhere. Don't want to get there, don't want to go home either.

Kirk   What do you wanna do?

Charlene How should I know!

(*To herself*) I want to look at my skin in a mirror. Want to see exactly what is happening to my pores. Want to scratch my name on things. Want a new nose. Want to smoke. Wanna have long hair. Wouldn't mind some Smarties actually.

(*Aloud*) The question is, why has she sent me away? What for? To Longbenton, to my nana and her stinkin Scottie dog, and her big nose, and her cluck-cluck noise, going, come along, Charlene, let's get you home, and off we'll go on the bus, through Eldon Square, and she'll say, there's your friends the vampire bats. And then, what a shame, they could be so nice looking. And back at her house, I'll sit on the end of her settee, and she'll say, how's school? Let's get some fat into you, could you just get the washing in? And all the time I'll be looking out of the window at the concrete road, and the little old Geordie men walking past in their brown hats, and I'll hear me nana on the phone talking to someone. Is she alright? How long? Things like that, and I'll go and stand in the kitchen with the radio on, and the checky tablecloth and the bird in the cage, Freddie the budgie, and I'll think about the meaning of life, and I'll wonder why my mother sent me to her mother, and what am I going to do in Longbenton for a week? Then my nana will get off the phone and come into the kitchen and she'll say, Charlene, pet lamb, you could clean out the budgie for me, then go to the shop and buy some Windolene. Then we'll have some chips. Windolene, the budgie, Longbenton, the checky tablecloth.

Who were you talking to? I'll say. Then she'll say, there's something I've got to tell you, pet lamb, your mam's having plastic surgery. Just like that. She's getting a new nose. Why didn't she tell me? I'll say, what's wrong with her nose? It's the same as my nose. She thought you'd be annoyed, says Nana. I am. Don't be

like that, says Nana. Get the Windolene, clean out the budgie. I
want to speak to her, I say. You can't. Why not? She's just coming
round from the anaesthetic. I see my nose in the mirror, and I
start to cry, because it's more important that I have a nice nose
than my mum, isn't it? I mean, who cares about her mouldy nose?
And another thing, it's not hers to change, she's my MOTHER.

Kirk   Oh Charlene, that's terrible. Fancy your mother
changing her appearance without even telling you. No wonder
you're so pale and sick and everything.

Charlene Am I? (*Pleased*) It's like abuse or something, isn't it?

Kirk   Thing is, Charlene, it hasn't actually happened yet.

Charlene I know!

Kirk   But if it did, Charlene, it would be terrible.

Charlene I would never speak to her again. That's what she's like,
Kirk. She just thinks about herself, her clothes, her face.

Kirk   Sounds like a monster.

Charlene She is. No, not exactly a monster.

Kirk   Oh no. I'm sure she's a lovely lady underneath.

Charlene She is. It's just she's very selfish, that's all. And she
doesn't realise what it's like to be me. No one knows what it's like
to be me. Can I have another Stella?

Kirk   Yeah, course you can. Thanks for sharing that with
me, Charlene. You've helped me understand something about
the human condition there. You know something? You're
really special.

Mellie Spangle You know, just sittin' here, thinking about life
an' all, you start thinkin' about your nearest an' dearest, the
ones who stayed, the ones who got away. An' I ask myself, does
anyone ever belong to us? Can you sign someone up on the
dotted line forever? I wrote this song when I was thinkin' about
this very thing.

SONG: Lost Property

Once I thought that you were mine,
That we were truly intertwined
That we would never ever fall apart
Like buddleia and butterfly
Or apples in an apple pie,
And then you turned around and broke my heart.

I feel abandoned, cut in two,
Like losing one of all my shoes
I'm half a person, quite at sea
Since I became lost property

And now I'm like an unclaimed case
Something precious that's misplaced
I'm waiting here for you to make a claim

Because can't you see, it's such a waste,
To sit about, inanimate,
When everything could be the same again

I feel abandoned, cut in two,
Like losing one of all my shoes
I'm half a person, quite at sea
Since I became lost property.

Mummy Natalie, don't you want to come and play I Spy, or
snuggle up with mumsy and have a nice yogurt? Leave the big
lady alone for a bit. Nats, that's my baby, you know. I'm her
mother.

Finola Hum humpph, I was wondering if anyone would mind
if I did a short piece from *Blood and Sex* by Kevin Barks. I am
playing The Slag.

Kirk Slugs? England's full of 'em. They come out at night,
leave slimy trails on the bed.

Finola I think you mean slugs.

Kirk Yes, slugs. Horrible things, all over the garden, ruining
the food.

Finola   I am a slag, not a slug. Shall I go on? Are you ready? In I come, I'm wearing a torn blouse thing with lipstick gashed all over my face, and I'm holding a hanky. Anyone got a hanky? Eugh, thanks... So here I come, lights down, you have to imagine there's this body on the stage with knives stuck into it, and there's this sawing sound. Could you?

Here I come, here I come... Oh boo hoo. In the play I would cry properly, but I'm not particularly moved at the moment. So you left me for that bitch, you bastard. I was BLIND BLIND! I can't see anything because in an earlier scene I had acid thrown in my face, and I'm hideously disfigured. It wasn't really acid, it was just water, that's theatre for you! BLIND with fear, lost in the distilling postmortem of my existence, all my life, fuck all of you!

Jimmy   Eh, watch your tongue! I have niver heard such filth, me mammy would twang you with a kettle. Little wee Natalie has had quite enough with Miss Tubby and her dorty university talk.

Finola   It's ACTING. Honestly!

Kirk   I think you're bloody fantastic! Bloody great, bloody marvellous, the way you came through the door like that, and the actions too. You're fantastic.

Finola   Really? Did you really? Is that a spare seat? Perhaps I could join you for a while.

Kirk   Help yourself. You remind me of someone with your red hair, doesn't she, Charlene? Doesn't matter. It was the way you moved your hands about all the time. Someone famous, who is it now?

Finola   Nicole Kidman?

Kirk   No, it's not her.

Finola   Tilda Swinton?

Kirk   Nah. Who is it?

Finola   Julianne Moore?

Kirk   Wait a minute, got it... FERGIE!

Finola   FERGIE! Oh no! (*Holds her head in her hands*)

Mellie Spangle News from headquarters! They've woken up the cow and things should be moving soon. I want to sing a song for all you lonely people out there, who think your journeys are worthwhile, and let's hope they are.

SONG: No Such Thing

There's no such thing as a straight line
To the place you're running to
For as soon as you start the ball rolling
You get a pebble in your shoe

And there's no such thing as a straight line

You lose your map, fall in a trap,
Get confused when the road forks
No such thing as plain sailing
In an ocean full of sharks

By the time you cross the border
You'll think you're at the end
But as soon as you start travelling
You have to learn to bend.

And there's no such thing as a straight line.

Go bravely, go with courage,
Hold your ticket in your hand
And hang on to your suitcase
For as long as you can

And there's no such thing as a straight line.

For a train is like a person,
Its heart may start to rust
It may speed through the tunnels
But one day it's going to bust.

And there's no such thing as a straight line.

Charlene How much longer?! We've been here at least five years. Help me, I need some drugs.

Mummy Charlene? Would you like to come and sit with me and I'll paint your fingernails, shall I, now Natalie's gone off with her friend and left me all alone.

Charlene I don't think so. I'm not ten, you know.

Kirk   She's not ten, you know.

Mummy I've got black nail polish.

Charlene I suppose so, if you're that bored.

Mummy Natalie seems to have forgotten how good I am at looking after children. Look at her showing that woman her tummy.

Prof   Yubba bubba. Oooh, she's really quite sweet, isn't she?

Charlene starts sucking her thumb. Jimmy McPhee suddenly clutches his head in agony.

Jimmy   I shouldna be on this train. I'm a coward! I couldn't face the game. I lost me nerve. Pride ruined me. The question is, what now? What will me mammy say? Do my skills transfer?

Finola   If you're psychic you should know if your skills transfer. That's what pisses me off about psychics. They always act as if they know everything. And maybe Audrey Thingumabob is just better at chess than you are.

Jimmy   Nooo, don't say that.

Finola   Load of fuss about bloody nothing. Huh. Go back there and fight, Jimmy.

Jimmy   Aye, but it's too late. What have I done? I've let down me mammy, and Motherwell, and Scotland. I just panicked. Mr Strang tried to stop me, but he could nee.

Mummy At least you've got skills. There you are, Charlene. We could do your toenails next. Look, Natalie's gone to sleep, with that woman. How sweet she looks, with all that felt-tip on her face. So content. I was never like that when I was young. My father kept on doing this (*brushes hair out of her eyes in a swooshy public school manner*) with his hair, and mummy did interior design using stuff like chicken wire and buttons and sheep's heads. Anyway, I hardly knew them as they sent me off to boarding school. I wasn't very clever but they didn't let you fail exams there. They wired you up so that you did automatic writing, so I made it to university, Durham, actually, met my darling Snooky, Lord Snooky of Northumberland, and married him! Just like that. Great wedding, designed by my mother, spoons everywhere, dangling from the ceiling. Anyway the point of marrying Snooks was to get pregnant. Even then I had imaginary babies that I pushed around in prams. When I was young I used to love to play at 'giving birth'. Sometimes I did it with real animal blood.

Finola   Oh dear.

Mummy We tried and tried to have a baby, but nothing happened. (*Pause*) But in the end, I had Natalie, and now I'm happy!

Jimmy   That's not true, now is it? I think you're telling us a little fib. I've been watching you. I'm sorry for your trouble and all, but aaach...

Mummy Of course it's true. What do you mean? Why are you all staring at me? I'm perfectly normal. I'm like a woman in a magazine. Look at all these toys.

Oh God. Snooky and I, we did our best. We even had tests in a hospital! A doctor put her hand up... but she couldn't find anything. Hopeless! Then Snooky started on the heroin. He would disappear for long periods. I think he's, er, in a clinic somewhere.

Finola   So Natalie's not your little girl then?

Mummy She is now. Oh God, I can't lie any longer. This morning, I was walking along just minding my own business, when I met someone, a little someone who was so pleased to see me. I spy, I thought, I spy with my little eye something beginning

with N. No, no, don't look like that, it's all fine. I know her
mother. She's called Fiona Blazingby and I said I would look
after Natalie for the day while she went shopping. Oh alright, I
didn't say anything about the train, or going to live in Durham
under a false identity. Why should I? Look, Natalie doesn't mind.
Oh stop looking so worried, you lot. Fiona will get over it. All she
cares about is clippy clopping round the shops with her little
handbags. Let's play another game! Let's have a séance or
something. Jimmy! Wink Murder? You can be the winker!

Jimmy   I BEG YOUR PARDON! I knew you was fishy, with
your I Spy and your weirdy colouring crayons!

Charlene So Natalie's not your little girl? You nicked her? But
she's not yours. You can't be her mum, you haven't got the same
noses. You're an imposter!

Kirk   Hang on, Charlene! I can see how you, she, felt...
Anyone would abduct a child under those circumstances!

Finola   No they wouldn't, Kirk! Perhaps it's time to let her
phone Natalie's mother to tell her she's alright.

Kirk   My phone, yeah.

Finola   Come on, Kirk.

Kirk   I could do that.

Finola   Give it here.

Kirk   It's not really a phone. It's just, er, a pretend thing. I
was just practising for when I really had a phone.

Finola   That's a joke. I've heard that joke. You've been talking
to Ramona. We all know about you and Ramona.

Kirk   There is no Ramona. It's just me and my pretend
phone going up and down the line. Meeting people and talking
and eating my sandwiches. It's nice. I've had a lovely day. A real
treat of a day. I'm going to give you all my phone number. We're
all friends now!

Charlene What's the point of giving us your phone number if it's not a real phone, stupid?

Kirk   It's the thought that counts though, isn't it?

Finola   Oh my GOD, this is too dramatic. I'll have to make a citizen's arrest!

Mellie Spangle (*Bursting into crackly life*) Hello hello, I am sad to say this train is now on track, delayed by only three hours. My name is Mellie Spangle, and I am the King of the North East Line!

Prof   (*Waking up. She doesn't know about Natalie*) We're bloody well moving. Finlay and I will soon collide.

Finola   Excuse me, madam. I am hereby arresting you for...

Jimmy   Wait, I'm seeing somethin', somethin' powerful that will change the course of our lives forever and ever!

If you look at the game of chess, it will tell you that every move yoos make is strategic, and will tek you somewhere else, but it may not be where you wanted, because you didn't see all the possible consequences of that move, or mebbes, like me, yoos are susceptible to interference and there are some things that yoos can't predict rationally.

Prof   (*Still struggling to wake up*) What on earth are you on about?

Jimmy   Hev yoos looked out tha winda ya stupid numpties? Train's going back the way it came. We've got a second chance.

Mellie Spangle Helloo helloo. We are very sorry to have to tell you that the train has had to terminate its journey and return to its point of departure. It's just the way the cookie crumbles today folks.

Finola   What a bummer.

Mummy What time is it? I could get her back by three. I suppose I'd better. She doesn't seem to like me that much. She seems to like big bouncy people.

Charlene I want my mum. I don't care about her nose. I just want my mum, and my nana. I LOVE MY MUM.

Prof   Finlay and me, we're not to be. No cakes, no things. Actually, I can't wait to get back to my room, to the smell of paper and ink. It fits me, you see, Nat. Oh, grrrrr from me!

Jimmy   It's a sign. I will return to play Audrey Damart tomorra. We shall lock, head to head, he will try to defeat me. Maybe he'll win, maybe I'll lose. At least there will be a buffet. I will hev courage. I may be beaten but I will hev learnt how te play I Spy and prevented a child abduction. That's the kind of wee man I am.

Kirk   I should be able to catch the 2.15 to Leeds. Think I'll go Virgin next time. (*Dials number*) Ramona! I still love ya, even though you're not there.

Mellie Spangle (*Terrible crackling, so that we only get the odd word*) Inconvenience... arriving soon... belongings... with... from me. Pleasant... (*The song sparks into action*)

SONG: Personal Belongings

Keep a hold of your stuff
Don't leave it there on the rack
I've had enough
Of giving stuff back

I don't want your pieces
Your personal clutter
Your crumples and creases
Your mumbles and mutters

I like a clean train,
Nothing left behind
You won't see me again
Don't lose your mind

Just take all your history
Hold it tight in your hands
Pack up your mysteries
And all of your plans

I'm not responsible,
I'm only a guard
Don't leave anything
Not even a calling card

Whatever you carry
That's your concern
What's yours is yours
Some people never learn.

Keep a hold of your stuff
Don't leave it there on the rack
I've had enough
Of giving stuff back

Lights down.

The End

Doughnuts Like Fanny's

The rude title of my play about TV cook Fanny Cradock raised a few eyebrows on the touring circuit. You had to know the reference, which is that Johnnie (Fanny's partner) once said, live on television: 'Perhaps you too can make doughnuts like Fanny's!' The touring play has a gentler title, *The Lives and Loves of a Kitchen She-Devil*.

This play was written for Quondam Arts Trust in 2003. It was really the idea of director and actor Fine Time Fontayne, who suggested Fanny as a great subject for a touring play, and who had collected some of the original footage of Fanny. I jumped at the idea of writing about one of my childhood phantoms. The image of Fanny Cradock staring out at me with black eyelashes from our small black and white television haunted me. I am sure we ate green mashed potato at some point in my childhood.

I researched the play through reading Fanny's own writing (her autobiography, *Something's Burning*, is a wonderful feat of self-deception) and watching her television shows, as a cook, then later being interviewed as an ageing celebrity by Parkinson and Jonathan Ross. She is a fascinating, yet awful personality. I struggled to find the good in her. Fanny always did whatever she liked. She lived her life joyously and selfishly, and although her last years were lonely and sad, she had some good times.

The play was later adapted into a one-woman show for the actor Sandra Hunt.

Julia Darling

Doughnuts Like Fanny's was first presented by Quondam Theatre Company at the Arts Centre, University of Central Lancashire, Preston, on 1 October 2002. It was directed by Fine Time Fontayne.

CAST

Fanny	Justine Adams
The men in her life	Neil Gore
The women in her life	Sandra Hunt

SONG: War Food

After years of tripe, and porridge oats
we look like puddings, smell like goats
WAR FOOD EVERY DAY
life's a cabbage, life is greens,
making stews with butter beans
war food night and day.
It's all WAR FOOD WAR FOOD
even a blancmange is rude (have a banana)
it slops about, it's often bland
even when it's contraband.
WAR FOOD NIGHT AND DAY

We've been boiling bones, counting eggs
chewing skin from chicken's legs.
We look like prunes, we're dull as soup
We've never heard of cantaloupe

Chorus

We don't have dinner, we have tea
with marmite, toast and Ovaltine,
mince and onions, corned beef hash
and everything is boiled or mashed

Chorus

ACT ONE

SCENE ONE

Husbands and babies

Fanny rises in camp splendour from behind a counter.

An end to mashed potato and Spam! To cut-price tins of condensed milk and paper packets of tea sweepings, and ticky snack pies, and thin soups. To hell with tripe and onions, pigs fry and sponges made of water and one egg. How wearying it is, when you dream of cooking exquisite, subtle dishes to be forced to work with damn leftovers, to scrimp and scrape and never to splash out on luxuries. Today we shall make sweet and savoury doves!

She goes flamboyantly to a cupboard to get a mixing bowl. We hear the sound of a baby wailing.

Oh no. There's always something! Children, husbands, always something. Ssh, I'm in the middle of a demonstration!

The baby cries even louder. Fanny goes and picks it up, but she's no good with it.

I was only sixteen when I married your father, Sydney, in Canterbury. Bijou, that's my mother, said, I don't want any soiled doves in my house! And I said, I'm not a soiled dove. I'm married. And she said, well, we'll have a ball! That was what she was like! She dressed me in a white gown, with white feathers everywhere. What am I going to do with this baby? Someone? Please?

The baby quietens down. Fanny puts it into a mixing bowl.

At the party, Bijou told the band not to play *Auld Lang Syne*. She said that every time they played that tune the man she stood next to got killed. So she stood next to my new husband, Sydney. His death was devastating. One moment he was flying over the house in his aeroplane. Next thing I knew he was being scraped off a cliff side. Ghastly. It was the only time in my life that I ever did any knitting. I knitted enough baby clothes to outfit a creche.

I loved him, you see. But there's no point going over it. I'm Fanny Cradock now. A remarkable success story. I'm a celebrity cook, an authoress, an interiors consultant, a psychic, which is why I know that Sydney is quite well. They say it's so light over there. It's always been a comfort, knowing that.

Don't worry about the baby. There's no need. He'll be fine. Someone will look after him. They always do. Same thing happened to me. Bijou was furious when she found out she was pregnant.

Now Fanny is beating egg whites, chatting as she cooks.

She was only sixteen. Same age I was. Daddy wanted a son to carry on the Pechey name. We're linked to royalty, you see. But she had me and I made her miserable. So she went to see her mother. Gran lived in a mansion in Essex. Apthorp. She got there about eleven o'clock. Ran upstairs to find her mother, wrapped in a turkish towel, brushing her teeth with a dry toothbrush. She couldn't stand spit, you see. She abandoned me, lying downstairs on the billiard table. Gran took a long time to get dressed. She had so many straps and buttons. By the time they came down I was screaming and rolling towards the edge of the billiard table, beneath me a marble floor! My grandmother grabbed me and said, Bijou, you are not fit to have a child. Have her! exclaimed my mother. For your birthday, Mumsy! And Gran said, Oh go on then. I accept. Yes. That's how I came to be brought up by my grandmother until I was ten.

You know, when I switch on an electric mixer to whip some egg whites, I still see Gran with her white ringed fingers curved over a thin, worn shard of carving knife, whipping egg whites on a Rockingham plate to a stiff peak with one lovely uninterrupted movement of the wrist. And now I'm a celebrity! I've got loads of money, loads and loads, and houses, and I travel all over the world! So let's proceed with our sweet and savoury doves, using choux pastry that I made earlier!

There is a loud knocking at the door.

Do excuse me!

She goes to open the door and is handed a second baby, which also cries.

Oh, for heaven's sake! Arthur! Come back! This isn't fair. I know
I married you... it was only four months after Sydney, but I was
grief-stricken. It was a terrible mistake. Please take baby
Christopher away.

She hands the baby back.

I'm sorry everyone. I'm going to have to cancel this performance
until a further date. (*She pulls out a trunk*) It's just not going to be
possible to carry on with these kinds of interruptions. In my line
of work, you always get stalkers, mad people who follow you
about. It's just something I have to cope with.

She pulls out a fireman's helmet.

Husband number three! Greg. It was just a quick thing. You
know, he was a firemen. Big biceps. The hose! No babies, thank
God. He was such a dish, charging into the flames! And he was
well off too, had a boat down on the river. But he was a whim.
Shame I married him. Let's forget all this now, shall we? It's not
important. There were two men in my life. That's all, darlings. I
mean, Greg was exquisite, but it was just before the war. Tripe
was exquisite. Let's just close this up, shall we?

She closes the trunk, putting the baby out of sight.

SCENE TWO

Poverty

(*Typing*) Consider a pink luncheon! At my grandmother's house
such occasions were commonplace. The mahogany would be
covered with pink damask, and little pink lampshades on pink
candles would enliven the light from those stained-glass windows.
Pink roses, sweet peas, London Pride and Gypsophila would
cascade from a silver and crystal peregne. There would be pink
sugared almonds, pink fondants (home-made) and pink icing-
coated Cape gooseberries in the bonbonniere. Hours would be
spent in folding pairs of pink table napkins into peacocks. All the
food would be pink, down to the inevitable pink ice bombe and
the china. This china, together with the glass, had a room of its
own, generally covered in dust, unlit, gloomy and down two very

steep steps. I can remember handing myself down these steps when very small, like a bird descending into the side of its cage, backside first, as Gran, list in hand, made her selection like a general arranging his logistics. You may ask, what am I doing in this bedsit with a young child and cardboard soles in my shoes? I am learning how the poor live. And I can tell you, it stinks. But unlike layabouts who expect charity from the state, I'm working night and day. Don't play with the gas, Peter!

I learned tout court that if you knock on enough doors you sell a vacuum cleaner. It's as simple as that. And when you have a small boy locked in a bedsitting room waiting to be fed and the only hope is a vacuum cleaner sale, of twenty-five shillings, you knock on doors and you go on knocking on doors. One way or another I have never stopped knocking on doors since.

She stops typing and starts sewing.

Pins, Peter. I said I needed pins! Stop whining, child. We had tea an hour ago! All you ever want to do is eat.

She holds up an impossible garment, all the wrong size.

It's not the dress that's the problem, sweetie, it's you. Let's face it, you look like the back of a London tram.

Fanny recites a poem.

It was a time of makeshift and make do.
I even went busking, I learnt how to queue
I made swiss rolls and pies, took up rich ladies' hems
Fluttered my eyes at unsuitable men.

And when I'd finished,
I limped back home
Sat by the gaslight
Wrote terrible poems

(*Spoken*) Alright, they got rejected from *Argosy* magazine! All great writers get rejected!

Fanny starts impatiently packing a case.

Peter, you're going to stay with your Grandpa and Grandma Evans dearest. Your father's mummy and daddy. They'll look after you, send you to a public school. You'll see me again when you're grown. They're stinking rich. They've said it's better if they bring you up themselves. You don't want lots of changes, do you, darling? You want to just grow up, like the rest of us. Mummy's got to earn a living, hasn't she? Mummy's going to be famous, you see, and that takes a lot of work. You won't be bored like you are here. Come along then. They're waiting at the door. They think I've neglected you. But we love each other, don't we, Peterkins?

Fanny passes the suitcase to invisible grandparents outside the door. She receives a letter in return, which she sits down and reads.

You may not contact him at any point until he reaches the age of twenty-one years. (*Aside*) Well, I can't say I'll miss him.

So what? Mother took me from Gran when I was ten and placed me in a distinguished boarding school where I learned nothing, forgot all I knew and hourly hoped to die. I remember eating a congealing date pudding that looked like operation scar tissue. Lesbian matrons who wrenched our ties straight and favoured little girls with pink cheeks and golden curls. Chalking my chilblained nose in a vain attempt to extinguish its all too fervent light. In the end they expelled me for holding seances with nice girls. They said I was warped.

She tears up the letter.

SCENE THREE

Fanny meets Johnnie

SONG: I Wanna Man

I wanna man who likes his food,
Doesn't need to be handsome
Doesn't need to be good.

But most chaps are pigs
They've all got flaws

Most of them turn out
Terrible bores

See, I wanna man with a pedigree
With a golden ring
And a family tree.

But there's no one there
Though they come in droves
They just make me yawn
And mark my clothes

I wanna man who's flexible
With a motor car
And sex appeal.

But there's no one there
Who fits the bill
After half an hour
I've had my fill

And I wanna man
Who's in control
Who's gonna do
What I tell him to

But there's no one there
Who understands
How I wanna man
With a cummerbund

Who's good in the kitchen
(A man of distinction
with perfect diction)

Fanny smokes, as if at a ball, eyeing up the talent.

Bloody Isle of Dogs. Helluva place to get to on public transport.
I got a lift in a utility truck. This is the Bore War, dear! Bore as in
boring. Some chap over there fancies me, I can tell, but I don't
like big fair Englishmen, and he's smoking a pipe. On the other
hand, I hear he's a major. Here he comes.

He, invisibly, asks her to dance.

I suppose I could.

She starts to dance alone, speaks as if talking over a man's shoulder.

He tells me that he's got four children and a dull wife in
Scotland. Easy to lose, I tell him. You've always been good at
losing things. I suddenly know everything about him. How he'll
treat his pipe like a dog does its bones, burying them into
armchairs, losing them in coat linings. Or lighters, around him
they will never work, and car door handles will break in his
hands, suitcase straps will disappear, tape recorders and luggage
zip fasteners and buttons will all magically fall away from him.
His name is Cradock. Major John Cradock. I like that. I'll do
something about his glasses, a monocle maybe. I want him in my
kitchen, licking out my bowls.

SCENE FOUR

London

Fanny is typing frantically.

(*Stops*) I'll write a cookery book! I've written God knows how
many novels and none of them make any money. I'm going to
phone my agent. Get me a glass of something, Johnnie. (*Snaps
fingers*) Champagne, I think.

She picks up the phone.

Hello. Dear, it's me! Yes. I'm going to write a cookery book.
It will be wonderful. What do you mean, the competition is
excessive? I don't think you heard me properly. I'm writing a
cookery book. Novelists don't make any money, do they? Not
good enough, sweetheart.

She slams the phone down.

Stupid fool. I'll sack her. I'll call it *Practical Cookery*, I think. Is that
good? I'll write about things you can make with dried eggs.
Mashed potato, that sort of thing, you know, for unimaginative

housewives. And after that I'll write another one called *The Ambitious Cook*. And we'll have a dinner party for Lady Chetwynd, Lady Daniel, and my publisher, John Lehman, Andrew Dakers and Captain Dudley Cutbill, André Simon. My most intimate friends, darling. André writes for the *Wine and Food Journal*.

This is the menu, Johnnie. Are you ready? Les canapés des gourmets. Little pies, with la crème forestière, that's a kind of green creamy sauce. Les coquilles St Jacques de Marquises, la poulard poêlée Massena, les petit pois Lucullus. Peas, basically. La salade verte. Green salad. And for the wine? Oh, let's say, a fino, a 1942 Charmes, Chateau Haut-Brion, Chateau Haut-Bailly. And a champagne. Can you sort that out, my love?

SCENE FIVE

Beginnings of fame

Fanny reads a newspaper article by André Simon, the food critic.

'Our American friends, who imagine that near starvation is all they can expect when they visit us, may well rub their eyes and read again the menu of this memorable dinner. Apart from the good food and wine served at just the right temperature, what was beyond belief was the fact that there was no cook in the kitchen. The cook was at the head of the table, beautifully gowned and attending to her guests. She prepared several dishes at the table, each one a masterpiece. This is Mrs John Cradock, or Frances Dale. All her books have so far been novels, but she has now written a practical cookery book, which is due to be published in June. I must have it!' André Simon, the food critic...

SCENE SIX

More work

Fanny is wearing a new hat and looking rather successful. The phone rings.

Johnnie, it's the *Daily Express*! He wants eight articles on 'My Kitchen, by Frances Gale'. Twenty guineas each!

She puts the phone down. It rings again.

It's Evelyn Garret from the *Daily Telegraph*. Evelyn, I'm so sorry, I'm already writing about food for the *Express*. Me? I can do anything. Clothes, interior design... Another name? How about Elsa Frances? Good. How much?

She puts the phone down.

They want a column on make do and mend. You'll have to do the diagrams, dear. You know, how to make a candelabra out of tin cans. Make a topless gown from an old dress. You can do that, dear.

The phone rings again.

It's the *Daily Graphic*. They're offering one month's trial, fifteen guineas a week and five guineas expenses. To do whatever I like.

The phone rings again.

I'm Philip Essex, writing about Atlantis, Mary Carden on beauty, and I'm Susan Leigh and Frances Dale, the children's author. I'm writing a book about ghosts as Phyllis Cradock. I'm Nan Sortain for the *Telegraph*, writing an agony column about acne and leg waxing. The origin of Easter eggs, a new approach to heat wave cookery. How to make six different bed heads for very little cash, the etiquette of tipping, how to plan your weekly menu, how to stop cakes splitting in the middle. A standard recipe for bramble jelly. How do I know all this stuff? My grandmother was a very resourceful woman, you see. She taught me everything I know.

SONG: Bon Viveur

At Charcos in Chelsea,
If you are gay and wealthy
You can eat chicken from a spit

And the White Hart in Essex
Is jolly and impressive
But the oysters were full of grit.

Oh we're bon viveur
You'd better call him sir
And bring me the best that you've got.

Because we're bon viveur,
You'd better make us purr
We can make or break you in a shot.

The Dragon in Cookham
Is certainly worth a look in
You can drink aperitifs by the lake.

But don't go to the Royston
They'll serve you poison
And horse meat dressed up as steak.

From Glasgow to Tooting
We know what you're cooking
We've got an eye on your sauces
And the quality of your courses.

SCENE SEVEN

Travels

Fanny puts on a travelling scarf. She's sitting in a car, with the scarf flying out behind her.

Friday afternoon. We drive through villages, rich with old brick and timber. It's all copy, darling. Twilight came and was replaced by the starlight of windows spattering the frosty darkness. There's an inn. Let's go for it!

She steps out of her car and goes to sit at a small table.

A small sediment of Brown Windsor greased the bottom of two chipped soup plates. A mean fire smoulders beneath a large Victorian looking glass. Two congealing rolls of fat enfolded a pap of coarse breadcrumbs and packet herbs. This mess masqueraded as rolled stuffed veal. A spoonful of custard powder custard clogged two leathery prunes.

We found that soiled towels and dirty lavatories were precursors of lukewarm food and laggard service. We rarely had a good meal at the end of a long winding drive. There would be fine paintings, valuable furniture, expensive carpets and curtains. But you can't eat curtains.

It was a huge success, darlings! Everyone was talking about it. They wondered if it was going to be their turn. We had to keep going. The age of the grand hotel was passing! It was in the small amateur places that we found quality, where the owners were cooks, see. The little touches mattered, like warmed ironed newspapers in the morning, for instance.

What days, Johnnie! What days! Spinning for mackerel across Cornish bays, drinking heather beer, eating undyed kippers. Or peeling off horrid nylon sheets and sleeping in our clothes, eating cold toast like damp flannel. Grapefruit segments that taste of tin cans! We were the critics of England's restaurants and inns. We *were* good taste. And even better, we were anonymous.

We learnt how to spin a spider's web of sugar and store it indefinitely. How to make Russian blood soup, the ancient Greek method of growing melons. We judged tripe competitions. We dined in pubs and palaces. We feasted on mountain plateaux and took trout from streams in the forests of the Savoie. We had supper a thousand feet below sea level in the Balearic caverns; drank from horns, goblets, tankards... haven't we, Johnnie? We have fished for baby octopus by moonlight in the Bay of Naples and cooked our catch on the sands at dawn, and roasted fish in sands so hot they scorched our feet. Bird's nest soup, fried worms, alsatian steaks. Kaffir beer, kangaroo soup, sea snails and hedgehogs, rooks, becfigues, larks, monkey, beetles... they have all gone down in their turn.

SCENE EIGHT

Back home. Peter

Home. Fanny drags a suitcase onto the stage. There's a huge pile of post that she starts to go through.

Can you get me some dry cornflakes? I'll start on this, love. Look at that washing up, did we leave it like that? Perhaps we should get another cleaner.

She opens a letter.

Another offer from a... Mr Dupont. Christ, that's a lot of money. He wants to buy the Bon Viveur name, to write nice things about his restaurant. They can stick it up their you know whats.

What's that funny smell? Johnnie, that parcel's moving. (*She pins it down with her foot and peers at it.*) Eugh, it's someone's blasted stew. I wish people wouldn't do that. She wants me to taste it! It must be two weeks old. Chuck it out. Chuck it all out.

She opens another letter.

What's this, a meat tenderiser? What rubbish! Just buy tender meat in the first place! Honestly.

There's a loud knocking at the door. Fanny looks up.

Shut up, dogs! Who on earth is it?

When he comes in I don't recognise him. He's rather good looking, but also scruffy, with a scarf round his neck and a duffle coat. He says, don't you know who I am? I don't. Well, he looks vaguely familiar. For a moment I think it must be a chef we've insulted! Then he says, I'm your son, Peter. Well, well, I say. I'm twenty-one, he says. I've just come down from university. I like the way he says that. Just come down... Mmmmm, have a seat, I say, sorry about the mess. Cleaner's left.

I expect you're terribly clever. Johnnie, go and get him a gin. Are you angry with me? Well don't be, I always knew you'd come back. As Kahlil Gibran said, 'Your children are not your children, Their souls dwell in the house of tomorrow, which you cannot visit, Even in your dreams.' So I didn't. I knew you were in good hands. I thought about you every day. But we're together now, and look at you, with your handsome face, and your nice jacket. I would shave off the moustache, sweetheart. Let's go out. I'll take you to a little restaurant I know in Chelsea. You can meet Henri, the chef there, one of my most intimate friends, darling. Can't he, Johnnie!

She walks through the audience.

Hilary, darling, this is my son, Peter, just come down from
university. Isn't he lovely? He's terribly clever! Evangeline! Peter,
this is my next-door neighbour, Evangeline, she's an actress,
darling! You must get to know her. Oh there's André. André,
guess who's come to stay? This is Peter. Peter, André is a brilliant
journalist and food critic. And there's Norman Hartnett, the
designer, sweetie. Go and talk to him, Peter. Tell him who you
are. Yes, this is my son, we've always been terribly close. He
phones me up all the time. We talk for hours. That's Pamela, one
of my assistants, like a daughter!

I live life to the full, you see, dear. But now you're with me, my
cup brimmeth over. Pamela, come over here, dear. This is Peter.
Doesn't he look like me?!

Interval

ACT TWO

SCENE ONE

Don't Cross Me

SONG: Don't Cross Me

I'm not the kind of girl to dwell
I speak my mind, and it's as well
I do, because the world is full of liars.
I can't bear cheats, I don't like crooks,
Or critics that don't like my books.
I damn the lot to eternal fire.

Don't cross me
Or I'll cross you.
I'm a river
That's too wide,
A wall you can't walk through.
Don't cross me,
Or I'll have you
You don't know what
It's like in my shoes.

All you snipes and underlings
That dare to tell me what you think
Can take a running jump into the Thames
And anyone who dares to say
They don't want it my way
I never ever want to see again

Don't cross me

I'm a broad who knows her mind
And I'm not known for being kind
I don't like it when life gets in the way
If you don't fit into my plan
You'd better go get on a tram
Because today won't be your lucky day.

Don't cross me

Yes, Pamela. I give Peter everything. I introduce him to my friends, I buy him clothes, I open up my heart to him, and what does he do? He seduces my assistant, Pamela, under my nose. He says he loves her... Honestly! I don't want to talk about it. I feel let down, and that's the truth. Children can be so hurtful. God knows where he is now. We had a row. Off he went, slamming the door. Don't come crawling back to me, I said. And as for Pamela, I can't be doing with girls like that. Tarts.

SCENE TWO

All the world's a stage

Fanny re-enters in a beautiful evening gown and a different wig.

I don't like the stage. God, my mother loved it. She was always dragging me along to things. Anyway, I used to say that I refused to belong to a profession which makes civilised dining an impossibility. But then Johnnie persuaded me, didn't you, darling sweetness? We decided to put on a live show. I would wear something like I've got on now. Invite the press. Start with a soufflé, and Johnnie would help me, be my assistant. We would call it *Kitchen Magic*.

SCENE THREE

Rehearsals

They are getting ready for the big Albert Hall show.

Do it again, Johnnie! Bring the sugar over and then turn and put the dish in the oven. Do it again! It's got to be right. Oh for heaven's sake. And this light above my head is giving me a headache. Who's in charge of it? And where's the damn cranberries? What's the point of putting the cranberries under the orchestra pit? I need them to stuff a pig, you stupid boy. This is the Albert Hall! It's not some amateur get up. Where are my sharp knives? I left them here! I can't see them. What are you doing now, Johnnie? You can't rest! It's tonight, not next week.

Don't you tell me to calm down. All of you, listen to me! We're going to go through this thing again. I've never met such a bunch of imbeciles in my life.

(*Changes voice to all sweetness*) And now, I will dust the petit gateaux with a frosting of WARM sugar, which I think Johnnie has over there. Where are you, my love? Keep to the script, Johnnie, for God's sake. And stop twitching! Then I pick up my knife, which is the WRONG knife. This is ridiculous.

She throws the knife at someone.

Perhaps that will make you sit up and take notice! Now! Again! What's the matter? I'll do it then. You just stand over there and smile. Don't move. I have to do everything round here.

A recorded announcement: 'The role of great names that has filled the Albert Hall is probably the greatest in the world, but never before, I think, have two people attempted to hold your attention with a couple of frying pans and a spit.'

Spotlight on Fanny.

And so with great pride and humility we dedicate this programme to George Auguste Escoffier.

Blare of trumpets. Fanny steps out, unbuttoning a pair of kid gloves. She's breathless.

Ladies and gentlemen, as you will see from your programmes, the first dish on our menu is onion soup with port wine!

Spotlight on her face.

Now, you beat the eggs – salt please, Johnnie – until they are light and fluffy. Come on, Johnnie, you're so slow! Think of that woman next door who you have never liked, but you were too nice to tell her what you really thought. So you whisk and whisk, you see! And that is the perfect way to make a soufflé. Egg whites please, Johnnie. These have been prepared earlier, but you will see that they are stiff, not flimsy. Fold the two together, adding two tins of peach and apricot junior foods, a great short cut. Now now, Johnnie, haven't you had enough wine, dear?

Is the dish ready? Very important that these little dishes are well greased. These are good enough for any dinner party! Vanish, Johnnie! When I have guests I always arrange a welcoming plate of raw vegetables, cut into these delightful flower shapes. Crudités is the proper name.

Her speech changes to natural.

After that it's just a montage. The oohs and aahs of the audience, as I pour champagne over a suckling pig, then pull the gougere out of the oven.

Afterwards the dressing room filled with friends, so many friends, howling mobs of people with flowers. We had six thousand five hundred people watching us. It was exhilarating! Incredible!

The lighting changes.

Mother, look at me now. Look at me, damn you. I have had people falling off their seats, enraptured by my voice, my skill. I'm somebody! Really somebody!

SCENE FOUR

TV

We hear recorded voices.

Woman   You could have warned me that your boss was coming to dinner!

Man   I didn't think he'd come. I'm up for promotion, darling, surely you can rattle something up?

Woman   But all we've got is fish fingers. I could make a sauce, I suppose.

Man   We can't give him fish fingers! It will ruin my career. You'll have to think of something.

Woman   I just don't know what to do!

Fanny enters, now dressed in slacks and a sixties hairband.

Fear not! You too can cook and be glamorous. Nothing could be simpler. Take off those awful slippers, dear, and get into the kitchen. You can't expect him to love you if you don't come up with the goods. What have you got? Eggs? Peas? We'll make a souffle a la petit pois.

Now the trick is to use your garnishes to lift the colour of the food, so you'll see here that I've taken these little bits of tissue paper and cut them into frills, and wound them round my finger... like so. Now if we can persuade it to go on, you'll see that that what would normally be a rather flat fish dish becomes something quite different.

In the same way, a melon, which, let's face it, can be very boring to look at, can be quite transformed! Take your fruit, remembering to test for ripeness by pushing the top with your fingers, and don't listen if the grocer tells you not to handle the fruit. Cut the top like this with a thin knife. Now, spoon out the pips, leaving this lovely basket shape. I use flowers and foliage to display this Corbet de Melon or Melon Basket, which is filled with seasonal berries. There! We have something for your dinner guests to admire immediately.

The lights go down.

That was terrible. Who's in charge of this microphone? It sticks out. I keep knocking into it. It's totally destroying my flow. Where is the sound engineer. Adrian? BRING HIM TO ME! I'll have his balls off and fry them in batter! He's gone home? Where does he live? I can't have this happening. I'm doing a goose next week, for God's sake.

As I have said, on many occasions, the only thing to do with those beastly birds is to eat them. Isn't it, Johnnie? I've done the script. Shall I read it out for you? I'll be wearing a blue gown with a white trim. Johnnie, where have you been? I was saying to Clive about the microphone. He says he'll get Adrian to call me. He'd better. I'll have him cut into pieces and fried on a skewer. Where do these people train? Do they train or do you just pluck them from public schools? It's my career we're talking about here. Yes, I was just about to read next week's script. Hmmm...

Another vexed question (*She stands up, starts to enact*) concerns the roasting of a goose. Its greasiness is indigestible and is very rightly frowned upon, so let us see now if we can get rid of the greasiness so that everyone enjoys a roast goose for dinner. First hang the bird in a draught for 24 hours, then truss it, like this one here, and stand it on a rack in a meat baking tin. Now, think of someone you don't like, for example, Adrian, the sound engineer, and take a fork and stab the goose viciously all over. Isn't that brilliant? Then roast him... it... dry at gas mark four. As Adrian cooks, the fat will ooze through the holes and trickle down the pan like lava flowing down Vesuvius's sides. Thus your sound engineer bastes himself.

She exits.

SCENE FIVE

Christopher

Fanny is typing like mad, with a flannel on her head. She takes it off. Her younger son, Christopher, has appeared, although we don't see him.

My God. You must be the other one. Christopher. Come here (*She stands to greet him*) Where have you been? What a lovely surprise. And good timing too, Chrissie love. It's just one of my girls has just walked out and I need someone to go and collect some raspberries from the market. Would you mind? Then when you come back we have a real conversation. I want to know ALL about you, but I just have to finish this article. It's the *Telegraph*. Just one thing, don't mention your father. I don't talk about him. Buy yourself a shirt, sweetie. Here. If you get back here at four you can sit in on rehearsals for *Kitchen Magic*. Everything is rehearsed, you see. It has to be. Everything has to be right. Now, I must finish this. Wonderful to see you!

SCENE SIX

More cooking

Another cooking show. Fanny is doing one of her TV classics, dressed in sixties stuff.

Hello again, everyone. How delightful to be with you again. Today we shall be cooking some really scrumptious food, that can be made either for a dinner party for up to ten guests, or maybe a romantic meal for two. Johnnie and I shall be giving you some tips as to how to present your food in an imaginative way. Now, where is he? Johnnie? (*To Johnnie*) How are you today?

I've asked Johnnie to prepare some of the ingredients for us, so let's hope he's done it. Today we shall be making iced beetroot soup, followed by stuffed chicken, Poulet St Michel, with casseroled peas, or petit pois en casserole, with duchesse potatoes. Let's start with the soup, which is a marvelous, refreshing beginning to any meal. Now, Johnnie, do get me some parsley, darling, while I get started.

You'll need a liquidiser for this soup. Any sort will do. Come on, Johnnie! Thank you sweetheart. Now, put the fat heads of the parsley, stalks too, into the blender, with stock, or milk... about 16 fluid ounces. Whir away. What are you doing POURING WINE, my love? I need the celery.

Now for a little talk about vegetables. All green vegetables should be crisp and firm. Reject anything wilted. Johnnie! Beetroot next. Celery should never be flabby or rust pocked! Into the blender! You must insist on small, tight cauliflowers, bulgey corn cobs, not long thin ones, hard, shining egg plants, moist globe artichokes with soft tips, hard crispy pimentos. Small leeks, moist mushrooms, drum-tight onions with paper-thin skins. Beans must snap when bent between finger and thumb. And the best swedes and turnips are as hard as cannon balls. Got it? Good!

Now, where was I? Yes, blend this all together, then beat in soured cream – thank you, Johnnie – seasoning... and there we are. Serve with two ice cubes in each bowl. Bright and glorious!

Now for the chicken. Johnnie has prepared some chopped mushrooms and gammon, and now I'm going to stuff the bird with these, pushing in the gammon, then the mushrooms. Doesn't do much for the bird's figure, lets face it, but on the other hand it wouldn't do much for ours either, would it ? There we are. Now I'll just give it to Johnnie to put in a medium oven and let it cook while I carry on talking to you.

This is terribly easy, you'll need fresh garden peas, lettuce leaves, line a dish with the lettuce, as I have done here. Johnnie! Thank you. Pour in the peas. Add an ounce of butter, a few scallions, chopped by Johnnie, slosh a bit of white wine in. Cover with more lettuce leaves, and put these in the oven with the chicken. Obviously, take out the lettuce leaves when you finally serve this, and add double cream, so that the peas swim in a green milky sauce. Marvelous.

Now, duchesse potatoes. The aristocrat of potato dishes! You can do these as a border, and can be made into any shape you like, can't it, Johnnie? I'm going to add colour, remember how we always tell you to use colour, to heighten your dishes, and surround the chicken with piped potato. I thought a green would be nice.

Cooking is like marriage, isn't it, Johnnie? Two things served together must match. So here is the mashed potato, and I'm adding a little food colouring, which is completely harmless, and stirring it in. Then, using a piping bag, I'm piping small blobs around the now cooked – Johnnie! This is of course one we cooked earlier – chicken. There you are! Isn't that fantastic? You can also use the potatoes as a base in which to stick flowers, or sprigs of herbs. Delightful!

She pulls her fixed smile, the classic pose. There is a glare of brightness, then dark.

SCENE SEVEN

Spooks

Fanny wakes up in the night with a hairnet on, looking like a ghost herself.

Who's there? You look familiar. Where's Johnnie? Why have you come now? Something's the matter with me? Is it serious? I'm afraid.

Lights up. Fanny looks dismayed and upset.

SONG: Spooks

I got plenty of friends
Come and have a look
They hang around in twilight
In every shadowed nook

Spooks in my bedroom,
Spooks at the door
Spooks on the telephone
Lying on the floor.

I've got a life out there
That no one else can see
Spooks from a dimension
Beyond reality

It's the real people
That cause all the trouble
Spooks understand me
Spooks are loveable.

They're always with me
They're all I know
They tell me what to wear
They whisper what to do.

Spooks in the attics,
Watching the TV
Spooks on the bus
Waiting for me.

Always waiting for me.

Kahlil Gibran said: 'Your pain is the breaking of the shell that
encloses your understanding. Even as the stone of the fruit must
break, that its heart may stand in the sun, so must you know pain.'

This is why I got (*Whispers*) cancer. Don't say it. If people knew then,
I can't bear to think of it. No one wants a cook with (*Whispered*)
bowel cancer. I had to have faith, to believe that I could get better.
I'd already made all kinds of things happen, just by believing them.

SCENE EIGHT

Christopher leaves

Fanny is back on form. At home, getting ready to go out.

I hope these sardines are fresh, Christopher. Did you check the eyes? I've got to rush out, dear. Must you wear that jacket? It looks so dingy. I gave you some money to buy a new one. What? You want to talk? I'm just so busy, dear. You can come with us if you like. We're going to a... what is it, Johnnie? Yes, dinner at the Mayfair Hotel.

Christopher, did you get my dress from the dry cleaners? How much did they charge? That's ridiculous. What do you think of this colour? Don't look like that. We'll have a little outing together soon, just you and me and Johnnie. Don't put on that silly face. Don't start, Christopher. I see you nearly every day. But you like doing things for me. Meeting all these grand people. What do you mean, you like Jane? She's not famous, is she? She's my assistant. Where is Jane? Honestly, I hire these girls, give them a roof over their heads, teach them how to cook, make them into women, and they treat me like dirt.

I beg your pardon? You love Jane? You must be joking. I forbid it! Don't talk to me about Peter. What do you think I am? A dating agency? It's all take, take, take with you boys, isn't it! Johnnie! Johnnie! Christopher's being rude.

My son said (*Deadpan, as if talking about someone who is mentally ill*) that colour doesn't suit you. In fact, nothing suits you. You're just a big dolled up nobody who cooks horrible food. I hate your food, it's all... FAKE. None of it even looks like food. I knew you wouldn't want me to marry Jane. You never like anyone having anything you can't have. Well, I'm sick of you, and him, hovering about in the background like an old pervert. You can stick your duchess potatoes up your arse. And you're not even married to your precious Johnnie. You're still married to my father, to Arthur. And you're also married to that poof fireman with the big biceps. You're a bigamist, mother.

I blame his father. Haven't I suffered enough? Get him away from me, Johnnie, before I kill him.

SCENE NINE

Gwen

This is the scene when Fanny makes her famous faux pas on TV with Gwen Trope, the housewife who won a cooking award. Fanny sits with Gwen on her right and another chef in a hat on her left.

Hello everyone, today we have the winner of our Cook of the Realm competition in the studio, the housewife, Gwen Trope. I've been invited to look over Gwen's recipes and to make some comments. So, Gwen, do you start with... seafood cocktail? That's frightfully rich... And then what? Straight into the duck?

She makes a terrible face, which is to be her TV downfall.

That's too much, too rich. What's this bramble with the duck? I know that's what you did for the Cook of the Realm, but my dear, now you're among professionals!

Blackout, with a spot on Fanny's face.

(*Little girl voice*) Johnnie, are you there? Johnnie, I'm home. They'll never give me a new series now. I've done a terrible thing. It's over. My television career. I was rude to the dumpy housewife who won that stupid competition. It's too late to apologise to all those viewers, impossible. What's the point of apologising to Gwen? I left her in tears at the studio. Silly little cow. Anyway, it's not her I care about. It was revolting, her menu. Duck and seafood!

Johnnie, why aren't you dressed? You were supposed to be writing a chapter for *Wine For Today*. You haven't even opened the letters. There's one here from the BBC. It's from the Parkinson show. They want me to be interviewed on my own. It's not my thing, interviews, and Parky's so... Bohemian. But he interviews all the greats, doesn't he, Johnnie? I must accept. I'm not at all happy. Hold me, Johnnie!

SCENE TEN

Parkinson

We hear the recorded voice of Michael Parkinson, or perhaps Fanny asks herself the questions. The focus is on Fanny's face.

Parkinson   Fanny, we've heard a lot about your cooking, and your marvellous travels and so on, but I wanted to ask you about something a little more serious. You've written about your interest in faith healing. Can you tell us about that?

Fanny   Yes, I am interested in it, but I don't particularly want to talk about it though.

Parkinson   Just let me ask you, you've admitted that you believe in faith healing.

Fanny   I believe in it, yes, but I just said that I don't particularly want to talk about it, as someone who has received and experienced it.

Parkinson   Was it a serious illness?

Fanny   Yes.

Parkinson   I see.

Fanny   Cancer. I was cured and my doctors will confirm this. Satisfied?

Parkinson   That's amazing.

Fanny   This is one of the most important things in my life, but I don't think it's right for chatsies. Do you?

Parkinson   No, of course not.

Fanny   Now it's over I don't mind saying it. You asked me and I won't tell fibs.

SCENE ELEVEN

Death

SONG: Out of the Limelight

When the phone doesn't ring
And the post is late
When you rise at ten
Go to bed at eight

You're out of the limelight
Away from the warmth
Of cheers and smiles

Lost in the dark
And the way back
Seems like miles

When your name isn't mentioned
No one cares what you think
Wants to know your opinion
Ask you round for drinks

Then you're out of the circle
Away from the flame
In the grey of the day

Just another woman
With nothing that is
Interesting to say

And all you can do
Is to try and get back
Put on your make-up
And hope it won't crack

Long for the feeling,
That wonderful feeling
Thousands of people
Your heart on the ceiling

But I'm out of the limelight
It's so far away
It's so quiet in the shadows
I'm just fading away

SCENE TWELVE

Alone

Fanny sits alone, with her typewriter. She's scruffy, in a dressing gown and slippers. Her eyes are made up with heavy black lashes. There is no sign of Johnnie.

I don't DO hospitals you see. Johnnie's gone. It's not the same man, in the hospital. Why would I want to see him lying there? It's finished. Fanny and Johnnie. The End.

Did I show you the wedding photographs? Amazing wedding, darlings, we had artichoke hearts, ritzy cheese tartlets, and two hundred individual cloches of filet de sole aux morilles sous cloche. Johnnie and I. Nineteen eighty-six. It was hush hush, just my most intimate friends.

A pause as she looks at a photo album, then casts it away.

I shall die soon. Well, there'll be the occasional TV show, Jonathan Ross and that kind of rubbish, but to be honest with you, I've had enough. I loved Johnnie. But he knows that. I loved our lives, and he loved them too. He loved being Johnnie Cradock.

My grandmother loathed old age. She stood there in her buckled slippers, she was only five foot high. She wore her white curls en brosse, lace at her throat. I can see her, pulling back the loose sleeves of her tea gown and saying as she looked at her arms, 'Old flesh is disgusting.'

She pulls back the sleeves of her dressing gown and grimaces.

Of course, I was an only child at Gran's house. I grew used to solitude, but then I was never really alone. I would lie on my bed next to Gran's in her bedroom with the vast lace covered bedstead, and the day bed, covered in gros point and the silver on her dressing table with cherubs' heads on the back of the hand glass and the hair brushes, and they would all be there, ghosts spirits, stroking my hair, telling me what would happen. Look at them! They're here now!

She pours a drink.

Oh, you can't see them! It's so alienating being psychic. No one understands!

I die in 1994, in a nursing home, seven years after Johnnie. Only twelve people come to my funeral. The bastards. Can you believe it?

But of course, I keep on coming back. You can't forget me, can you? I'm not the sort of woman who just disappears. You're hoping that I have regrets, that I wish I had been kinder to my children, nicer. Well, darlings, let me confide in you. I would like to be remembered as a woman who wasn't sorry. Do you hear me? I'm not sorry for anything. I've had my cake, and I've eaten it. And I've enjoyed it.

I'm going to draw a bath.

SONG

I can make mutton into lamb
A flower arrangement from an old tin can
A bird out of flour,
A sugar spun tower
A pâté from last week's ham.
I can dress like a queen
My soufflé's a dream
Make sour lemons sweet
Cut a gown from a sheet

I can garnish a suckling pig
Pluck a thrush, trim a wig
Make salmon spread
Lay a bridal bed
And a pudding from Christmas figs
I can stir and whisk
Be delightfully brisk

Dance a graceful waltz
make a hollandaise sauce

I can stuff a hefty goose
Whisk up a mousse
I can give advice
On cooking rice
Squeeze a man til he has no juice.
I'm the cherry on the top
You couldn't buy me in a shop
Without me there would be no crème!
I'm a princess, I'm a dame.

The End

Attachments

This play was commissioned by Live Theatre in 2002, when Sean O'Brien and I were each asked to write a play for Charlie Hardwick and Trevor Fox, creating an evening entitled *Double Lives*. At the time Sean and I were both writers in residence with the company.

A friend of mine, Alison Stringer, had once told me about an awful day she had experienced with a hoover salesman who just wouldn't go away. She had ended up buying the hoover. This story had been hanging around for years, but I couldn't work out what to do with it. Then I met a hoover salesman who told me that he had been in prison and that it was the only work he could get. He told me about the training and how intense it all was.

Trevor and Charlie work so well together. They create a kind of electric charge! I don't know where the rest of the story came from. I was thinking about death a lot I think. I know that as soon as we got into rehearsals the play became tighter and wittier and altogether livelier thanks to Charlie, Trevor and Jeremy Herrin, the director.

I really enjoyed working on it. It's also one of my most dramatic pieces, full of movement and conflict and all those things that theatre is supposed to have, whereas some of my other works show the definite preoccupations of a poet and a fiction writer. Later it was made into a half-hour television comedy and broadcast on Tyne Tees, but personally I preferred the stage play.

Julia Darling

Attachments was first performed as part of *Double Lives* at
Live Theatre, Newcastle upon Tyne, on 13 November 2002.
It was directed by Jeremy Herrin and designed by Perry John
Hudson.

CAST

Davina   Charlie Hardwick
Bobby   Trevor Fox

A woman, Davina, stands with her back to us. She's making sandwiches, using a large knife to cut them into squares, listening to Alanis Morisette, which is playing very loudly. A doorbell rings, but she doesn't answer it, just carries on cutting. A man walks in carrying a hoover and a case. She turns, holding the knife, jumps out of her skin, and screams.

Bobby   Good morning! Do you have a moment? I assure you that this won't take long, but it could change your life!

Davina turns the music off.

Davina   Who the hell are you?

Bobby   Good morning! Do you have a....

Davina   How did you get in?

Bobby   I rang, but no one answered. The door was open.

Davina   That doesn't mean you can just walk in.

Bobby   You had the music on.

Davina   What do you want?

Bobby   I've got something to show you.

Davina   No thanks.

Bobby   That you'll be very interested in.

Davina   I'm not interested in anything.

Bobby   I think you might be.

Davina   I'm not.

Bobby   Just you wait!

Davina   No!

Bobby   The Platinum Deluxe!

Davina   What?

Bobby   It's a hoover.

Davina   A hoover?

Bobby   Well, more than a hoover.

Davina   I don't know what you're talking about.

Bobby   I've got a card, here!

Davina   (*She doesn't read it*) So what! (*Hands it back*)

Bobby   It won't take a moment.

Davina   I haven't got a moment.

Bobby   How do you know that you don't want anything? You haven't seen what it is you don't want.

Davina   I know that I won't want what you're selling.

Bobby   You haven't even seen it yet.

Davina   Get lost.

Bobby   There's no need to be rude.

Davina   I'm just being assertive.

Bobby   Did you do a course?

Davina   That's enough!

Bobby   Perhaps we could make another appointment?

Davina   Out! Out! Out!

Bobby   Alright. Keep your hair on.

Davina   You shouldn't walk into women's houses, making them jump like that. I'll report you.

Bobby   I was given your name by a friend.

Davina   What friend?

Bobby   Michael.

Davina is clearly shocked.

Davina   Michael?

Bobby   I mean Mr Heart. Mr Michael Heart.

Davina   Michael sent you?

She sits down. Then laughs.

Davina   Michael told you I wanted to buy a hoover?

Bobby   Not exactly. He suggested that...

Davina   You come and call on me. I don't think so.

Bobby   In fact I've got something here belonging to your friend.

Davina   My partner.

Bobby   Oh, I didn't realise. You don't live together then?

Davina   No.

Bobby   There's a lot to be said for living separately, I think.

Davina   What have you got that belongs to Michael?

Bobby   Hang on. Can I just put this vacuum somewhere?

Davina   Don't get comfortable, you're not staying.

Bobby   Um. Could you put that down?

Davina   What?

Bobby   The knife.

Davina   I'm not a murderer, you know!

Bobby   It's a bit scary. You feel a bit vulnerable, like, when you do door to door.

Davina   *You* feel vulnerable?

Bobby   You get some nutters, see. Not that you're a nutter.

She puts the knife down.

Davina   Well?

Bobby   This!

He holds up a see-through bag full of dust.

Davina   What is it?

Bobby   It's the residue that the Platinum Deluxe sucked out of Mr Heart's abode.

Davina   You mean his flat? Why do you use such stupid words? Give it to me.

Davina takes the sealed plastic bag and looks at it with a horrified expression.

Davina   That's Michael's dust?

Bobby   Yup!

Davina   You hoovered his carpets?

Bobby   I gave a demo, yes.

Davina   Can I smell it?

Bobby   The bag is sealed, for hygiene purposes.

Davina   I want it.

Bobby   I suppose...

Davina   I'm in that bag. I spent a lot of time on that carpet.

Bobby   I'm sure you did.

Davina   I want it.

Bobby   Please yourself.

Pause. Davina stares at the bag.

Bobby   Shall I carry on?

Davina   Sorry?

Bobby   With the demonstration. It's only the Platinum Deluxe that does that. A normal hoover would only pick up the surface matter. Do you want to know how it works?

Davina   Not really.

Bobby   Mr Heart found it fascinating.

Davina   Did he now?

Bobby   No charge or anything. You just keep on making sandwiches. I'll just do the mat, shall I?

Davina   Oh christ. Ten minutes maximum.

Bobby   I'll just get the display ready. You just carry on. I can see you're busy.

When Davina's back is turned, Bobby clumsily tries to assemble the hoover. He is obviously hopeless at his job. She turns.

Bobby   It's so easy to assemble, even a five-year-old could do it!

Davina sighs helplessly, goes back to her sandwiches. Bobby frantically fiddles.

Bobby   I'm new to this myself. I only started a week ago.

Davina   Really.

Bobby   Do you work?

Davina   I'm an anaesthetist.

Bobby   I bet you have to be brainy to do that.

Davina   Yes.

Bobby   Did you do a degree?

Davina   Er, yes.

Bobby   Is that where you met Mr Heart? University?

Davina   Yes. He was doing history of art.

Bobby   Bit of art and a bit of science. Nice combination.

Davina   Yes.

Bobby   Is he coming to your party?

Davina   What party?

Bobby   The sandwiches and everything.

Davina   Oh yes, he'll be here.

Bobby   Birthday, is it?

Davina   Will you stop asking questions and get on with it.

Bobby   Sorry. I'm nearly ready. I'm just making conversation.

Davina   I'm not in the mood.

Bobby   Funny you should mention science and art, because that's what the Platinum Deluxe is all about, a blending of superb modern design with an engine that has the power of a racing car.

Davina   Oh for God's sake.

Bobby   Hang on a minute! I never even asked you your name. I've only been doing this a week, see. I'm Bobby.

Davina   Davina. Just hurry up.

Bobby   Shall I start again, Davina?

Davina   I don't want to know about the rigging, do I?

Bobby   What rigging? It's a hoover, not a ship.

Davina   Men just want to talk about numbers and watts and turbos and kinds of knots. I don't want to know.

Bobby   It's got a seventeen-foot power cord, with an automatic cord rewinder. A dustbag full indicator. Includes a non-electric air-driven turbo brush that rotates at over 2000rpm.

Davina   Stop it! You could tell me how much it costs if you like, for a laugh.

Bobby   I do that at the end.

Davina   Let's cut to the end then.

Bobby   (*Gets out a pad and pen*) This is the shop price.

Davina   That's ridiculous.

Bobby   This is the factory price.

Davina   Hilarious.

Bobby   And because I like you...

Davina   Oh sure.

Bobby   This is my price! With a free guarantee thrown in.

Davina   Two thousand pounds!

Bobby   It lasts for a lifetime. It will be the last vacuum you ever buy. You get a set of attachments as well.

Davina   Are you mad? Who would want a hoover that badly? You'd have to be ill.

Bobby   Depends on how much you value your home.

Davina   Who writes your scripts?

Bobby   You're not listening to me, Davina.

Davina   Seriously. Why would anyone want to spend that much on a hoover? You could go on holiday, you could have plastic surgery. Not that I want plastic surgery.

Bobby   You don't need plastic surgery.

Davina   I know I don't need plastic surgery. But two thousand pounds! I could get in caterers for parties, so I wouldn't have to chop up stupid cucumbers.

Bobby   Are you doing dips? Crudités?

Davina   Them as well.

Bobby   I'd rather have pineapple cheesy sticks.

Davina   What?

Bobby   Me mam used to make them. Those sandwiches look bloody awful. You haven't even cut the crusts off.

Davina   What do you know about it?

Bobby   Presentation is everything.

Davina   Is that what they teach you at hoover-selling school?

Bobby   You're very sarcastic.

Davina   Two thousand pounds! You must be mental. It's only a pile of plastic. Look at it! It's not even attractive.

Bobby   I think it's very attractive.

Davina   It's ugly.

Bobby   It isn't! It's shiny and sleek.

Davina   Well, you can just go off together, can't you and enjoy the rest of the day. Why don't you take the Platinum Deluxe to the cinema? Goodbye. Thanks for the entertainment.

Bobby   Can I just tell you something, Davina?

Davina   Don't keep on saying my name. It gets on my nerves.

Bobby   Do you ever think about dust? About all the bits coming off people every day? Do you ever think about that?

Davina   Probably, when I was twelve.

Bobby   Like an aura, clouds of dust, little organisms, and live mites, and tiny fleas and bits of skin, and flecks of people, trailing behind them everywhere they go, leaving traces on everything they touch. Well, the Platinum Deluxe sucks them all up. It cleans around people, so you can see them more clearly. So they shine, Davina.

Davina   Don't be silly. You can't see it.

Bobby   I can. I can see the difference. Since I've been doing this job.

Davina   You've only been doing it for a week.

Bobby   Exactly. The difference after I've hoovered. You feel it. You can breathe again. It's the absence of crap. Excuse my language, but there's no other word for it. And so many people's lives are full of it. They look sort of blurred. I get a feeling when I walk into a house, of all the matter in the air, and this house, Davina, is crawling.

Davina   No, it isn't.

Bobby   Yeah, it is.

Davina   Cheeky sod.

Bobby   How often do you hoover?

Davina   Michael does it, once a week.

Bobby   Tut tut. Once a week? Is that all?

Davina   I don't like the noise. It's stressful.

Bobby   You can hardly hear the Del Plat. It whispers around the rooms, like a deep breath, like a slow marine creature, sucking plankton from the sea.

He prowls about.

Davina   Stop doing that! It's creepy.

Bobby   And all the little mites and creatures, if you could turn their volume up they'd be screaming their heads off, knowing the happy multiplying days are gone.

Davina   Rubbish.

Bobby   Happy days of squirming and procreating everywhere, on your mattress, inside your pillow, in the forests of your fabrics, because that's what it's like for a mite in this house, like a lovely happy forest. And you an... an... whatever, doctor.

Davina   Anaesthetist!

Bobby   Working all day with disease, skin cells, and germy breath, breathing it in.

Davina   I wear a protective mask and gloves. It's very clean, my job. All I do is watch people slide into oblivion.

Bobby   The little mites still get through, wriggling round the sides of your mask. I've seen it all under ultra-violet cameras. Gives me bad dreams.

Silence.

Davina   I wash.

Bobby   Washing! Huh!

Davina   How often do you wash?

Bobby   I don't need to wash. I hoover with the Plat Del morning and night. I get free use, see. I can hardly bear to think of my former life.

Davina   A bit of dirt never did anyone any harm.

Bobby   You'd be surprised.

Davina   Dirt's there for a reason.

Bobby   Yeah, to kill us.

Davina   No. We have to get used to it. It builds up your immune system.

Bobby   Well, Doctor Davina, in scientifically proven laboratory tests they've shown that households who use the Plat Del have less illness than those who use an ordinary hoover. I think it should be compulsory, myself. Like inoculations.

Davina   Well, I'm not dead, am I?

Bobby   A lot of deaths are unexplained. Cot deaths, freak things. No one knows why they happen, but they do. You got children?

Davina   (*Upset*) No!

Bobby   I expect you want children.

Davina   Why do you expect I want children?

Bobby   A lot of women your age do.

Davina   It's none of your business.

Bobby   I do.

Davina   Good for you.

Bobby   You'd want to protect them if you did have children. I would.

Davina   I happen to believe in disinfectant.

Bobby   And you an an...

Davina   Anaesthetist!

Bobby   Yeah, I know.

Davina   We all live with germs and dust. Native Americans don't hoover their bloody wigwams, do they?

Bobby   Look what happened to them!

Pause. Davina looks worried. Bobby is pleased with himself.

Bobby   The Plat Del is a very scientific invention. Your friend, sorry, your partner, Mr Heart was interested in the various components, but I won't bother you with those. It's just rigging to you. We talked and talked. I showed him the filter system and everything. He knew what I was talking about.

Davina   He was having you on! He doesn't care about hoovers. He's about the most undomesticated man I've ever known. He's never bought a new toothbrush. All his mugs are stained round the rim. He wouldn't put bleach down the toilet in case it disagreed with a dolphin.

Bobby   You'd be surprised! We went through all the attachments. He was very receptive.

Davina   Was he?

Bobby   Alright, he was a bit cynical. I'll give you that. But he loved the demo. When I showed him all the stuff in that bag, he couldn't believe his eyes. I mean, you can't fail to be impressed with that, can you?

Davina   He was laughing at you.

Bobby   I'm very sensitive and I'd know if he was laughing at me.

Davina   You probably didn't understand his sense of humour. He's very dry.

Bobby   Oh well, you know him a lot better than I do. I'm just saying, he was interested in the health aspect. He liked the idea of clean air.

Davina   He smoked!

Bobby   Perhaps that's why. So, which room shall I do?

Davina   What?

Bobby   Which carpet?

Davina   I don't want any of them doing.

Bobby   I could start in here.

Davina   You're not starting anywhere. Oh God. You can do that little mat and that's the end of it. How did I get into this? I must be mad.

Bobby   It's free.

Davina   I can't believe that Michael sent you round here.

Bobby   I expect he thought it would be a surprise.

Davina   A joke. It must have been a joke.

Bobby   Do you want to know a joke?

Davina   Not really.

Bobby   A hoover salesman calls round at an old woman's house.

Davina   Did you tell Michael this joke?

Bobby   I expect so. Anyway, she won't let him in. So he goes off and gets a pile of horse manure and shoves it through her letterbox. Then he shouts through: 'DON'T WORRY. You'll find that the hoover I'm selling can leave your hallway IMMACULATE.' 'I don't think so,' she says. 'I think it will,' he says, pleased with himself. 'I don't think so,' she says, 'I've just had the electricity cut off!'

Davina   Ha ha.

Bobby   Do you smoke?

Davina   No. I hate smoking. I told Michael he couldn't smoke here. You'll have to go out in the back yard, I said. He didn't like that at all. That was the main reason he didn't move in. Him and his fags.

Bobby   The Plat Del could clear up that argument.

Davina   Cheaper to give up smoking.

Bobby   Couple of minutes and you'd never know there had been a smoker in the room.

Davina   You don't know when to stop, do you? I'm not buying one.

Bobby   You said ten minutes and I've only had seven.

Davina   Get on with it then.

Bobby   See this? (*He holds up a weird-looking attachment*)

Davina   Looks gynaecological.

Bobby   I wouldn't know. It's for really stubborn stains. You put the cleaning fluid provided in here, then you squirt it onto the stain and then apply the suction module to it. Shall I demonstrate?

Davina   If you must.

Bobby   Give us that ketchup.

Davina   I'm having people round!

Bobby   Got some kitchen wipes? Here I go, having a little dab.

Davina   But, oh! (*Cynical*) The stubborn stain is still there! What specification do you have on your suction module?

Bobby   You've tried your old hoover and it won't work. Looks like you'll have to throw out the old mat but...

He turns on the hoover.

Bobby   Hey! It's disappeared!

Davina   Like in a pantomime!

Bobby   Impressed?

Davina   For two thousand quid I could buy a Persian rug.

Bobby   You don't want one of them. Disgusting. Come on! It's amazing!

Davina   I suppose so. But who cares?

Bobby   Don't you want to be clean?

Davina   You make it sound religious.

Bobby   I can't believe that a clever woman like you, an, an... doctor, for God's sake, wants to live like a pig.

Davina   That's enough. Look, Bobby. Listen to me. I don't want anything. I don't want you here and I don't want the Plat Del. I want an ordinary, messy life.

Bobby   So you're not interested?

Davina   You've got it, Bobby! You finally got it! Hoorah!

Bobby starts packing up.

Bobby   I'll be off then.

Davina   Don't forget your squirter.

Bobby   Can I just get you sign my list.

Davina   What for?

Bobby   It's just to show how many places I've called at.

She signs.

Davina   Off you go then!

Bobby   (*Reading signature*) I've just realised something.

Davina   What?

Bobby   Your surname.

Davina   Here we go.

Bobby   And you a... an, an...

Davina   Anaesthetist!

Bobby   Davina Number! A woman who numbs all pain! My number's up when I see Doctor Number.

Davina   Why do people always think they're the first person to think of that joke? It happens all the time. My doctor is called Doctor Pain, and there's Mr Orchard, the greengrocer. Mrs Snarley, the dog trainer next door. What's your surname?

Bobby   You'll laugh.

Davina   I doubt it. Tell me anyway.

Bobby   Bottomley.

Davina   Ha ha. What a happy note to end on! Bye bye, Bobby Bottomley.

Bobby   Ha ha, nice to meet you Davina. Hope the party goes well.

Davina   It's not a party.

She shows him to the door.

Davina   By the way, when did you see Michael?

Bobby   About a week ago.

Davina   Tell me about it.

Bobby   I thought you were busy.

Davina   I just want to know.

Bobby   I rang the doorbell. He let me in. I showed him the hoover. Then I left.

Davina   What was he wearing?

Bobby   A red shirt, with white flecks in.

Davina   I gave him that shirt.

Bobby   He's got a cat.

Davina   Leonardo da Vinci.

Bobby   Yeah, that's the one.

Davina   It stinks.

Bobby   Yeah.

Davina   Oh God. The cat. Who's feeding the cat?

Bobby   I expect he is.

Davina   He's not there.

Bobby   Where is he?

Davina   Oh, doesn't matter.

Bobby   Is he on holiday or something?

Davina   No.

Bobby   Say hello from me when you see him.

Davina   I won't see him.

Bobby   Have you split up or something?

Davina   No. He's dead, damn it!

Bobby looks horrified.

Bobby   What did you say?

Davina   Michael's dead.

Bobby   No, he's not. He can't be.

Davina   Yes, he is. That's why I'm making sandwiches. That's what you do when people die. For the mourners.

Bobby   Why didn't you say?

Davina   I couldn't get a word in edgeways, with your stupid attachments.

Bobby sits down and is very upset. Davina also starts to cry.

Davina   I mean, here I am (*Sobs*) chopping up sodding boiled eggs, and the love of my life has been blotted out, and what happens? A salesman comes round and tries to sell me a hoover, tells me that my house is dirty and that I live like a pig.

Bobby   I'm sorry, I'm really really sorry.

Davina   How stupid is that!

Bobby   But I didn't know.

Davina   No. Course you didn't.

Bobby   How did he die?

Davina   He just collapsed. An explosion in his brain. It's called an aneurysm.

Bobby   An an...?

Davina   It's alright, don't try and say it!

Bobby   Where?

Davina   In the car.

Bobby   He was driving?

Davina   No, I was driving. He was sitting next to me. We were arguing about smoking. He said, 'More people die from car accidents than smoking' and I said something like, 'Oh come on, not that old chestnut!' Then he sort of fell forward and jerked. I said, stop messing about, Michael, it's not funny. I don't want to have kids with someone who smokes. What kind of example does it set? And he's just lolling, so I push him, and he falls sideways, and there's blood coming out of his ear.

Bobby   Oh my God.

Davina   So I jam on the brakes, and we're just coming down over the Tyne Bridge. It's teatime, really busy, and I sat there, feeling his pulse, all the cars behind us hooting and drivers shouting, shaking their fists at me.

Bobby   Was he dead?

Davina   Yes. Just like that.

Bobby   That's terrible.

Davina   It's all so unfinished.

Bobby   You shouldn't be all alone. Someone should be looking after you. Lucky I called.

Davina   I'm sick of talking. People phone up and they want you to tell them all about it, but I'd rather make sandwiches. I don't like kindness much. It makes me feel uncomfortable.

Bobby   And then I come in trying to sell you a Plat Del!

Davina   I could have said...

Bobby   It's the kind of thing you laugh about later, isn't it? (*Pause*) But not now.

Long silence. She eats a sandwich, offering him one too. They chew in a desultory kind of way.

Davina   You're not going to sell any Plat Dels this way, are you?

Bobby   I'll get back to it. Theory is, if you knock on enough doors you'll sell a hoover eventually.

Davina   Must be hard.

Bobby   Yeah, well, I couldn't get another job.

Davina   What were you doing before?

Bobby   Nothing much.

Davina   What?

Bobby   Do you really want to know? I suppose it doesn't matter now.

Davina   What?

Bobby   You won't like it.

Davina   Oh, come on. Spit it out.

Bobby   Prison. A lot of salesmen have been in prison.

Davina   What for?

Bobby   Fraud.

Davina   Anything clever?

Bobby   Not really. Embezzling.

Davina   How much?

Bobby   Quite a lot.

Davina   Where from?

Bobby   A charity.

Davina   What kind of charity?

Bobby   A little kids with disabilities charity.

Davina   You're a monster!

Bobby   I'm having you on! I nicked cars.

Davina   That wasn't funny at all. It was extremely tasteless.

Bobby   I know. I don't know why I said that. I was trying to cheer you up.

Davina   Really!

Bobby   Sorry. (*Pause*) I expect you'll get some time off work?

Davina   I don't know if I want time off. I mean, what am I going to do? I'll just think about Michael. Think about what I haven't got.

Bobby   You can't depend on anything, can you?

Davina   Everything was planned. He was going to give up smoking. I was going to get pregnant. I even decorated the spare room.

Bobby   What, for a kid?

Davina   Yes. Why am I telling you this?

Bobby   Someone else will come along. I mean, when you've got over this.

Davina   Will they?

Bobby   Course they will!

Davina   I'm a thirty-eight-year-old anaesthetist.

Bobby   What's wrong with that?

Davina   It's boring. People can't think of anything to say about it. They just say, oooh, and your name is Davina Number, fancy!

Bobby   When you feel better, someone will come along.

Davina   It takes so long to get to know anyone.

Bobby   Yeah, it takes a long time to know someone properly. I mean, people aren't what they seem. Look at me, I'm more than a vacuum cleaner salesman.

Davina   Yes, you're also a convicted thief.

Bobby   I didn't mean that. I'm an artist. I paint ceilings.

Davina   What ceilings?

Bobby   I paint skies onto people's ceilings.

Davina   Like the Sistine chapel?

Bobby   Sunsets, golden skies, cherubim, silver linings and that sort of thing.

Davina   I could do with a silver lining.

Bobby   You've probably got all kinds of hidden depths, haven't you? What do you do in your spare time?

Davina   Well, I'm a belly dancer. I've been going to an evening class for years. We've got a group together. We do weddings and conferences and things. We're called The Swinging Navels.

They're coming tonight, the other Swinging Navels.

Bobby   See, I never would have thought of that, looking at you.

Davina   I wear a veil and bells and silk scarves and fake tan.

Bobby   Fantastic.

Davina   Michael used to like it.

Bobby   Did he?

Davina   He used to say, give us a belly roll, and I'd do a little performance for him. He used to join in sometimes.

Bobby   I can imagine.

Davina   It's good for child bearing. (*Close to tears again*) Develops the muscles.

Bobby   Don't think about that now. I'll make some more sandwiches. Got any tuna?

Davina   I know you didn't know Michael, but first impressions, did you think he'd be a good father?

Bobby   Pepper? He had a nice smile.

Davina   Yes, he did. (*Tearful*) So, when you went to his flat, what did you think of him?

Bobby   I don't really know. Where's the brown bread? I was doing my spiel, you know.

Davina   Did you like the flat? The decor?

Bobby   Aye, canny.

Davina   Mmm.

Bobby   I mean, I didn't really look.

The atmosphere turns chilly again.

Davina   Where did you sit?

Bobby   In the sitting room.

Davina   On the sofa?

Bobby   Yes, I think so.

Davina   Did he offer you a drink?

Bobby   No.

Davina   So you sat in the sitting room. At what point did he give you my name?

Bobby   At the end.

Davina   By the way, how did you get his address?

Bobby   It's a computer thing... random.

Davina   Which day was it?

Bobby   Last Wednesday afternoon.

Davina   Ah.

Pause. Then Davina grabs him, her face very close.

Davina   No, it wasn't.

Bobby   Could have been the morning actually.

Davina   He was with me last Wednesday.

Bobby   Must have been Thursday.

Davina   He died on Thursday.

Bobby   Tell you the truth, I'm terrible with my memory. It could have been Tuesday.

Davina   You never went to the flat, did you? He hasn't got a sofa.

Bobby   What are you on about?

Davina   The front room hasn't got anything in it. Michael didn't like furniture.

Bobby   Does it matter?

Davina   Course it matters. I want to know where you met him. You never met him at all, did you?

Bobby   Course I met him.

Davina   So where?

Bobby   God, where was it?

Davina   (*Very angry*) Where did you meet him?

Bobby   In a bar.

Davina   In a bar. Which one?

Bobby   Raphael's Bar. I did a ceiling in there.

Davina   Where's that?

Bobby   By the station.

Davina   What was he doing there?

Bobby   He must have popped in for a night cap. It was a quiet night. It's my local so I was just propping up the bar, talking to anyone who came in.

Davina   Why didn't you say that in the first place?

Bobby   The bag of dust.

Davina   It's not Michael's dust?

Bobby   No. It's just a sample. We all get one when we do the training. It's part of the script.

Davina   And you let me believe it was.

Bobby   I didn't know he was dead, Davina!

Davina   So how did this conversation in Raphael's Bar go?

Bobby   He just comes into the bar, and I start telling him about what I do, about the ceilings, and he says he knows someone who might be interested.

Davina   In a ceiling? Not a hoover.

Bobby   Yeah. I never told him about the hoover job. He told me all about you though.

Davina   What did he say?

Bobby   About how much he loved you, and la de da and moving in. And having to give up smoking. He wasn't pleased about that.

Davina   He talked about our relationship to a stranger in a bar near the station? I find that hard to believe.

Bobby   Well he did.

Davina   How odd.

Bobby   It's not odd at all. It happens to me all the time. Maybe I've got an open face, but somehow people want to confide in me. It works well in the hoover business. Women feel sorry for me. I know all about the women in this street. They tell me everything.

Davina   Don't change the subject.

Bobby   Mad women, agoraphobics, women with too many cats, with Alanis Morisette playing.

Pause.

Bobby   I'm off.

Davina   No, you're not, come here. You knew Michael, didn't you?

Bobby   You're stretching my pullover.

Davina   Tell me!

Bobby   What are you doing?

She turns on the Plat Del, which roars into action.

Davina   I'll hoover your face off!

Bobby   You're a cracker. I mean, I know you're bereaved and everything.

Davina   Tell me!

Bobby   Get off me with that thing. It's lethal.

Davina   Can it suck up lies? That would be a useful appliance, wouldn't it? A vacuum that could get the shit out of men.

Bobby   Help!

Davina   TELL ME EVERYTHING!

Bobby   I WILL. I WILL!

She turns it off, but holds the nozzle to his head like a gun, prodding him.

Davina   Well?

Bobby   I knew him.

Davina   How?

Bobby   We used to meet up, in Raphael's, to talk.

Davina   How long?

Bobby   A while.

Davina   You met him in the bar?

Bobby   Yeah.

She prods him.

Bobby   No, before that.

Davina   When?

Bobby   He visited me in prison.

Davina   Oh.

Bobby   Did he tell you about that?

Davina   I knew he did prison visits. I didn't think he met people outside though.

Bobby   Well, he did. I've known him for years.

Davina   Why would he want to meet you?

Bobby   Why not?

Davina   Did you like him?

Bobby   Yes. Course I liked him. I wouldn't have kept on meeting him otherwise.

Davina   And he told you I would like a silver lining painted on my ceiling?

Bobby   That was later, last week, in Raphael's. For your birthday. I'll do a free estimate if you want.

Davina   It doesn't make sense.

Bobby   Yes it does.

Davina   There's something wrong.

Bobby   Davina, you're just upset.

Davina   I've seen that bar, driven past it.

Bobby   It's just a little place.

Davina   What do they call it round there?

Bobby   I don't know. A street?

Davina   It's a gay area, isn't it?

Bobby   Some of it, yeah.

Davina   Are you gay?

Bobby   That's none of your business.

Davina   It's all my business now, Bobby.

Bobby   Maybe I am.

Davina   I said, are you gay?

Bobby   Yes. Usually.

Davina   Usually?

Bobby   YES! Apart from once with Barbara Cranky when I was sixteen. YES.

Davina   So you met Michael in a gay bar. You'd been meeting him for some time.

Bobby   On and off.

Davina   But you never went to his flat?

Bobby   No, I didn't know him that well. It wasn't that kind of thing. He wouldn't have invited me round or anything. It was casual.

Davina   And Michael never mentioned this to me. Why do you think that was?

Bobby   Don't ask me.

Davina   But he told you about me.

Bobby   Coz he loved you and everything. He was mad about you. It was quite boring actually.

Davina   It doesn't fit in, with who I thought he was.

Bobby   Michael Heart. Your partner.

Davina   This is just the start of it, isn't it?

Bobby   You've got to have some secrets in a relationship. Bit of mystery.

Davina   There's more. It's like tugging at a tiny hole in a nylon stocking, and soon it's all hole.

Bobby   I don't know why you're getting so upset, apart from the fact he's dead, of course.

Davina   The whole thing is cracking open.

Bobby   It was only a quiet drink every now and again.

Davina   You're lying.

Bobby   Why would I lie?

Davina   I'm not stupid.

Bobby   I can see that. I mean, you're an an... a doctor. Look, Davina. I'm really shocked to know he's gone. I had no idea. It's a blow. He was really young.

Davina   Forty. He was forty. Or was he?

Bobby   Quite young.

Davina   How old are you, Bobby?

Bobby   Thirty-five.

Davina   A younger man.

Bobby   Not that young.

Davina   Have you got a partner, Bobby?

Bobby   No.

Davina   Why not? You're nice looking.

Bobby   I split up with someone quite recently.

Davina   Who was that?

Bobby   Karl.

Davina   Karl?

Bobby   Will you get off my back. I'm sick of you going on at me. I'm sorry about Mr Heart and everything, but it's not my fault he had an an...

Davina   Aneurysm. Did you sleep with him?

Bobby   What? Course I didn't.

Davina   Just tell me the truth.

She prods him with the hoover again.

Bobby   You're being ridiculous now. You're in shock.

Davina   You did. Didn't you? You were lovers. Look at me, Bobby. Look me in the eye and deny it.

Bobby   I never.

Davina   You can't look at me, can you?

Bobby   Oh God.

Davina   You did! Where?

Bobby   My flat.

Davina   How often?

Bobby   Put the hoover down. I can't talk while you're holding that thing.

She puts the hoover down.

Davina   Here. Sit down. Have an egg sandwich and sit. Let's hear it from the top.

Bobby   I wish I'd never come here.

Davina   Why did you come?

Bobby   To sell you a fucking hoover.

Davina   I don't think that's why you came. You came to meet me.

Bobby   I haven't done anything wrong, have I? It's not my fault.

Davina   What do you want exactly?

Bobby   I don't want anything. It would help if you bought a hoover, but otherwise...

Davina   Did you know he was dead?

Bobby   These sandwiches have hardly got any fillings in.

Davina   Did you?

Bobby   Yes! Yes! It was in the bloody journal, stupid! Man collapses in car on Tyne Bridge! His partner, Doctor Davina Number battles to save his life to no avail! Everyone knows. You want the truth Davina? Your life is falling apart. Everything was ready, and now it's not. It's all in pieces. You wanted kids. He was just about to move in. You've even decorated the kid's room upstairs. But, oh dear, there's one little snag, he's gay and he's got a boyfriend who he's known for years, and a whole other life out there in the dark lands round by the station, and he never said a word about any of it. And instead of disappearing into his dingy life, the boyfriend won't go away. In fact, I'm in your house. I couldn't keep away see, it was too easy. Why should you get all the grieving? I want some! I deserve to be seen! I want...

Davina   What?

Bobby   I want people to know I exist!

Davina   I don't care. He was going to move in, for God's sake. He wouldn't even let you through his front door!

Bobby   But he spent plenty of time at my house. Couple of nights a week sometimes, when you were working.

Davina   Stop it!

Bobby   And now Michael's dead you can't even have a go at him.

Davina   No. (*Puts her hands over her ears*)

Bobby   At least he was honest with me. I knew he had another life. Christ, we talked about you enough. You can't have both, I told him. She'll find out sooner or later. I said he should be open with you, but he said it would break your heart. Now I've met you I think he was wrong. I think your heart is in perfectly good condition. I think you might have killed him though.

Davina   No.

Bobby   It's much easier than you think to live two lives.

Davina   The bastard, the lying bastard.

Bobby   He had a lot to lose. A whole life, or half a life.

Davina   The bastard cowardy shite.

Bobby   Do you hate him?

Davina   Yes. I do. I really hate him.

Bobby   I really hate him too. He's left a hell of a mess.

Davina   I'll kill him!

Bobby   Where are you going?

Davina   I'm getting him.

Bobby   But he's dead! You haven't got a corpse in there, have you?

Sounds of crashing and the dragging of something heavy from off stage.
Davina runs out of the room and comes back with an urn of ashes that she chucks onto the mat.

Davina   Have him! Go on, Bobby. Hoover him up. Take him away from here. He's all yours.

Bobby   Is that him?

Davina   Get rid of him. Put him in a sealed bag. I don't want to think about him again.

Bobby   You can't do that.

Davina   Oh yes I can. What are you waiting for?

Bobby   That's Michael. I can't.

Davina   Give me that thing!

Bobby   No! It's not right!

Davina   Give it to me!

Davina grabs the hoover, turns it on and starts to suck up the ashes. Then she panics, and changes her mind.

Davina   What am I doing?

Bobby   I told you.

Davina   Turn it off!

Bobby   Alright, I'm trying.

Davina   Stop it, I've got to put him back. I didn't mean it.

Bobby   He's in the bag now.

Davina   Get him out again!

She pushes a switch and Michael's ashes come whooshing back out of the hoover, covering them both. They brush at themselves madly, hysterically.

Bobby   He's everywhere. He's all down me neck!

Davina   What have I done? Get him off me.

Bobby   Stop shouting, Davina. Stop it. I'll get a cloth or something. What did you do that for?

Davina slumps into a chair.

Davina   I loved him.

Bobby   Bloody Plat Del. It's fucking useless.

Davina   I didn't mean it.

Bobby   He's everywhere now.

Davina   Look at us! We'll never get clean.

She starts to laugh, then he laughs too. But then the laughter subsides.

Davina   I remember him dancing, you know, the belly dancing. He'd get dressed up in my costume, and once...

Bobby   Go on.

Davina   I was watching him standing over there, just where you're standing, rolling his hips, giggling, and I knew it, like a brick in my stomach. He's gay, I thought. He doesn't even like kissing me, not on the mouth anyway. But I stopped myself. I thought, does it matter? Does it really matter? He's a nice man. He's kind. He's got a nice smile. And I wanted kids, Bobby. I wanted them really badly. You don't know what it's like at work with everyone talking about their children all the time.

Bobby   He should have been open. I would have told you, if I was him.

Davina   But he didn't, and now it's too late.

Bobby   It's true, I wanted to meet you. I couldn't just disappear. I mean, no one's making me sandwiches.

Davina   Help yourself. So what do you think?

Bobby   I can see why he liked you.

Davina   Can you?

Bobby   But I shouldn't have come.

Davina   I could have carried on deluding myself.

Bobby   Now what?

Davina   I'll get back to numbing people. Did you know that anaesthetists are generally fun-loving people? It's because we have to make jokes all the time, to relax the patients before they go under. But they never hear the punchlines.

Bobby   I would, listen to the punchlines.

Davina   What do you mean?

Bobby   I could come round again.

Davina   What for?

Bobby   We could get to know each other.

Davina   You and me?

Bobby   We could help each other.

Davina   You help me?

Bobby   Yeah.

Davina   How?

Bobby   If you still want children, I'm here. I mean, what have I got? A bedsit, a crap job and a broken heart. I'd be a good father. I know I would.

Davina   You and me?

Bobby   I don't mean sex.

Davina   Artificial insemination?

Bobby   Yes. But I'd help. I'd be a father. Think about it.

Davina picks up the 'gynaecological' attachment and looks at it.

Davina   It's a bit cold.

Bobby   You could warm it up in the microwave.

Davina   I didn't mean that. It's a cold arrangement.

Bobby   I don't think so. I would say it was clean. Honest.

Davina   Honesty? Is that what you're selling?

Bobby   I'm a better bet than Michael was.

Davina   I loved him, you know.

Bobby   I loved him too. And he loved both of us. Now look at us. We've both got nothing and we're covered in crap.

Davina   I don't think I want children any more.

Bobby   Well, it's early days.

Davina   Why do I want them?

Bobby   They stop you being selfish.

Davina   I like being selfish. Maybe I only want kids like an accessory?

Bobby   You know it's more than that.

Davina   I want someone to love me.

Bobby   You don't want to be alone.

Davina   But I am.

Bobby   Think about it.

Davina   I think you'd better go.

Bobby   What about the mess?

Davina   Leave it. I'll brush up what's left and put it back in the urn, ready for the party.

Bobby   I didn't come here to upset you. I wasn't going to say anything. I was going to do the demo. I just wanted to...

Davina   It's alright. I'm glad you came round. But I don't want to see you again. I don't want what you're selling, Bobby.

Bobby   I see. Is it because I'm a hoover salesman and you're an an... an.

Davina   No.

Bobby   Anaesthetist.

Davina   Well done.

Bobby   I'll be off then.

Davina doesn't answer. Bobby picks up the hoover and leaves. When he's gone, Davina notices he's left the squirter behind. There's a hint of belly dancing music in the background.

Davina   Bobby! You've left your bloody attachment behind. Come back!

She stares at the thing, then holds it as if it's a dancing partner. The music gets louder, then fades into darkness.

The End

Julia Darling's radio plays

By Sue Roberts

Over the past few years as a producer at the BBC I have had the pleasure of directing two series of Julia's plays for Radio 4, *Posties* and *Appointments*, which were both broadcast in the *Woman's Hour* drama slot in May 2004 and February 2005 respectively. Writers often find these 14-minute plays difficult to write, but the form seems made for Julia, appealing to the poet and short-story writer in her. They are the radio version of the short story.

Julia's radio plays are peopled by ordinary folk who become special through dialogue and story. She has a gift for extracting every last drop of drama and emotion out of the most everyday situations, by giving them an unusual twist; two old friends meeting in the local Turkish baths for gossip – one has a tumour behind her eye. A retired postmistress reluctantly takes delivery of a computer from her son in Australia – she falls in love with the woman who has literally walked into her life and her living room with it. An appointment with a clairvoyant transforms into a reunion with the deceased members of a women's football team. The canvass may be small but the emotional journey is huge.

This is radio drama at its best. Tight stories. Strong characters. Real dialogue delivered with rhythm and poise. Streets we know. The drama of a life next door we can all recognise and relate to.

A strong vein of humour runs through all Julia's writing. It is as though the sun shines into even the darkest corners of her work. Even though she writes about potentially difficult subjects, anorexia, cancer, mugging, asylum – her tone is always optimistic. You leave a Julia Darling piece the better for hearing it.

One of the first big pieces of radio Julia and I made together was a documentary, *Home Truths*, exploring how elderly people felt about giving up their independence when going to live in a residential home. During the recordings I remember the endless patience Julia had with the people we talked to, and the strong attachments she made with them. There are many older characters in Julia's radio plays, all embracing life as fully as their younger stage partners. Julia has real empathy with these characters. They are sharply observed and drawn with great respect, often taking us by surprise. They celebrate life. They are defiant.

Julia seems very at home in radio. It is clear that she writes with an authentic living vocabulary which is not at all page bound. This is true not only of her radio work, but also of her poetry and prose, and her theatre work too. A generosity of spirit infuses all her work, creating heroes out of those who win everyday battles against the odds. She speaks upon behalf of the silent and the unsung.

Spring 2005

Sea Life

The BBC and Live Theatre commissioned myself and fellow writers Peter Straughan, Lee Hall and Sean O'Brien to write short plays based around the ideas of philosophers.

This play gave me a chance to meet and talk with the inspirational writer and philosopher Mary Midgely, who lived in the North East. Mary talked to me about her theory of the world as a kind of aquarium, where we can only see events through one pane of glass, when we need to be looking at the whole picture. I mulled over this idea, spending some time at the Sea Life Centre at Tynemouth, thinking about octopus. It seems to me that plays often emerge from a gathering of images and ideas. Writers need to be exploring something, rather than just telling us what they know.

Julia Darling

First broadcast on 7 December 2001 on BBC Radio 4 from a live performance at Live Theatre. Produced by Sue Roberts.

CAST

Billy	Bridie Hales
Mother	Libby Davison
Ray	Stephen Moore
Steve	Trevor Fox

We hear Ray muttering, fiddling, setting up a camera. Billy runs into the Sea Life Centre, making a hell of a racket. She runs into Ray, who is in the middle of a very delicate study of a birthing octopus.

Billy   Aye aye aye aye.

Ray   Who? What the hell?

Billy   Aye aye aye.

Ray   Are you with a school par... The aquarium's closed.

Crash.

Ray back.   Who are you? You've knocked over the sign. Come

Billy   What what what? (*Sounds like a bird skimming past*)

Ray   Hang on a minute. (*He walks to the foyer*) Shirley, there's someone in here, ran in out of nowhere. Shirley?

Shirley   (*We only hear her voice*) I've hurt my toe on a plastic lobster wastepaper basket. I've got to go to the RVI for an X-ray. Lena's coming in.

Ray   But there's someone here. We're supposed to be closed.

Shirley   I'm sorry, Ray. I'm in agony here.

Ray   What am I supposed to do?

Shirley   Tell them to go away, Ray. They shouldn't be in there. We're closed, tell him. It must be some kid just ran in. The door was closed.

Ray   I'm on my own here, Shirley?

Shirley   There's the taxi. Ouch!

Ray   For God's sake. Who's there? Where are you?

Billy   I'm in the dark.

Ray   That's why I can't see you.

Billy   That's because I'm hiding.

Ray   Where are you hiding?

Billy   You're cold.

Ray   I haven't got time for this. I'm very busy. In the middle of something.

Billy   Why don't you pretend I'm not here?

Ray   Because you are here, whoever you are. I'm filming.

Billy   I won't say anything.

Ray   Look, you'll have to leave. Now!

Billy   I don't think so.

Ray   I'm sorry! Where have you come from?

Billy   Outside.

Ray   You should be at school by the sound of it.

Billy   I don't go to school.

Ray   What's your name?

Billy   Billy. I'm difficult. I'm a girl.

Ray   I can see that... Billy.

Billy   Very difficult. That's why I don't go to school. My mum teaches me.

Ray   And where is your mum, Billy?

Billy   Calling me. Calling and calling.

Ray   Why don't you go to her then?

Billy   She's cross.

Ray   We're all cross, Billy. I'm cross.

Billy   I'm not cross.

Ray   Why don't you come out and say hello?

Billy   Because you're cross. You'll send me away.

Ray   Alright. I won't be cross.

Sound of Billy creeping out.

Billy   You're ugly. You got no hair.

Ray   That's because I'm bald.

Billy   Hmmm. What is this place anyway?

Ray   A closed aquarium. Come on, Billy, let's go and see if your mother's outside.

Billy   She's not. She's miles off.

Ray   You said she was calling you.

Billy   She's right down the other end of the beach, looking in rockpools.

Ray   You can run back and find her then.

He tries to grab Billy, but she scampers off.

Billy   I'm too young.

Ray   Too young for what?

Billy   To be alone. You're looking after me now, Ray.

Ray   No, I'm not. I'm filming.

Billy   Filming what? Doing what? What are you doing?

Ray   The octopus vulgaris is laying her eggs. I'm a scientist. I don't work with children.

Billy   Where?

She comes closer.

Ray   There.

Billy   Doesn't look like anything's happening. It's all dark. Like a cave.

Ray   She's watching us. They're very clever, octopuses, very clever indeed. She needs a dark place. She's very shy. And cautious. She doesn't like noise, or interruptions.

Billy   I'm clever too.

Ray   At some point she'll start pushing out eggs and attaching them to the ceiling of her tank, 200,000 eggs perhaps, tiny eggs. Then she'll caress them with her suckers to keep the algae and bacteria growing on them.

Billy   That happened to me.

Ray   No, it didn't.

Billy   Yes, it did. My mum caressed me with her suckers.

Ray   No, Billy. You were just born, unfortunately.

Billy   Nothing's happening now. Let's go and look at the seahorses.

Ray   Does your mum have a mobile phone?

Billy   You can see the seahorses round the corner. Come on, Ray.

Ray   Does your mother have a phone?

Billy   Let's tell each other about amazing things that have happened to our mothers.

Ray   I said, does she have a mobile phone?

Billy   Like my mother nearly got her ear chopped off.

Ray   How?

Billy   She was acting out a Viking battle.

Ray   I see. Does she have a mobile phone, Billy?

Billy   Course. She'd have to, wouldn't she? I'm always running off. She has to call the police. What happened to your mother?

Ray   Nothing happened to her. What's the number?

Billy   Have you ever looked at a seahorse?

Ray   The number.

Billy   Numbers bumbers... (*Starts running round*) Seahorses love each other forever. They wind their tails together.

She starts running about again.

Ray   Don't, Billy, don't make a noise. Careful of the camera.

Billy   Aye aye aye fish pie! Fish look like people. People look like fish. We're looking through the windows.

Ray   Billy, please, the fish don't like it. They're delicate organisms.

Billy   Where?

Ray   What?

Billy   Where's the delicate organisms?

Ray   Everywhere, Billy.

Billy   Where's the dolphins?

Ray God help me. I'm going to phone the police.

Billy Where are you going?

Ray To the office.

Billy Why?

Ray Because I need to make a phone call.

Billy About me?

Ray Maybe. I'm going to phone my wife.

Billy What for?

Ray About the dinner.

Billy Can I have some? I'm hungry.

Ray I'll ask her.

The door slams.

Billy (*Running*) Octopus, jellyfish, shark, sting ray, starfish, crab, an enemy, anemone. Conger eel, plaice, brill, thornback ray, smooth hound, skate, cuckoo wrasse, sea horse, seahorse, John Dory... round and round and round.

In the office.

Ray Is that the police? I'm a marine scientist working at the Sea Life Aquarium. The aquarium's actually closed. This girl's run in from nowhere... Her name? Billy... Don't know the surname. Oh, you know her. Billy Cray. Famous, is she? Well, I've got her and I need her taking away. How long? Could you get here sooner? I'm filming, you see, I can't get on. Please. Thank you.

Billy Can't see them all at once, too many walls. Why can't it be all windows? Octop, jelly, shar sting, cra, enemy, conga, plaice, brill, ray, smoothieskate, cuckoo, John...

As Ray walks back, his phone rings.

Ray   Yes? Ellie, what? The ante-natal? Of course. I was about to ring. How did it go? Oh working, there's been a few disturbances. I won't have time, love. I'll be all day at this. Don't be... I'll try and get something from the supermarket. Why not rest up, eh?

Billy   What did she say, your wife?

Ray   She said she wants to have a rest.

Billy   Why? What's the matter with her? You can sleep when you're dead.

Ray   She's having a baby.

Billy   How many eggs?

Ray   Only one.

Billy   You should put her in the tank and watch her with your camera thing. Keep her company.

Ray   She wouldn't like that.

Billy   Neither does the octopus. It wants to be left alone. Is that an expensive camera?

Ray   Yes.

Billy   Can it see in the dark?

Ray   Yes, it can. Your mother will be here soon. Why don't you go and sit in the lobby and wait for her. I could get you a fizzy drink from the machine if you like, Billy.

Billy   I'm not allowed fizzy drinks.

Ray   I see. Well, can you just have a look round while I sort out the camera?

Billy   Will you look at it all day?

Ray   Yes, all day. And tomorrow too. All week.

Billy   Do you know everything?

Ray   Me? No, not at all. I know a lot about octopuses.

Billy   What for?

Ray   It's my subject. That's what I do.

Billy   Octopus man. Who am I?

Ray   I don't know, Billy.

Billy   I know a lot.

Ray   I'm sure you do.

Billy   You know what? The trouble with school is they do one thing at a time. They should do everything at the same time. They say, now it's time for maths, get out your maths books. Then they say, put away your maths books and let's look at maps.

Ray   It's the only way to learn, that's why. You can only do one thing at a time, or you get in a muddle.

Billy   I can do everything at the same time. But it's too hard for most people. Not many people can do it.

Ray   It's not very satisfying, is it? To do everything at the same time.

Billy   I've got concentration deficit. But I can do lots of things at the same time. Look, I run round, and see everything at the same time.

Ray   Don't start running again, Billy.

Billy   I can see you, Ray. If I look through this window. I can see you in the glass, all wobbly and baldy and blue.

Ray   Stay over there.

Billy   You're looking at me, Ray. Wave at me!

Ray   I'm waving.

Billy   But if I run back I can be where you are. And if I ran quickly enough I could see myself looking at you.

Ray   Don't run, Billy.

Billy   If you ran too, then you could be me and I could be you.

Ray   No!

Sound of terrible crash as the camera is knocked over. There is an awful silence.

Ray   What have you done? The lens... I don't believe this.

Billy   It wasn't me.

Ray   Come here!

He starts chasing Billy and grabs him.

Billy   Stop pulling me!

Ray   Ow, ow, ow!

Ray's mobile phone rings.

Billy   Get off, that's my mum.

Ray   You bit me, you little....

Billy   Shouldn't have pulled me along.

Ray   Hello? Hello? Christ, Ellie... I'm sorry... out of breath. It's this child, broke into the Sea Life Centre, knocked over the camera. Oh God, it might be broken, Ellie. What's that? I don't care about the supper, Ellie. We'll get a takeaway. Or a restaurant. I just want to get on, love. It's all going wrong here. What do you mean, heartburn? It's not my fault, is it? I'm just doing my job. It's WORK, Ellie.

Billy   You can fix that camera thing, Ray, but you can't fix wives. That's what my mum said. You'll have to go home.

Ray   I can't go home. I'm working. Or I would be working if it wasn't for you.

Billy   Octopuses don't work. Seahorses don't work.

Ray   But people do.

Billy   I don't.

Ray   Well that's your problem, isn't it.

Billy   I'm only nine.

Ray   How does she cope with you? Your mother must be a saint.

Billy   I'm difficult.

Ray   I'm surprised she hasn't killed you by now.

Billy   She wouldn't do that.

Ray   I would.

Billy   She loves me. You don't.

Ray   No, I don't.

Billy   But you would love me, if you knew me better.

Ray   I doubt it.

Billy   I've got gifts.

Ray   Oh yes, what gifts?

Billy   I've told you. I can be everywhere at once. I don't have to do everything one thing at a time.

Ray   That's not what I'd call a gift.

Billy   I can draw things.

Ray   Draw things?

Billy   DRAW things.

Ray   Where is everyone?

Billy   I expect they're in a traffic jam. They're always in a traffic jam. Jammed up. Give me your paper.

Ray   You're not having my notebook. Look, here's a pencil. You can draw on the back of the dot to dots.

Billy   What shall I draw?

Ray   Why don't you draw the octopus vulgaris? I can't film her anymore. I'll have to try and get a new camera. Your mother is going to have to pay for it, you know.

Billy   Sorry, sorry, boo hoo.

Ray   The lens is shattered. It will cost hundreds.

Billy   I said I was sorry.

Ray   You don't look sorry.

He stomps off to the office.

Ray   Is that Whitley Bay Camera Club. You wouldn't have a XV 2Y4 lens, would you? Oh, great. I'll come over in an hour or so then. It's Ray Spence. Good news at last!

Billy   Done it.

Ray   Done what?

Billy   Drawn the octopus.

Ray   Let's see. Christ. Did you do this?

Billy   Yes. Course I did. Can we do something else now?

Ray   This is beautiful. How did you do that?

Billy   With the pencil. It just comes out. Shall we look at the seahorses?

Ray   Can I have it?

Billy   Alright. If you come and look at the seahorses holding tails.

Ray   This is extraordinary. How did you do that?

Billy   I've got special powers. But it hurts.

Ray   What hurts?

Billy   All the things. All crowding in.

Ray   I can't imagine what it's like to be you, Billy.

Billy   There's not enough space, all the things happening at the same time. And she takes me to the doctor and they say I need calming down and she says, you're not giving my Billy drugs! She's a Viking, you see, and she's a midwife. So they say, please, Mrs Cray, sit down, Mrs Cray.

Ray   But perhaps you do need calming down?

Billy   It's not calming down I need. It's space.

Ray   What kind of space?

Billy   Like a fish. Space to swim in. The doctor men. When they look at me, they only see me through one window. Like I'm a fish. They don't see where I'm going.

Ray   Where are you going?

Billy   They don't see me and my mum on the beach, running along. Or laughing, getting dressed up.

Ray   But you run away from your mum.

Billy   I'm missing her now. I didn't run away because I was cross. I just did it because I could. Because I was fast, and she was slow. Because I saw a blue sign with a fish on that said come here. And that was how I came to see you.

Ray   She'll be here soon, Billy. I can't get over this drawing.

Billy   They always say that. They hate me then they like me again, when they see the drawings.

Ray   You broke my camera, Billy.

Billy   You wouldn't come away from your octopus window.

Ray   That's because I was trying to see something.

Billy   But you just look all the time at one thing.

Ray   Yes.

Billy   Well, you shouldn't.

Ray   I'll get a dustpan and brush.

Billy   I expect the octopus looks at you and thinks, I wish he'd go away for a bit. I expect she thinks you should go and get some food from the supermarket for your wife, get her some vitamins or something for the the little baby person. I expect.

Ray   Octopuses don't know about supermarkets.

Billy   You said they were clever.

Ray   She's never seen a supermarket.

Billy   Bet you've never seen a newborn baby coming out.

Ray   Do you think I'll make a good father?

Billy   No.

Ray   Why not?

Billy   Because, because... you're a bit of a know-all.

Ray   That doesn't mean I won't be a good father.

Billy   You don't know how to be surprised.

Ray   What's that got to do with it?

Billy   Children like you to be surprised, that's all. They like to teach you things. What will you do when the baby cries?

Ray   I'll look after it. Sing it a song or something.

Billy   You'll be too busy.

Ray   No I won't, not when the baby's born.

Billy   Yes you will. You'll be looking at the octopus. Your baby and the octopus baby might come out at the same time.

Ray   I hope not.

Billy   Because then you'll have to choose. Why do you keep on looking at your watch?

Ray   Because it's getting late.

Billy   07700 900657. That's her number.

Ray   Say it again.

Billy   I only say it once.

Ray   Why don't you call her on my phone? Here. Tell her where you are.

Billy   She'll be walking along the beach. Going, Billy, Billy, all happening at the same time, while your camera breaks and your wife and the octopus have babies. All together.

Ray   But... it doesn't all happen in the same room, does it?

Billy   Yes it does.

Ray   Go on, phone her up.

Billy   Alright then. Give me the phone then. She'll tell you.

Ray   Tell me what?

Billy   About looking after babies. (*She dials*) Mum, Mum. I'm with an octopus and a man. In the dark. You can come and help. The octopus is having a baby. Bye.

Ray   Will she know where you mean?

Billy   Yes, she'll know. There's only one octopus in Whitley Bay.

Ray   That's good.

Billy   Does your wife like it here?

Ray   My wife doesn't like octopuses. She thinks they're sinister.

Billy   I expect she likes looking into another window. She can see you through it, all funny looking. I expect she likes looking at the seahorses, with their little heads and manes and tails. And I expect she wishes you were like a seahorse, because they never leave each other. And if one dies, then the other one gets sadder and sadder until it dies.

Ray   You know a lot about seahorses.

Billy   My mum talks about them, down at the rock pools, but we never see one. We just imagine them.

Ray   Why don't you do a picture of one?

Billy   No thanks. I've got one in my head all the time.

Ray   That's nice, Billy.

Billy   There's lots of things in there actually.

Ray   Yes, I'm sure there are... swimming about.

Billy   I quite like you, but I think you've got problems.

Ray   Problems? You, for instance.

Billy   I'm helping. I'm always helping. You're looking in the wrong window.

Ray   This is the most important window for me at the moment, Billy.

Billy   That's why your wife doesn't like it.

Ray   Where is everyone?

Billy   Swimming along, slowly, slowly.

Ray   It's just I've got so much work to do.

Billy   Fish don't work.

Ray   No.

Billy   Fish just do.

Ray   That must be nice.

Billy   Let's be fishes.

Ray   How?

Billy   I'm tired.

Ray   Really?

Billy   Let's pretend that we're in the tank.

Ray   What are you doing now?

Billy   Lying down. In the dark. Like babies do, with all the water lapping round. You can be an octopus if you like.

Ray   Thanks.

Billy   And I'll be a seahorse. But we're in the same sea. You're over in your bit, and I'll be over here. Go on.

Ray   Why not?

Billy   Are you ready? Close your eyes, and we'll just be.

Ray   I'm closing my eyes.

Billy   And it doesn't matter.

Ray   No, it doesn't matter.

A few seconds of silence. Of 'glug glug' and the sounds of the real sea. Then loads of voices.

Shirley   Ray, are you there? I'm back. Waited for hours at the hospital. Hello, who are you?

The sound of a police walkie talkie.

Mother   I'm looking for my daughter. Billy Cray. She's in there somewhere. It's alright, inspector. I'll take over now. Thanks. Can I go through?

Sounds of Ray and Billy giggling as they lie in the dark.

Voiceover of Mary Midgley:

You see, human life is like an enormous, ill-lit aquarium, which we never see fully from above, but only through various small windows unevenly distributed around it. Scientific windows, like historical ones, are just one important set among these. Fish and other strange creatures constantly swim away from particular windows, reappearing where different lighting can make them hard to recognise. Long experience, along with constant dashing between windows, does give us a good deal of skill in tracking them. But if we refuse to put together the data from different windows, then we can be in real trouble.

The End

Posties

These plays emerged from the play *The Last Post*, and several of the themes and characters that I explored in that drama told their stories in these five short pieces for BBC Radio 4's *Woman's Hour*. However, two new themes arose which are featured here. One was the idea of lost letters, which came from a newspaper clipping about a letter that had been delivered 37 years after being posted. In my play, *Lost Letters*, the letter would have changed someone's life had it arrived.

The other play included in this collection, *Letters Home,* looks at the breakdown of communication between an anorexic daughter and her stressed mother, and how letters can help you cross a difficult bridge. This play has been used by Newcastle University's Medical School to show trainee doctors the human story behind eating disorders. I am so pleased when my work is used in this way.

Julia Darling

Lost Letters

First broadcast on 19 May 2003 on BBC Radio 4. Produced by Sue Roberts.

CAST

Tilly (a 19-year-old Post Office worker)   Grace Stillgrove
Amy Herd (a 70-year-old house mother of a girl's school)
                                                    Val McLane
Mr Peas (a postman of retirement age)   Donald McBride
Assorted voices   Various cast members

The sound of postal machinery. Tilly is sorting through envelopes, yawning. We hear her thoughts.

Tilly   And I'm walking along. My hair's blonde and I'm wearing a leather jacket with a turned-up collar, and dark glasses. This man comes running up to me, and he says, 'Excuse me, but I'm making a film, and your face is just right.' I wave him away, like he's an insect. 'Please,' he says, 'Please, my card.' 'All right,' I say, then he says: 'Can you sing?' And I'll open my mouth, right there on the street and start singing, and everyone will stop and look at me. WOW.

She sings, really out of tune.

Mr Peas   Tilly!

Tilly   What now?

Mr Peas   I've got something EXTREMELY interesting for you.

Tilly   *(Mutters)* Oh great, have the Post Office choir brought out a commemorative CD? Can't wait!

Mr Peas   Look at this.

Tilly   A letter.

Mr Peas   Look closely.

Tilly   An OLD letter.

Mr Peas   Look at the postmark.

Tilly   1960. Oh.

Mr Peas   It's been bricked up in a postbox for nearly fifty years.

Tilly   How can someone brick up a postbox. They're red!

Mr Peas   They found it in Scotswood. Must have happened in the slum clearances.

Tilly   Fancy.

Mr Peas   It's got to be delivered.

Tilly   I think you're a bit late, Mr Peas.

Mr Peas   We have to try. I thought it could be a project for you.

Tilly   Me?

Mr Peas   Yes, you.

Tilly   I bet it's not even important. It will just say something like, thanks for the weekend in Scarborough, or, Auntie Lu Lu has passed away. Why don't we open it and see?

Mr Peas   It's a crime to open someone else's post. You know that.

Tilly   The person's probably dead anyway. (*Reads*) Amy Herd.

Mr Peas   Not necessarily.

Tilly   She'll be too old to care.

Mr Peas   I'll leave it with you, shall I?

Tilly   But Mr Peas...

The sound of a doorbell and a barking dog.

Tilly   I'm looking for Amy Herd.

Man   Who?

Tilly   Amy Herd.

Man   I heard you! She's not here, pet.

Tilly   Oh, GREAT.

The sound of Tilly leafing through a directory.

Tilly   Hampton, Halliday, Healy, Hebble, Henderson, Hepplewhite, Herd, Herd, Herd, herds of Herds. This is SO pointless.

Tilly   (*On the phone*) Is there a Mrs A Herd there?

Sylvia   This is Sylvia.

Tilly   It's Amy I'm after.

Sylvia   I'm Sylvia Herd.

Tilly   Well, you're not the right one, are you?

Another phone call.

Tilly   Are you Amy?

Foreign voice   Sorry, sorry.

Tilly   Mrs Herd?

Foreign voice   I don't understand.

Tilly   Forget it.

New phone call. She speaks too quickly.

Tilly   I'mlookingframissusherd.

Amy   I heard.

Tilly   Well?

Amy   What do you want?

Tilly   Amy Herd?

Amy   Yes?

Tilly   Are you joking?

Amy   Not at all.

Tilly   You're Amy Herd?

Amy   Who is this?

Tilly   I've got a letter for you.

Amy   Who is this?

Tilly   The Post Office.

Fades.

Tilly   Of course she lives miles away. I have to get a bus, then another bus. On the way there, I think about having plastic surgery and if it would hurt. I start replacing different bits of me, until I've got a new nose, new lips, new legs, new clothes, new voice box. I wonder if they can do that, give you a new voice? By the time I arrive I've almost forgotten what I'm there for. It's a house all by itself, with a driveway and a long garden full of dripping laurel bushes. There's a rusty playground next to the house that looks as if no one plays in it. I ring the bell and a small untidy woman opens the door and stares at me. She's got a blue smudge on her lip as if she's been sucking a biro.

Amy   Are you the girl from the PO?

Tilly   Yeah.

Amy   Come on in. Sorry about the boxes.

Tilly   I've got your letter.

Amy   Yes.

Tilly   Sorry it's late, er, very late. It got bricked up apparently.

Amy   How can a postbox get bricked up? They're red!

Tilly   That's what I said.

I follow her down a hallway that's full of boxes with things spilling out of them. I'm holding the letter. I think, she should have got this fifty years ago. I try to see her as a young girl, but I can't. She looks like she's always been dumpy and round-shouldered with wispy hair.

Amy   So!

Tilly   Could you sign here? I'll be off.

Amy   Don't you want a cup of tea?

Tilly   I don't drink tea.

Amy   Squash?

Tilly   Alright.

Sounds of Amy clinking about in a kitchen.

Tilly   If that was my letter I'd open it straight away!

Amy   I expect you're curious.

Tilly   I've been looking for you for weeks.

Amy   Do you want ginger nuts or chocolate digestives?

Tilly   Er, both.

Amy   Here we are. Now, let me see.

Tilly   She goes over to the window and frowns at the letter, as if she's not really sure what to do with it. I feel like screaming OPEN IT! The room is filled with stuff. There's photographs everywhere of groups of girls clustered around Amy Herd. Girls in gymslips with bobbed hair and cards on a mantelpiece that say GOOD LUCK and THINKING OF YOU. There's a pile of sheet music on the floor. I eat two biscuits and let them mix up with the squash in my mouth.

Tilly   (*With her mouth full*) Nice handwriting on the envelope.

Amy   I know who sent it.

Tilly   Was it important?

Amy   At the time.

Tilly   I thought it would be some little note. You know, would you like to come to tea on Saturday? I said to Mr Peas.

Amy   Who's he?

Tilly   Mr Peas at the post office. He looks like a stringy parcel. I said, it will be nothing but he said it was our duty to deliver it.

Amy   It smells funny.

Tilly   So would you if you'd been buried for nearly fifty years.

Amy   True.

Tilly   She puts the letter on the table and sits down, pokes a fire in the grate with a poker and sighs. I wonder if I'm going to be here all day

Tilly   Are you a teacher?

Amy   No, I was a house mother. This was a boarding school for girls, girls who had been in some sort of trouble. It's closed now. I've got to move. You only just caught me.

Tilly   That's lucky.

Amy   It's going to be converted into a health spa. Imagine it! This room might be a Turkish bath, or a massage salon.

Tilly   She walks around the room, touching things, as if she's trying to remind herself that they exist. The letter looks annoyed that she's ignoring it.

Is that your piano?

Amy   Yes. I taught the girls singing sometimes.

Tilly   I want to be a singer.

Amy   Can you sing?

Tilly   Er, not really.

Amy   You have to learn how to breathe.

Tilly   What do you mean?

Amy   To breathe deeply.

Tilly   I can do that.

Amy   It's more difficult than you think.

Pause.

I can't bring myself to open it. I'm sorry.

Tilly   Why not?

Amy   It's a bit of a shock, that's all.

Tilly   I'll take it away again if you want.

Amy   No. Perhaps you'd like to...

Tilly   Open it? I don't mind.

Amy   Go on then.

Sound of ripping.

Tilly   Glue's still strong.

Amy   Glue was good in 1960.

Tilly   There it is.

Amy   Go on, read it out loud.

Tilly   Me?

Amy   There's no one else here, is there?

Tilly   I suppose so.

My Darling Amy,
Here is a train ticket. I'll meet you at King's Cross on Friday at
4.00 pm. I've got tickets for Sydney. The crossing only costs ten

pounds. Please come. If I don't hear from you I'll understand, but my heart will be broken. Your Joe

Aaaah! That's terrible.

Amy   I waited and waited for that letter.

Tilly   You could have done with email really.

Amy   I thought he'd left me.

Tilly   Joe?

Amy   Yes, Joe.

Tilly   Who was he?

Amy   A milliner. A hat maker. I worked at the hat shop too. It was a boring job. I just sewed on feathers and stitched rims. He was older, and he made fantastic hats, with birds and flowers on them. I was your age, about nineteen. After work we would stay behind. He had white silky fingers and he was very artistic. He would stroke my head and my whole scalp would tingle.

Tilly   Eugh.

Amy   But he was married.

Tilly   Oh.

Amy   I didn't care.

Tilly   I bet his wife did.

Amy   Yes, she tried to stab me with a hatpin, after he'd left. That's why I left the hat shop.

Tilly   He must have waited for you at King's Cross.

Amy   I wonder how long he waited?

Tilly   How long did you wait?

Amy   Years.

Tilly   He'll be all old and wrinkly now.

Amy   I wonder if he's still got his teeth?

Tilly   I didn't like the sound of him, with his slithery fingers and fancy hats. I pictured him like a lizard with a slippery tongue. I didn't think he matched the Amy Herd in the photographs with the fishing net in her hands, or holding a football trophy.

Amy   It's not fair!

Tilly   Maybe you had a lucky escape?

Amy   I wouldn't mind so much if I'd had a choice.

Tilly   It's not my fault!

Amy   I could have gone to Australia!

Tilly   It's not that nice.

Amy   How do you know?

Tilly   I had an uncle come from there. His skin was all cracked and red. He looked like a burnt chop. They get a lot of skin cancer there.

Amy   I would have worn a hat!

Tilly   There's no need to be sarky!

Amy   It would have changed my life, this letter.

Tilly   Didn't you like working here?

Amy   I suppose so.

Tilly   I bet you were nice to the naughty girls.

Amy   They weren't that naughty. Most of them were just lost.

Tilly   I'm sure you helped them, with the breathing and everything.

Amy   It's just knowing that I could have been someone else, that there was another possibility, another Amy, in Australia. How would you feel?

Tilly   I didn't answer. I looked at her sitting there, all slumped and sad. I tried to imagine her being someone else, but I couldn't see it. She picked up the letter again and stared at it.

Amy   Why's it turned up NOW? Just as I'm retiring and I've got to move out, and you know, I feel so ALONE.

Tilly   What are you going to do?

Amy   I'm moving into sheltered housing. It's got two little overheated rooms, with too many armchairs in. I'll get little single meals on a tray, and have to go to sing-songs in the community room on Friday nights.

Tilly   It might have been worse in Australia. You'd have had to sing *Waltzing Matilda*.

Amy   I hate that song.

Tilly   So do I. They made us sing it at Brownies.

Amy   They do, don't they! And that other one about the cookaburra in the old gum tree.

Tilly   You see! It's all turned out for the best!

Amy   Bless you.

Pause.

Tilly   I'd like to be someone else.

Amy   Would you?

Tilly   A different version of myself.

Amy   At least you've got time.

Tilly   Have I?

I see a terrace that goes on and on, with identical doors and chimneys, stretching down a hill, with me trudging down it, posting letters.

Amy   Of course you have.

Tilly   She picks up the letter again and looks at it as if it's a faded photograph. Then she chucks it onto the fire. We both sit there watching it curl up into black flakes that glow red at the edges.

Amy   And that's the end of that!

Fade with music.

Tilly   When I leave her house it's raining. I look back and she's waving at me through the window. One of the swings in the playground creaks in the wind, like there's the ghost of a girl swinging back and forth. On the way back I feel empty, as if I've lost something. I suppose I got so used to carrying that letter around, and now it's delivered and things are back to normal.

At home that night I do a strange thing. After everyone else has gone to bed I turn off the telly and I write a letter. I write a letter to Amy Herd. In it I say that I'm sorry about her lost letter, and it must have been due to some idiot colour-blind labourer. I say how I've been thinking about how there are different versions of each of us, just waiting to be occupied, like there's a burnt chop of a woman in Sydney hanging out her washing in a dusty garden. Then I say I hope her move goes alright and if she wants some help shifting boxes, well it's the least I can do. I sign my name and underline it.

Then I write, PS, I would really like to know how to breathe if you have time.

The End

Letters Home

First broadcast on 21 May 2003 on BBC Radio 4. Produced by
Sue Roberts.

CAST

Grace (a single mother)   Siobhan Finneran
Janie (Grace's teenage daughter)   Tara Prendergast
Mel (Grace's friend from work)   Jo-Anne Knowles

Grace What's happening? I feel like shouting I'M NOT
QUALIFIED! I just want to walk away. You do. Put it this way,
it's not what I signed up for when I got pregnant. This. Four of
us, living in a terrace, sandwiched between a house full of
Alsatian dogs and an old lady who won't stop washing her step.
It's winter. I just got divorced. It feels like everything's an effort.

I'm a dinner lady. All day I am surrounded by food, heaps of
it. Limp chips, gooey pizzas, mountains of wrinkled peas,
waterlogged carrots.

And there's my two younger kids, Jackie and Claire, who gobble
up what I put in front of them like little birds, mouths open,
scraping the plates with their forks and spoons, calling for more.
And then there's Janie, who doesn't eat any bloody thing at all,
who pushes it all away with a look on her face as if I'm trying to
poison her. What are you supposed to do when your daughter
won't eat?

This is my method. SHOUT VERY LOUDLY. THROW
SOMETHING. CRY. Let's face it, I'm as much use as a
chocolate fireguard.

Janie (*Whispered, as she writes a letter*) Dear Anna,
I have decided to write to you. I feel like I've got a new friend.
You're a better mother than her downstairs. All she does is shout.
We understand each other, don't we? We like the same things.
Soon I'll be just like a feather, floating. Nothing will hold us
down then, will it?
Your Janie

Sounds of Grace at work, heaving saucepans with her co-worker, Mel.

Mel It's a phase.

Grace But how long should you put up with a phase, Mel?

Mel It will pass.

Grace I hate slimming.

Mel Lots of famous people don't eat.

Grace   Is she ill?

Mel   No! Are you ready with that custard?

Grace   It looks revolting. Everything looks repulsive when there's too much of it, doesn't it?

Mel   What about your doctor?

Grace   (*To herself*) My doctor is like a mechanical man. He reminds me of the cobbler in the window of the shoe shop who endlessly bangs a nail into the heel of a boot. They should make a model of my doctor, writing out prescriptions again and again. I can never get to see the nice doctors. They're always busy, nice people.

I was wondering, shall we go to the doctors about your eating? I say to Janie. What do you mean? she shouts. Too loud. Too sudden. Why would I want to go to a doctor? There's nothing the matter with me. I'm just trying to slim down a bit. But you're thin enough, I say. No I'm not, she says, and she squeezes her stick thighs. Look at that she says. Blubber. It's no good starving yourself, is it? You'll end up fatter than you were in the first place. Soon as I say the word FATTER I regret it. Words like that fill the room, words like weight gain, you look nice, that top suits you.

What is going on? What would you do? Well? It's been like this since Christmas. All right, since the divorce. It's my fault. I know it is.

Janie   Dear Anna,
Look, if you let me eat that apple then I'll run all the way up the hill. As you know, I ate a triangle of toast. I could feel it moving through my body, like a bit of grit. I regretted it all day long. At least at the call centre no one looks at me. When will I be perfect, Anna?
Love Janie

Grace   I go to the library with Jackie and Claire. I can only find one book about eating disorders. It's sandwiched between books about different diets and ways you can change your life INSTANTLY. My fingers hesitate around the spine of a book called *How To Be Rich, Thin And Beautiful*. The book about anorexia is modest and green. Keep talking to the sufferer, don't get angry, says the book. How are you supposed to talk to someone who won't speak, I wonder? Then it says, if your child won't discuss things with you, write a letter.

When I get home, Janie is upstairs. I can hear music throbbing through the house. I go and knock on the door. JANIE, I shout. HAVE YOU HAD TEA? But there's only a muffled reply. I find some writing paper and I sit by myself in the kitchen with a blank sheet in front of me. I never write letters. I keep getting up and sitting down. In the end I write:

Dear Janie, I wish you would eat something. Love Mum

That's the truth. I wish she would just sit down with a plate of food and eat it. That would be enough to keep me happy for the time being. I go upstairs and I put the letter under her door. There's no answer from inside. I'm so tired. I just want to lie on the settee and stop worrying about things.

The next morning I go to Janie's room and open the door. It's dark in there. The floor is covered with clothes and make-up and mess. I don't know what I'm looking for. There's my letter, ripped open and lying next to the bed. Stuck on the wall next to the bed is a list. The heading is WHAT I HAVE EATEN TODAY. Underneath it says: one cracker. Apple. Diet Coke.

Downstairs I get out the writing paper again.

Dear Janie, I write. Please tell me how you feel. I don't know what to do.

Then I rush to work, run into the kitchen, slip on a chip and end up in hospital with a broken ankle. Can you believe it?

Janie   When I get home there's another of Mum's stupid notes propped up on the kitchen table. The house smells of cooking fat. My mother is a lump of lard. I find it hard to be near her, she smells so bad. I feel like retching.

But there's a message to phone the school. I ring the number and the receptionist tells me that Mum's in hospital, and could someone collect Jackie and Claire. This is the last thing I want, but there's no one around but me, so I go up to the school. Jackie and Claire are all on their own with the teacher. They look bored and worried at the same time. Come on, I say, Mum's bust her stupid leg.

I phone up the hospital. Mum's voice is small and desperate. You could ask Mel to come round, she says. Someone will have to step in. I don't know what we're going to do.

I cook Jackie and Claire's supper and put them to bed. I read them a story from a library book about a princess who's so sensitive that she could even feel a pea through twenty mattresses. I feel like her. If I ate a pea I would know it. After the kids are asleep, I sit down and feel like Mum in the kitchen. Mum, with her fat ankles and her messy hair, trying to make everyone do things. I'm trying to keep my mind off eating. I start to write a letter.

Dear Mum, I write. You want to know how I feel? Enormous. I don't like my life. I hate the job at the call centre. We all sit in rows. I feel like a battery chicken. Sometimes I want to pretend there's a bomb scare just to get out of the place. I miss Dad. I feel like I'll never see him again because of you. I just want to lose weight and get out of here. Love Janie. PS Hope you are OK.

Grace I come home the next day in crutches. I'll be off work for weeks. No one's there when I get in. The kitchen sink is piled up with pans. There's toast crusts all over the sitting room carpet. But there on the kitchen table is a letter from Janie. As I open it, I'm afraid. I lie on the sofa and read it again and again. Then I write back.

Dear Janie, I'm sorry you miss your dad, but we couldn't live together any more. It was a nightmare at the end, and I know you suffered. The thing is, you're just punishing yourself with not eating. I've been reading a book about it. It's all about trying to be in control. I know you don't like your job at the call centre. I don't much like mine at the school. I hate smelling of food all the time. The thing is, we've got to survive somehow.

Then I grit my teeth and write another letter.

Dear Brian, Could you get in touch with Janie? I'm worried about her... (*Fades out*)

A door slams.

Grace Janie, is that you?

Janie Yeah.

Grace Have you picked up Jackie and Claire?

Janie Course I have.

Grace Come in here. I can't get up.

Janie I'm busy.

Grace Oh.

Janie's room.

Janie Dear Anna, When I woke up this morning there was hair all over my pillow. I ate a bowl of cereal today. I did it because I felt I couldn't walk up the hill without something, but now I feel that you're angry with me. Then Dad phoned up. He's living in Carlisle. He wants to meet up. I hope he won't expect me to eat anything. I'll have to tell him that I've got a stomach upset or something. Love Janie

Grace Dear Janie, I've been finding out about anorexia. I phoned up a helpline. It won't go away, you need help. I know now it's no good telling you to eat. It's like telling someone to drink poison, isn't it? We can fight this thing, Janie. Let me help you. Thanks for helping with J and C. What would I do without you? Mum

Janie Dear Mum, I would rather die than eat a biscuit. I love being light and thin. It makes me feel better. I hate my body when it's got food inside it. I don't want to upset you, but to me, being better means being fat.

Grace Dear Janie, It's killing you. Why don't you come and talk to me? Pauline at the helpline says you can phone her any time.

This is her number... (*Fades out*)

And so the letters go on. As my ankle heals, letters are pushed beneath doors and propped up against work bags, stampless, urgent, full of declarations of love and hate. But when we see each other, nothing is said. We don't even look at each other. I wonder how long it can go on. Janie is as thin as ever, although she disguises it underneath thick jumpers and coats. I can see her wrists, sharp and fragile, the shape of her skull beneath her thin hair. I long to force food into that pale mouth, but Pauline says no, wait, keep writing the letters. So I do.

Janie   Dear Anna, Last night my dad came over. He didn't come into the house, just stood on the step. We went for a drink. He kept on looking at me and I was expecting him to say something, but he didn't. I sipped my Diet Coke, while he asked me about my job and told me about some new girlfriend he's got. Then he kissed me before he went home and he smelt of beer and love. He squeezed me really tight, so I could hardly breathe, and he never said anything about how I looked. Not once. Sometimes, Anna, I wish I had never met you. From Janie

Grace   Brian phones up in a state. He says that he couldn't get over how thin Janie was, that we should get her to a doctor. Maybe, I said. But perhaps we need to get her to talk to someone else. Someone who knows about eating disorders. You sound calm, said Brian. Well, I've had to lie still for nearly a month, I said. It does things to you, lying still.

Dear Janie, Did you speak to Pauline?

Janie   Dear Mum, She just wants me to get fat, Mum. I can't bear the thought of being fat.

Grace   Dear Janie, She'll help you work it out.

Janie   Dear Mum, I wish you didn't have to go back to work.

Grace   Dear Janie, I'm not going back yet. Come down and see me, love. I know you're upstairs on your own. It must be lonely. I would be lonely if I was you. I'm all alone too, watching women crying on daytime telly. I've never seen so many women cry. What's happening to us all? Would you come and keep me company?

Late at night.

Janie   Dear Anna, I think I'm going to go downstairs. I want something else. I want a life, Anna. You can't have me. Thanks for the good times. There have been good times. I'm letting you go.

Sound of someone knocking on a door.

Janie   Mum?

Grace   Is that Janie?

Janie   Yeah. Can I come in for a while?

Grace   Hang on a minute.

Sound of her sitting up, arranging herself.

Come in. I'm ready. I'm ready now.

The End

Appointments

Again, I wanted to write about an older woman, and I also wanted to write about a week of appointments in a woman's life. My own life is increasingly filled by trips to masseurs, acupuncturists and hospitals. Maureen, in her late seventies, is diagnosed with a brain tumour on Monday. For the rest of the week she visits clairvoyants, friends, beauty parlours, and talks to a Macmillan nurse, trying to make sense of her condition. She also finds herself being haunted by a women's football team she played with during the war.

Sue Roberts produced these five short dramas at BBC Radio in Manchester in January 2005. Working with Sue is like being driven around in a limousine. Things happen smoothly and seamlessly. She has an impeccable ear and way of understanding what the writer intended.

Julia Darling

First broadcast from 21-25 February 2005 on BBC Radio 4.
Produced by Sue Roberts.

Maureen	Val McLane
Carla/Receptionist	Carol McGuigan
Nurse	Janet Hampson
Doctor Merrily/Driver	Rob Pickavance
Rusty/Nurse (Hilary)	Grace Stilgrove
Old woman/Maude	Madeleine Moffat
Theresa (fortune teller)	Jane Holman

MONDAY

Diagnosis

Interior. Day.

Maureen   (*Whispered, to herself*) I would rather not attend. I said that to my dog, Harry. I don't really want to go, but you feel bad if you don't. As if you are letting someone down. As if you should be grateful that anyone wants you to attend at all. It would be much easier not to. It takes a long time to get dressed and ready, just the stockings and the shoes take a lot of heaving, bending and squeezing, and you have to have several layers at this time of year. Then there's all the turning off and locking up, and settling the dog in the basket.

Exterior, day.

Maureen   Then down the lift and through the houses, with the kicked-about gardens and harsh little windows, down to the bent bus stop. The steps are steep down to Moss Road, and the wind blows harder than it used to in the last century. I'm still not used to the two thousands. It's so dirty everywhere. Hospital days are usually wet, and you have to travel right across the city. It reminds me of the war sometimes. All the grey faces and the puddles, and the bewildered town streets. And the bus seats are hard, and the driver swings round the corner, and the bus screams like it's never going to stop, like a horse being beaten. And of course, I haven't been well, with my headache, and the eye, and the shadow.

Interior, day. The phone is ringing.

Carla   Mum, Mum, it's Carla. I was wondering if you wanted a lift to the hospital. You said you didn't but it's so cold I thought you might have changed your mind. I've booked you in for Friday by the way. Give us a ring.

Exterior, day. Maureen plods along.

Maureen   I don't know why I go to see Doctor Merrily, as it's never a barrelful of laughs, and I know it won't improve things. Doctor Merrily!

Sound of bus screeching to a halt.

Maureen   Then when I get there I can smell the worry in the air, and I totter through the swing doors, and down the long corridor, past the paintings of wild animals and then the potted plants.

Interior, hospital. Day.

Maureen   And every so often you pass someone lying on a stretcher, all swathed in white, and with that alarmed, 'whatever happened to me?' look, with the dark caves around their eyes, and the linoleum stretching in every direction, and it's a funny thing, because I know I am sort of invisible, that no one sees me clumping along in my furry boots and green coat, and nobody knows that I was once the best striker in a women's football team, or that I had a dress shop on the Shields Road, or that I am Maureen!

I plod up to the desk and say my name – Maureen Wetherby – and the receptionist runs her fingers over a pile of files in front of her. I whisper inside, Maureen Wetherby for Doctor Merrily. It rhymes, see. Go on, smile, Mrs Receptionist, with your make-up all stiff. Can't you see I'm exhausted?

Receptionist GP's name?

Maureen   Doctor Clips.

Receptionist Date of birth?

Maureen   Twenty first of the eighth, nineteen thirty. (*To herself*) That was a long time ago. It's like looking down a well at a black and white world. I'd love to tell you about it, about the goal I scored in Sunderland.

Sound of muffled cheering like at a football match.

Receptionist Waiting Area C. Just over there.

Maureen   Aye aye. Waiting area C. I've been here before. Three rows of grey chairs, fixed to the floor. There's a print of an Italian villa on the wall. Here's somewhere you'll not be going!

A large sign saying PLEASE TURN OFF YOUR MOBILE PHONE. And it smells of tomato soup. The other ones are nearly all old, looking bleakly out from under their white fringes, hands curled round their handbags. Why are we so quiet?

And why I am here? I went to Doctor Clips because I kept seeing something out of the corner of my eye. It was a sort of a round blue shape, bouncing. Dr Clips is long and stringy and she's half German. Her husband left her for a younger woman. She looks as if she's cried a lot. She looked in my ear and my eye. She asked me if I got headaches. I told her yes, and they were like someone was holding an icy iron to the back of my head, or sometimes like a devil was hammering nails into my forehead. Then she said I'd need to have tests, so up I came for the scans, like lying in the middle of a giant whizzing polo mint, and now it's time for the results of the scans. That's why I am here, at least I have got that straight. But d'you know what? I'm not sure I want to know. I've still got the one good eye. I'd rather be watching the footie at home with the dog.

Nurse   Maureen Wetherby!

Maureen   My name sounds so shocking, so out loud in this place. It's the same name that I had when I was a child, but now I'm a different person. I get up nervously, follow the woman with flat shoes to a door into the room with no windows with the paper on the bed, ready to catch the spills... tears, blood, saliva, sweat.

Nurse   Just sit there for a moment, Maureen. The Doctor will be with you in a moment.

Maureen   Off she goes. There's the hand basin. Sign says, Very hot water. The bin, with the yellow plastic lining, the pink walls, the little trolley with hypodermics and cotton wool. Here's me, sitting, a bit flustered, waiting.

There's a big swish and commotion as Dr Merrily comes in.

Maureen   Doctor Merrily is very tall, with small hands and feet, and long awkward arms. He usually wears a suit, but today he's got a white coat on. His hair is brown and quite long, and he pushes it behind his ears. He smiles, but he looks uneasy. He's not old, but he acts as if he is older than me. He's carrying my file. It looks swollen with information. He's got poor skin, but he looks at me with his face very stiff, and I can see he's not looking forward to the conversation.

Doctor   Aaah, good, hello there, Mrs Wetherby.

Maureen   Busy are you? (*To herself*) He makes a great business of looking in the files, pushing his hair back, frowning. He looks as if he is acting the part of a doctor. I sit waiting, patiently.

Doctor   We have your results here.

Maureen   I'm all right now. It's best forgotten, whatever it was.

Doctor   The tests are quite positive.

Maureen   That's good, isn't it?

Doctor   I mean definite, indisputable.

Maureen   He holds up an X-ray and waves it in front of me. Looks like a weather chart, all misty and squirling. That's my head, is it?

Doctor   Yes, that's your head. Notice the abrasions.

Maureen   I politely look at the grey and black. The shadow on the left of my eye leans over too. It doesn't mean much.

Doctor   Maureen. There's a malignant tumour behind the right lobe that's been pressing on your eye.

Maureen   Uh huh. Doctor Merrily shakes his head. He can see I am not interested. I expect he wishes that I was a scientist and we could talk about things properly.

Doctor   It's inoperable.

Maureen   You can't cut it out then?

Doctor   No.

Maureen   So?

Doctor   It's very serious.

Maureen   He says this with his face all stiff. I smile at him then. I don't know what to do, so I look down at my shoes, and play with my buttons. Then I hum, for a while. Heaven, I'm in heaven, la la, out together dancing cheek to cheek...

Doctor   Are you all right, Maureen?

Maureen   Where are you from?

Doctor   Portsmouth.

Maureen   Do you miss it?

Doctor   Yes. Mrs Wetherby, I am arranging...

Maureen   The bus here took forty minutes!

Doctor   I'm going to put you in touch with a nurse, who'll come to your house. This nurse, she's trained in caring for patients in their homes. She'll make sure you get your entitlements, and pain, of course, she'll deal with pain.

Maureen   I don't get pain, just shadows.

Doctor   But you might.

Maureen   Is it compulsory?

Doctor   Not at all but...

Maureen   How old are you?

Doctor   Forty-three.

Maureen   Is your mother still alive?

Doctor   No. I miss her. More than I can say. Life is cruel, isn't it?

Maureen	Is it?
Doctor	She had a stroke.
Maureen	Have you got children?
Doctor	Yes, three.
Maureen	I've got one daughter. Carla. She's a beautician.
Doctor	Really.
Maureen	My husband's dead. Bobby.
Doctor	You can talk about your feelings with the special nurse.
Maureen	Do I have to?
Doctor	Of course not.
Maureen	What does your wife do?
Doctor	She's a paediatrician.
Maureen	Doctors clump together, don't they?
Doctor	I know it's a shock, Maureen.
Maureen	Oh well.
Doctor	Perhaps we can get you a cup of tea?
Maureen	It's the bus. I just don't enjoy it on the bus anymore.
Doctor	I'm giving you a prescription for pain killers. Do you drive?
Maureen	Me? Never.
Doctor	It's just that you might get drowsy.

Maureen   I've left the dog. I need to get home.

Doctor   Good. I mean, I'm sorry it's not better news.

The door slams.

Maureen   And off he scurries. See, what was the point of coming all this way to hear that? Inoperable brain tumour. Very cheerful. What now? I do up the buttons of my coat. I bought this coat ten years ago from Binns. It is my last coat. I get up and walk out into the waiting room. The air is thick with too much patience. They sit in rows waiting for Dr Merrily. I walk back down the looming corridor, past the swift receptionist with her long nails and squeaky voice, through the glass doors and out into the wet car park.

Exterior, hospital. Day.

Maureen   There is a plastic shelter built especially for smokers. A line of people with drips stand in it, smoking happily, watching the drips roll down the sides. I walk up to the street, to the bus stop, where a whole cluster of people are waiting wistfully, looking up the hill with hope still in their eyes. I want to get home to my dog. I want to turn the fire up. I shall never pay another bill. I feel very alone, suddenly, and deserted. I'm an old lady waiting for a bus. I'm invisible. In the distance I can see St James's Park. An ugly building, I always thought. When the match is on, it sounds like a huge sea, roaring and crashing against the rocks. I need something big to happen. Something that will drown out Dr Merrily's sad voice.

A bus screeches up.

Driver   Come on, pet. Make way for the lady!

Maureen   The bus driver smiles at me, a great sloppy, roguish grin. It quite bowls me over, that smile. I clamber towards it. Someone gets up and offers me their seat. I pull my hat over my ears. There is always tomorrow, I think. Don't look back.

TUESDAY

The House of Spirits

Interior, flat. Day. Maureen is waking up. We hear a dog barking, a kettle boiling, her shuffling around her flat.

Maureen   Ssssh, Harry. Ssssh. Go on, eat it, will you? I'll take you out later. Foggy. Yellow sky, lights on in the flats, as if the air is soaked in iodine, and it's not early. Two vests today, and thick socks. I don't need to take much. My purse, a notebook, in case she says anything I might forget. I don't usually forget. There's that shape again, just to the left. Sometimes it's as if it wants to say something, but when I turn, it's gone. Here we go. Fur gloves, zippy boots, so many things to put on. Look in the mirror. What do you see? A woman with a face like crumpled tissue paper. Hair cut grey and short, rather like a centurion, two gold earrings, spot of lipstick. I don't know why. Habit, I expect. Sit, Harry! Shut the kitchen door. Make sure the gas is turned off, and the fire in the sitting room. I feel like a snail leaving its shell. Here I go. Here I go.

We hear her leaving the house, locking doors.

Exterior, day. Street.

The estate is still asleep. The trees look undernourished, hunched, with the leaves hanging on miserably to twigs. I walk down the steep steps, slow, very slow, to Moss Road, but today I'm walking, so I turn left and go down the hill towards the river, passing the corner shop which blazes with light, and I peep in and see all the bright packets and tins piled up, and wave at Mr Casbari, who waves back with a smile that could launch ships. Smiles light up my days. Slow down the hill. Maude slipped down here and broke her hip. Be careful. I can see the river winding along, a black snake. I pass the doctor's surgery, with its green railings and ramp. There's a dog tied up outside. I consider setting it free, but of course I don't. I hope Harry isn't on my bed. Now we're at the main road. Cars bomb along. Roads belittle us, I think. Soon it will be all road, everywhere. No one will walk anymore, which makes me think how glad I am that I lived through a time when the earth was still beautiful, when the bicycle was queen, when there was still enough air for everyone. Everyone seems to be smoking in their cars, trapped inside a private room of smoke. I used to love cigarettes, but now they seem so unnecessary, so silly really. There's the bed shop.

Interior, flat. The phone rings.

Carla   Mum, it's me. How did it go at the hospital? Where are you today? Mum? Oh for heaven's sake! (*She puts the phone down*)

Exterior, day.

Maureen   I bought my last mattress from there, a long time ago. A mattress for Bobby and I. Slow, very slow. Avoid dog mess. So many mattresses, all piled up. Cheap pine beds. I will never buy another bed. Cross the road. There's a taxi rank, a battered door and a shop selling double glazing. I go to a small door between the two and ring a bell. A voice rasps through the intercom.

Voice   Yes?

Maureen   Maureen. To see Theresa.

Voice   Push the door, Maureen. Up the stairs, love, first door on the right.

Interior, House of Zodiac.

Maureen   I've been here before, about two years ago. I've always had a weakness. The stairs are long and narrow and the walls are painted dirty light blue. There's a naked bulb and you would think someone would get a lampshade, but you forgive a lot in these kinds of places. Up I go, knees creaking, the shadow in the corner of my eye lingering just behind me. One step at a time. I push open the door and there's a damp, warm waiting room, a few brown armchairs, a table with magazines like *Zodiac Weekly* and the *Astral Times*. There's a woman, think she's called Shirley, sitting at a desk smoking and drinking tea. She's all rusty looking, red hair, prickly cardigan, florid skin. I sit down. A man in a blue duffel coat with his hair plastered neatly in a side parting sits in the corner. He fiddles with the toggles. His skin is very doughy. I wonder what he's come for. What have I come for?

Rusty   It's you next. Mr Moody's waiting for his mam. She's in with Theresa now. You can pay now if you like. Saves time after.

Maureen   I take out my baggy leather purse and pull out a twenty-pound note, and she writes it down in careful biro on a pad, then puts it in a drawer, clipped to other notes. I can see she's an efficient receptionist. I sit down again. I could drop off sitting here. The chair is wide and soft. I feel a long way from anything, and my head buzzes. The shadow on my left bounces, then settles. Sometimes I think it hums.

There is a commotion as woman comes out.

Mr Moody   All right, Mam?

Mrs Moody   Much better. I spoke to Charlie. He says hello.

Mr Moody   That's nice. Come on now. We'll get a bowl of soup on the Shields Road.

Rusty   (*To Maureen*) In you go, darlin'.

Maureen   I go through a door, then across a hallway and into a small room. Theresa sits behind a desk. She's very large. Her arms balloon out from tight sleeves. Her pudding face is perspiring, and her eyes are very sharp and coaly. The curtains are half drawn, but I can still glimpse a bit of the yellow sky. She's got a pack of cards and some crystals on her desk, but she doesn't look exotic. She looks like a working woman, a lorry driver. She gestures to the chair opposite her.

Theresa   Sit down, Maureen, pet lamb.

Maureen   I'm impressed that she knows my name. She eyes me critically, as if she's trying to catch me out. I came after Bobby died and she told me that he was happy in heaven and that I wasn't to be sad. I wasn't sad at all. I wanted to know if he'd hidden any money in the flat.

Theresa   I can see you're a bit down today, Maureen. Well, don't be.

Maureen   Her voice is flat, her eyes a bit glazed. She shuffles her cards and winks at me. She starts talking in a soft monotone. I catch bits and pieces, but it's a bit strange.

Theresa   He's still waiting for you, but you're not ready yet, you've got a big surprise in store. Don't believe the man with the long hair. I see, I see. You've got a cloud around your heart, but that's alright, you'll blow that away, always a strong woman. There's a man here works in a rope factory. Does that ring a bell?

Maureen   That's Bobby.

She keeps on, flipping over cards, pushing them about on the table. I feel a bit tired. I wish she'd stop talking.

Theresa   He's your husband, is he? He says he misses you. He's standing right behind you.

Maureen   He always did that. It got on me nerves.

Theresa   Is there something you want to tell him?

Maureen   Not really. I wanted to ask you about...

Theresa   Oh no.

Maureen   What is it?

Theresa   The girls are coming in.

Maureen   Which girls?

Theresa's glancing around, looking a bit nervous, wiping her forehead with a tissue. She's looking above my head.

Theresa   Oh Lord! Bobby's not pleased. He's gone off in a huff.

Maureen   Theresa stops talking. She pulls a pack of fags out from a drawer and lights one. I feel like saying, did you know they've banned smoking in most places? But I don't. She inhales, watching something happen behind me. She looks affronted, as if she's been interrupted by something. I clear my throat. I wanted to ask her about death. I wanted to say, will I be somewhere comfortable, because that's what is really bothering me? I don't want a public death. I don't want to pass out in a queue, or halfway up some steps. She hasn't mentioned the shadow person yet, but surely she knows that it's here. Theresa looks exhausted. She swivels around in her chair, and sighs.

Theresa   It's getting rid of them afterwards. Were you in a football team?

Maureen   Years ago. The Byker Belles.

Theresa   They're all here, or most of them.

In the background, there's a sound of cheering as if from a football field.

Theresa   Cheering, and walking their mud onto my carpet.

Maureen   She points at the floor. The carpet is dark and filthy. I can't see any mud. I turn and look at the empty room.

Theresa   (*To the invisible footballers*) Sit down, will you! Keep your voices down.

Maureen   They're not all dead.

Theresa   There's at least ten women here.

Maureen   Is Nancy there?

Theresa   Irish woman, red knees, long blonde hair?

Maureen   That's her.

Theresa   Sally, and Freda and Melanie, and Florrie... All come to have a kick around in my office. God forbid.

Maureen   What do they want?

Theresa   They want you to play with them, Maureen. Florrie says that time is an illusion. Nothing ever really ends. They say you were the best striker and always will be.

Maureen   No, not really. I wasn't as good as Sally.

Theresa   Sally says you were.

Maureen   That's nice of her, but...

Theresa   They'll be here all day if they don't leave with you. I'm not having them.

Maureen   Theresa stands up, making sweeping movements with her arms.

Theresa   OUT! All of you!

Maureen   Haven't they come for a reason?

Theresa   No, they just want a party!

Maureen   Could you ask them if there is anything particular I should know? Ask them if I'm going to die soon? Is that why they're here?

Theresa   They won't say. They're a rough lot.

Maureen   Theresa walks to the door, holds it open. Aye, she says, aye, I'll tell her. She stomps back. I catch a whiff of something in the air. Wartime sweat, I think, or some cheap hair stuff. I get a lump in my throat. I mean, she's a great performer, Theresa. I don't really think an entire women's football team just came back to visit me. I mean, I'm not that gullible.

Theresa   They say, see you Friday.

Maureen   This Friday?

Theresa   Or thereabouts.

Maureen   Do they mean...?

Theresa   I don't know everything, Maureen.

Maureen   I'm not sure I want to...

Theresa   Don't let them boss you about.

Maureen   I'm worried about how and where. I don't want to embarrass myself.

Theresa   She doesn't want to make a fool of herself!

Maureen   Tell them. Tell Sally and Nancy and Florrie.

Theresa   They're just laughing at you. I think they've gone beyond embarrassment. Anyway, they've gone outside now, thank goodness. They frightened Bobby off.

Maureen   He never appreciated the football. No one did.

Theresa   Well, Maureen, the girls are back in town. Maybe not in my office, but they'll be dribbling right behind you.

Maureen   Then she's escorting me to the door, pushing me firmly out. I don't go back to the waiting room. I walk down the narrow stairs and into the street. I imagine the team waiting for me, jostling down the road like in the old days, all lazy and easy-limbed. I feel cushioned by them as I climb the hill back to the flat. One paper described us as the most degrading spectacle connected with football ever witnessed. They said the female body wasn't the right shape and that we shouldn't be showing our knees, that we would not be able to have children. But they didn't mind us hauling hay bales around on the farms, or making guns in the armaments factories. I was nearly divorced over it.

These are the thoughts that follow me home after my appointment with Theresa and the dark shadow receded to a little dot, way out on the horizon. And by the time I got home, my headache had quite disappeared.

WEDNESDAY

The nurse

Maureen's dog barks. She is shambling around in her flat. We hear a low murmur of women's voices. The football team has followed Maureen home.

Interior, day. Maureen's flat.

Maureen   I wake up with my head pounding. The rooms feel busy, although I am the only person here. The shadow keeps rolling around on the edge of my vision. Carpets are crumpled and chairs pulled close together. The atmosphere is, I don't know, sort of different, as if there's been a party going on.

I get the old football cups out and put them along the mantelpiece, along with a couple of photographs of the team. My, we were a handsome bunch of lasses. Great raw knees and thick necks, and wide, hairy shins. I sit by the fire chuckling away, spitting, then polishing the trophies with my sleeve. God, we had some times, honest to God.

The doorbell rings and we hear her shushing the dog and opening the door. It's the Macmillan nurse, Hilary.

Nurse   (*Through the letterbox*) Mrs Wetherby?

Maureen   Yes?

What now? Some big-boned, red-cheeked woman peering through the letterbox. She looks as if she knows everything. There were girls like her at school. They had the best sandwiches in their lunchboxes. They won prizes. She fills up the doorway. I'm busy. I'm thinking about being in a women's football team. She can't come in.

Nurse   (*Loud, through letterbox*) Your consultant, Dr Merrily, suggested I get in touch. Can I come in for a moment?

Maureen   I'm in the middle of me housework. Quiet, Harry.

Nurse   I love dogs.

Maureen   No you don't. I can see you eyeing my hallway, inhaling my life.

Nurse   It won't take long.

We hear the door opening and the nurse coming in. There's a distant sound of a group of women, the football team, giggling and whispering.

Maureen   I'm in the sitting room.

Nurse   We can make another appointment if you like.

Maureen   She beams at me with her red cheeks. I can see her making mental lists about me. I realise I am still wearing my dressing gown and that it's ripped around the sleeve.

Maureen   What for?

Nurse   Your assessment.

Maureen   Do I have to have an assessment?

Nurse   Of course you do!

Maureen   Get on with it then. Do you want me date of birth?

Nurse   Do you have any pain?

Maureen   Sometimes. A bit of a headache.

Nurse   I can get you aromatherapy, or an Indian head massage.

Maureen   I see.

Nurse   Or we could talk.

Maureen   What about?

Nurse   Anything you want. Shall I call you Maureen?

Maureen   I suppose.

Nurse   I'm Hilary.

Maureen   It's just I'm very busy.

Nurse   Busy doing what, dear?

Maureen   I've got people to see.

Nurse   I expect you're feeling a bit shocked.

Maureen   Why?

Nurse   With the scan results.

Maureen   Oh that.

Nurse   Some people go into a state of denial.

Maureen   She reaches out and squeezes my wrist, as if she's secretly feeling my pulse. I pull my hand away.

Is that the time?

Can't she see? I don't want to discuss it. I don't want words like scan or inoperable in my house. She's making me anxious.

Nurse   Shall I put the kettle on?

Maureen   I suppose.

She makes herself at home, looking at everything, opening the fridge, the cupboards.

We hear Hilary putting on a kettle.

Football team   (*Whispering*) Kick her out, Maureen. Remember who you are.

Maureen   She's only young. She doesn't know any better.

Football team   The best striker in the Byker Belles. Maureen Wetherby! Send her packing!

Maureen   Who is that?

Silence.

Nurse   Who are you talking to?

Maureen   No one. I've got blocked ears.

Nurse   I'll write that down. You might need to be dewaxed. What lovely photographs.

Maureen   She starts picking photographs up and staring at them.

Nurse   Is that your daughter?

Maureen   Yes, Carla. That's my husband, Bobby. He's dead.

Nurse   Aaaah, and he looks lovely there, doesn't he?

Maureen   He wasn't lovely. Lovely is one thing Bobby wasn't. He was witty sometimes, he could hold a tune, he liked a drink, but lovely, no, he wasn't.

Football team   No, he wasn't.

Nurse   I see.

Maureen   He didn't like me doing my own thing. Always had to know where I was, followed me up the street sometimes.

Nurse   When did he die?

Maureen   Three years ago. Actually, in that chair you're sitting in.

Nurse   Oh.

Maureen   I had to have it cleaned.

Nurse   That must have been a shock.

Maureen   Not really. He was yellow. Alcoholic.

Nurse   Hmmm. I meet a lot of characters in my work. You know, people like you with interesting pasts.

Maureen   What do you mean?

Nurse   You should write down your memories.

Football team   Ssssshhhhhhh... Don't let her get you down... the best striker.

Maureen   I can't.

Nurse   Why not?

Maureen   I'm illiterate.

Nurse   I could write it down for you.

Maureen   No thanks.

Nurse   I keep a diary about everyone I meet.

Maureen   Do you?

Nurse   I love my job.

Maureen   Visiting ill people?

Nurse   Helping them find solutions.

Maureen   But I haven't got a problem.

Nurse   That's OK, that's OK.

Maureen   Unless you know how to get rid of pigeons? Do ya? They poo on the roof of my porch. Do you want to see?

Nurse   That's not my department.

Maureen   What is your department then?

Nurse   Palliative care.

Maureen   You help with death?

Nurse   You could put it like that.

Maureen   Come and look at this.

Nurse   Well...

Maureen   It's not very hygienic. It falls on my head. Look. Pigeon poo in me hair.

Nurse   I could phone the council.

Maureen   Would you? I haven't got the time meself.

Nurse   I can't imagine what you do all day, Maureen.

Maureen   I have appointments. I meet me friends. I catch buses. I keep an eye on things.

Nurse   You might want to come along one day and meet everyone at the hospice?

Maureen   Why would I want to do that?

Nurse   Free treatments! It's a lovely place. There's a brass band plays there on Sundays. You might make friends.

Maureen   I've got friends.

Nurse   You can never have enough friends. Tell me about your support systems.

Maureen   Support systems?

Nurse   Do you have someone coming to cook your meals.

Maureen   No, of course not.

Nurse   What about cleaning?

Maureen   It's just me and the dog. We do our own cleaning.

Nurse   We can do something about that.

Maureen   It's not dirty!

Nurse   What if you feel poorly? Who would you call?

Maureen   My daughter, Carla. She's a beautician. Or Maudie, she was on the team.

Nurse   On the team?

Football team   On the team...

Maureen   Lady's football. The Byker Belles.

Nurse   So you were a footballer, eh?

Maureen   In the war.

Nurse   Fancy that. Is that a picture?

Maureen   That's us in 1950.

Nurse   Did you win?

Maureen   Oh yes, we won.

Nurse   Against the other lasses?

Maureen   The Sunderland Slappers.

Nurse   That's not very nice, Maureen. I'm from Sunderland.

Maureen   Beg your pardon. There's only me and Maudie left. We meet every Thursday, at the Turkish usually.

Nurse   Are you sure that's a good idea?

Maureen   Have you ever been to the Turkish?

Nurse   No. I'm just worrying about the heat, at your age.

Maureen   Because you don't like taking your clothes off, that's why. You like to be the one with the clothes on while everyone else is in their underwear. I know you. I know.

Nurse   This is my card, Maureen.

Maureen   It's pink.

Nurse   Pink is my favourite colour.

Maureen   So am I supposed to phone you up, like?

Nurse   I am here for you. I'll be visiting you regularly.

Maureen   Why's that?

Nurse   Because you're ill.

Maureen   I don't feel ill.

Nurse   But you will soon, dear. Sadly.

Maureen   Ha ha.

Nurse   When would you like to go to the hospice?

Maureen   I don't want to go at all.

Nurse   Are you sure?

Football team   Tell her, Maureen.

Maureen   I don't need a nurse.

Nurse   Well, have a think about it, dear.

Maureen   I'll phone you. If I need you.

Football team   Go! Go!

Nurse   Well, I'm here if you need me.

Maureen   I don't need you.

Nurse   (*Icily*) I see.

We hear Hilary being shown out. A dog growls and the door slams. A big roar of laughter is unleashed, as if the entire football team has been hiding in the cupboards.

Maureen   I think I'm going mad. I'm living with the Byker Belles. Quiet!

And that's how it was for the rest of Wednesday, with the rustle and thick breaths of half a dozen ghostly footballers, opening the fridge, and pulling photographs off the mantelpiece, whistling in my ear and changing the channels on the TV. I'm feeling overwhelmed. I'm too old for this. I don't know what they want.

THURSDAY

The Turkish bath

Interior, flat. Day. The phone is ringing.

Maureen   Yes?

Carla   Mum? Are you OK? I've been phoning all week.

Maureen   I'm fine, darlin', just going out now. Are we still on for tomorrow?

Carla   Course. But where have you been?

Maureen   Out and about.

Carla   By yourself?

Maureen   Not always. Look, Carla, I'll see you tomorrow, pet. Got to rush now.

She puts the phone down.

Exterior, day. Maureen walking.

Maureen   In the morning it's quiet again, thank goodness.

A lightly frothed sky. Swift frilly clouds passing over it, like the day we played against Leicester City and I scored a hat trick. Remember that, Harry? Now look at my legs. Purple and blue, swollen at the ankle. I spent the morning writing a list of things I want to do. Yes, I know I told the nurse I was illiterate, well, I'm not. I won first prize in English at school. I want to go to the Stadium of Light. I've never been. I want to travel first class on a train. I want to hire a punt on the River Wear and hear the Edinburgh Tattoo.

The shadow on the left of my eye is almost a companion now, a quiet friend. I wear a red wool hat pulled right down so that the wind can't whistle in my ears. I leave the heating on and trudge down to Moss Road and head for the city. It's only a ten-minute walk to where I'm going, over the Byker Bridge, where you can see right over the river, and the criss-crosses of other bridges arching over River Ouseburn and the whisky warehouse. And I feel happy, happy in an airy, walking over bridges sort of way, happy that I haven't got a headache and that my feet still step forward, that I can still lift my feet. I reach a street of shops that all seem to have letters missing, quariums and urniture, and I am the only person walking along the pavement, as if no one walks here anymore. I cross the motorway using a spindly concrete bridge that takes me into the city, to cafes and building societies and libraries. I stop for a rest. My bag is heavy and I put it on the pavement for a moment. I wonder if I am likely to collapse? Then I plod on for the last hundred yards, through a sudden swarm of students emerging from a university building, hair and bags and thin little arms. Then I am outside the grand municipal building that smells of chlorine and floor polish. I buy my ticket from the heavy-faced woman with gritty eyes behind a glass counter. It's an all-day ticket. As you walk down the marble stairs it gets hotter and hotter. You can smell the baths coming towards you, like warm arms pulling you into a soft room.

Interior, day. The Turkish bath.

Maureen   Brenda. Brenda is the doorkeeper, who guards the towels and the tea machine. She has tattoos down both her arms and wears a black bathing costume. She points me inside, nodding but not acknowledging that she's seen me many times before. Maude is already there. She's lying on a marble slab with two cotton wool pads on her eyes, with a towel wrapped around her ample, sweating bosom. I prod her fleshy arm and she lifts up one eye patch and grins.

Maude   Get your clothes off then.

Maureen   Don't hurry us.

Maude   Jacuzzi's broke again.

Maureen   Things never broke in the old days. Or they fixed them.

Maude   They served you poached eggs here.

Maureen   Poached eggs, and tea on a silver tray.

Maude   Poached eggs, tea on a silver tray, and please and thank you.

Maureen   Poached eggs, silver tray, please, thank you and can I do anything else for you, madam? I'd sit in here and I'd be so happy, I wouldn't call the Queen me auntie.

Maude tries to think of something else but can't.

Maude   Aye. (*Pause*) What happened to your eye, Maureen?

Maureen   I'm having a hell of a week, Maudie.

Maude   Are you under the doctor?

Maureen   Doctor Merrily.

Maude   I'm with Doctor Garonin.

Maureen   Doctor Merrily, he's from Portsmouth. I saw him on Monday. He says I've got a tumour in me eye.

Maude   Never. I can't see it! I don't know much about Portsmouth. Garonin's from the east. He's large, and often too hot. He's got three children, but he's divorced. That's all I know. You try to make conversation, don't you?

Maureen   God almighty, I try. Dr Merrily's slow in coming forward if you know what I mean.

Maude   So what does he suggest?

Maureen   I dunno.

Maude   Is it sore?

Maureen   Not really. I don't know what to make of it all. I was worn out, with getting to the hospital. And you have to get the bus after 9.30 to use your pass, or the driver says...

Maude   TWIRLY! Cheeky sod.

Maureen   Aye, TWIRLY. So I have to beg him, as the appointment is at nine. Begging in the street at my age!

Maude   If they had legs like these.

Maureen   It's been hellish, Maude. Can I put me feet up on your slab?

Maude   Aye aye. Carry on. It's the same with bowels, exactly the same. A sign on the wall saying 'The doctor is very busy as all the other doctors are sick'. By the time you get to see the doctor you've lost the will to live.

Maureen   I know, I know.

Maude   So what are you going to do?

Maureen   What can I do, Maudie?

Maude   Doctors like to show off, don't they? I'd rather not know, I say. Keep your fancy illness names to yourself.

Maureen   Well, on the Tuesday I went to see Christine at the House of Spirits.

Maude   I went to her once. I wanted to know if I'd find true love, but she kept on about me mother. Twenty quid!

Maureen   Well, guess who turned up?

Maude   Bobby?

Maureen   He was first in, but he got overwhelmed.

Maude   What do you mean?

Maureen   The Byker Belles turned up, loads of them. Florrie and Melanie and Freda and Sally and Nancy. And the thing is, Maudie, they followed me home.

Maude   Don't be daft.

Maureen   I think they've come to get me, Maudie.

Maude   I think you're being over sensitive.

Maureen   I mean, it's not that I'm not pleased to see them. I am. But I'm a bit frightened. I don't want to die yet, Maudie.

Maude   Don't worry, pet lamb. They can't make you go if you don't want to.

Maureen   You know what they were like. They wouldn't take no for an answer.

Maude   Are they hostile, like?

Maureen   No, they're just everywhere.

Maude   Here?

Maureen   Hang on a minute. Listen.

Maude   I can't hear anything.

Maureen   We both sit there, red faces, listening to the water running down walls, to the gurgle of underwater pipes below the baths, to the muted conversations of other women come to spend the day in these warm rooms.

No, I can't hear them. Phew.

Maude   So how did you leave things with Doctor Merrily?

Maureen   Sad. Doctor Merrily is not a happy man. He wouldn't see a joke if it slapped him on the bum. All he can talk about is bad news.

Maude   Doctor Garonin's not a barrel load of laughs. He's all bum. At least you've got two eyes. I've only got the one bowel.

Maureen   True. Then on Wednesday, yesterday, a big school girl dressed up like a nurse who demands a cup of tea, she wants me to go to the hospice, for the free aromatherapy massage.

Maude   I never heard of massaging an eye.

Maureen   Exactly. She kept on holding my wrist, like this, as if I needed comfort. There were balls of dog fluff everywhere, all on the carpets. I thought Harry might bite her. She looked as if she wanted something, but I'm buggered if I know what. She didn't know anything about pigeons and that's the biggest problem in my life. And the Byker Belles kept on whispering in me ears. To be honest with you, Maude, she's neither use nor ornament.

Maude   You don't have to see her if you don't like her, pet.

Maureen   No. You're right.

I look at Maude. She's a golden colour, all wrinkles and caverns and glinting gold teeth. She was a defender, always there when you needed her. Maude lives with her son in Forest Hall. She bakes most days, and she's a wonderful cake decorator. I feel this huge surge of love for her, for her big living body and all its flaws.

Maude   What are you thinking about?

Maureen   You're a nice woman, Maude.

Maude   Aye.

Maureen   What shall I do about the Byker Belles?

Maude   They'll go home eventually.

Maureen   I've called up the dead.

Maude   You know what they were like. I mean, they were a force to contend with on a night out.

Maureen   What shall I say to them?

Maude   Tell them straight.

Maureen   Ssshhhh.

We hear a distant sound of women laughing in the shower.

That's them! They're here now. I can hear them sloshing about in the showers, laughing and making jokes. They're big ghost women, Maudie.

Maude   Oh, I know, but you were the best striker.

Maureen   I'm scared.

Maude   Hey, Maureen, it will be all right. Ssssh, remember, we were a team. Nothing frightened us. Even the Sunderland Slappers. Come on, pet lamb. It's that Doctor Merrily and his nurse have upset you. Hey, WE SHALL OVERCOME!

Maureen   She leans over and takes hold of my hand. Funny how one person can try and hold your hand and you want to run ten miles, but Maudie's hand is steady and it's a comfort. I'm grateful. I can see I've been getting stressed.

Pause. The sound of bubbles.

Maude   They've fixed the jacuzzi!

Maureen   Have you got time for one?

Maude   I've got all day, me.

Maureen   Me too. I'm here until teatime.

Maude   Thought I'd see if the manicurist's in?

Maureen   I'm seeing Carla for a massage tomorrow. I don't need to go to the hospice, do I?

Maude   Course you don't.

Maureen   There's nothing a good steam won't cure, is there, Maude?

Maude   Nothing at all.

The sound of a women's football team laughing in a distant steam room.

FRIDAY

Carla's facial

Exterior, day. Maureen walking.

Maureen   The taste of mud in my mouth. I liked that. The way I ran and exceeded meself. I can't describe it. I felt alive. I woke up this morning, Friday, just thinking it, half out of a dream of falling down and cheering in the middle of a match. Harry's been sleeping on my bed. I don't care about the hairs anymore. The dark shadow in my head is almost like a friend now. I wake up with it next to me. It looms larger and larger. I even catch its face sometimes, a young face, a face that's moving very fast.

So today I have a lie in, which I don't often do. I get up at ten, and let the dog out for ten minutes and I frown at the sky, which is loose and wispy. I go back in and I make myself a bowl of porridge, God's food, and feel it weighting me to the ground. I dress myself in a lilac dress that I've kept since the dress shop days. It's made of woolly stuff. I put a spot of powder on my cheeks, and a sweep of red lipstick. I brush the bramble of my hair and tie it down with a purple scarf. I sing while I'm getting ready. I sing, 'We shall overcome, we shall overcome, we shall overcome some day!' I feel strong by the time I leave the flat. I walk with a purpose. After the war, the football authorities took the game back from us. They didn't like us playing. They said it was dangerous for women. Our wombs would drop out, they said. They put us back in the kitchens. Well, that's not true in my case. I opened a dress shop on the Shields Road. But that doesn't mean I didn't miss the game. I starved. I got thin. I missed the other girls. We would meet in the High Street and be almost awkward with each other. We couldn't fit the parts of ourselves together, one part that whooped and sweated and ran and kicked and the other part that was supposed to live in rooms, small little rooms with sinks and taps and cake tins.

I take a taxi into town. New Byker Cabs. It's a treat. Why not? I think. The driver is immense. He fills up the whole of the front seat. When I tell him where we're going, he sighs. It's only a short ride. Just into town. But I ignore him and I sit in the back of the cab like a queen, and when I get out I give him a tip.

Interior, shop.

The department store is full of well-upholstered ladies. This is a place you would meet for afternoon tea, where you can buy the best ham in Newcastle, where the teapots are silver. I take the soundless lift up to the third floor, to beauty and hair. That's where I'm going. I'm going to see Carla, my only daughter. I come every week, for a facial. It's half price.

Yes, every week I have an appointment to see my only daughter, who is forty-five. She's been in beauty ever since she was young. She wears thick foundation and her face is like a mask. She never married. She lives on her own in a housing estate full of couples and business people. She's got fluffy toys on her bed. She enters competitions in magazines. I wish we were closer. There she is, in her white coat, coming towards me. I trouble her, I know that. I don't think I approve of beauty. I only come for facials because that's the only way we get to be alone, talking.

Oh, Carla.

We hear the sound of the lift and the chatter of receptionists.

Carla   Hello, Mum. Just go on through. I've been so busy, body tans, bikini waxing, everyone's on holiday but me. Trudy's got a poorly ear, So she's gone home. I'm on my own again.

Maureen   I can wait around a bit.

Carla   I'm ready now.

Maureen   You look too thin.

Carla   What do you mean?

Maureen   And pale. You don't look after yourself.

Carla   (*To herself*) Here we go!

Carla is getting all her creams ready, looking at Maureen's skin. They are in a small beauty room.

Carla   How was it at hospital? Did you have a scan or something?

Maureen   Oh you know, waiting, then everyone asking me my date of birth, then the results.

Carla   Which were?

Maureen   Usual gobbledegook. I've got some pills.

Carla   Now, close your eyes, mum. I'll rub this on. It's new, it's made from jasmine flowers from New Zealand and almond oil from Spain.

Maureen   My skin's felt old this week, Carla.

Carla   Your skin's a miracle, Mum. It's the best I've ever seen. Like putting my fingers into a bowl of dandelion fluff. We get some terrible skins in here. Some skin is horrible to touch, corrugated, rough as Artex. They come to me, but it's too late. Not like you, Mum.

Maureen   Oh shush.

Soft sounds of the football team.

Carla   That door keeps on opening all by itself.

Maureen sighs. She knows the football team is coming in.

Maureen   Did I tell you I once played football in the war? There was a team of us, Florrie, Nancy Sally... and we were friends.

Carla   You told me loads of times. I've seen the photos, and the cups. I remember Dad pontificating in his chair about bloody women in their strips. Keep still a moment.

Maureen   I miss them sometimes.

Football team   (*Whispering*) Morning, Maureen. What's with the ylang ylang? Eh?

Carla   Tell me about the hospital, Mum? What did the doctor say?

Maureen   Nothing worth repeating.

Carla   What's wrong with your eye?

Maureen   It's just a bit sore.

Carla   There, I'll put a cold pad on it.

Maureen   Have you been eating properly.

Carla   Of course.

Maureen   You're so thin.

Carla   Don't start. Shut your eyes.

Maureen   I can hear them in the room, gathering around me, leaning against the couch. I smell beer and smoke. There's the rumble of laughter, of women together.

Football team   Are you coming back with us today, Maureen? We're ready for you.

Maureen   No!

Carla   No what?

Maureen   Everyone's dead but Maude, from the team.

Carla   Well it was a long time ago, wasn't it?

Maureen   It doesn't seem like that. I can still taste it, Carla.

Carla   Was it great?

Maureen   It was just that I was so alive then, pet. I could feel the blood inside my veins and the wind against my face. I wish you had something like that in your life.

Carla   I do.

Maureen   What?

Carla   I walk by the sea. I do Pilates.

Maureen   It's not the same.

Carla   Don't criticise. Smell that! It's rosemary!

We hear the sounds of people playing football in the distance.

Maureen   Do you believe in ghosts, Carla?

Carla   I think I do. Why's that?

Maureen   It's just they're with me now, the team. I feel them in the room.

Carla   You're joking!

Maureen   I think so. They're waiting for me. Down at the end.

Carla   The end of what?

Maureen   The pitch. Look.

Carla   You're in a funny mood today. You're worrying me. Try to stop thinking. There's no football teams in here. Just me and you.

(*To herself*) And the usual conversation. You're too thin... The trouble with you, Carla... When are you going to...?

Do you want the whales, or the bubbly brook? The bamboo chimes are broken, but they made me jumpy anyway. I'll put on the whales. You can't go wrong with whales. I'll just pluck that eyebrow. There! Much better.

Maureen   I'm tired.

Carla   I bet you are. If you'd phoned I would have driven you to the hospital. Why do you always do everything by yourself?

Maureen   Do I?

Carla   Breathe in and out slowly, Mum. Try to relax.

Sounds of whales, and Carla fiddling about with her creams.

But I'm not surprised you're a bit glum. These winter nights are far too long. I'm not so fond of darkness either. And there's far too much of it. I think I may have become a creature of the dark, I've been so long inside. And I worry about you.

We can hear Maureen breathing deeply.

She's gone to sleep. Oh Mum, if only we were all as strong and beautiful as you! But I get on your nerves. I'm not the daughter you imagined. I'm shy and slow. I've got no children. There's nothing bright about me.

We hear the sounds of football again.

Yes, I've been sad all week. What should I do, Mum? I'm thinking of moving house. St Peter's Basin's got no plug. It's full of empty balconies. At night the cupboards rattle. Oh well, mustn't grumble. It's just sometimes I feel so SINGLE. I know you'd say something like, have an adventure, be braver, but where do I find that bravery, Mum?

Pause. She looks intently at Maureen, who doesn't seem to be breathing.

Carla   MUM?

Football team   Come over here, Maureen. Over here.

Maureen   (*In dream*) I'm in Bradford, I'm dribbling down the pitch. Where are they all? I pass to Florrie and she passes the ball right back. This woman, like a lorry she was, arms like a gorilla, came galloping up behind, but I sidestepped and caught the ball around my foot and sent it sailing to the goal. Yes!

Sounds of cheering.

Maureen   I hear the crowds, calling out my name, across the grass. I hear Maureen Florrie, Nancy Sal. I hear our songs across the sky. I'm running like the wind, arms in the air! And I am not alone, like I'm not now.

Carla   (*Tearful*) Mum? Are you all right? (*Starting to panic*) MUM? Wake up!

Maureen   (*Startled*) What's that? Where am I?

Carla   Oh God, I'm sorry. For a moment you seemed so still. I'm sorry.

Maureen   (*Chuckles*) Did you think I'd gone?

Carla   Just for a second. And it's cold in here, though the fire is on.

Maureen   You're right. They were calling. It's been like that all week. I'm haunted by a football team, and there's this shadow, travelling with me. It's right there now.

Carla   You should have called me, Mum. Why don't you?

Maureen   I don't want to get in the way, Carla. Why don't you?

Carla   You never want to listen.

Maureen   Is that true?

Carla   You want me to be someone else.

Maureen   No. I don't.

Carla   And what would you be getting in the way of? There's nothing here. Just me and you living at opposite ends of this dark city. It's not right.

Maureen   But I don't want to interfere.

Carla   What is there to interfere with in my life? I'm just a woman who spends her days in quiet rooms talking to women. Someone who doesn't do much harm, I suppose. What about you?

Maureen   I see a girl who one minute was roaring and leaping in the air, and the next thing she was living in a small flat wearing tight dresses. I'm not sure how it happened. I let myself down.

Carla goes up very close.

Carla   Go on, smile. You hardly ever do.

Maureen   You're right. Sometimes I feel as if my forehead's full of clouds.

Carla   You could move in with me. I'd drive you to the Turkish baths in my car. I'd take you on a punt down the River Wear. We could go to the Stadium of Light. You'd like that. We'd get videos of epic football games.

Maureen   I'd like to hear the Edinburgh tattoo.

Carla   Me too!

Maureen   I thought you'd never ask.

Carla   I'm asking now.

Maureen   Maybe for a few days, a trial?

Carla   Why not? You could always change your mind.

Maureen   I know what the shadow is, pet. It's the ball, the thing I am trying to catch. I've got it now. It's in my hands. I can pass it anywhere.

Carla   I don't know what you mean.

Maureen   I've got the ball, Carla! I mean, I think the world isn't safe, but I'm still in it for a while. I'll come and live with you. The team can have my flat.

Football team   A flat! Get some beer in! Wa-hay!

Maureen   Can I bring the dog?

Carla   Harry? Oh God, I suppose so.

Maureen sits up, but she's a bit wobbly.

Maureen   I'm passing it to you, Sally. The ball's for you. You need to run with it, right down to the end. I don't want it.

Carla   What are you on about, Mum?

Maureen   Carla, it's time you stepped out of your skin and into daylight. Beauty's made you miserable. I've wanted to say that for years. I'm going home to pack.

Carla   I'll drive down after work then! Your bed's all ready.

Maureen   Come on, girls, let's walk through Newcastle arm in arm, along the streets we own. Just one last time. Then you can carry on a while without me. Let's sing our hearts out.

Women singing I seem to find the happiness I seek, When we're out together dancing cheek to cheek!

The End

About Julia Darling

1956-2005

Julia Darling moved to the North East in 1980, and lived and worked as a writer in Newcastle from that point on, drawing inspiration from the region and its people. She produced many plays, for youth theatres and regional companies, as well as writing novels, short fiction, songs and poetry.

Her first plays (*Growing Pains*, *Mother of Invention*, *Gone with the Lettuce*) were mainly produced by youth and theatre-in-education companies. Later she developed a number of touring plays with Quondam Arts Trust, including *Rafferty's Café*, *Head of Steel*, *Black Diamonds* and *Doughnuts Like Fanny's* (a play about the life of Fanny Cradock). *Eating the Elephant* was written for the Ashton Group, a touring theatre company based in Barrow in Furness.

Julia had a long and fruitful relationship with Live Theatre in Newcastle upon Tyne, where many of her plays were premiered. In 2000 Julia took up a position as writer in residence with Live Theatre, along with the playwright and poet Sean O'Brien. This collaboration produced many plays for Live and for BBC Radio Four.

The Last Post was produced by Live Theatre in 2002, after an artist's residency with the Post Office as part of the Arts Council's Year of the Artist scheme. Using the theme of letters, Julia adapted some of the stories from *The Last Post* for BBC Radio 4's *Woman's Hour* under the title of *Posties*. She also wrote a further five plays, *Appointments*, for the same radio slot. The play *Sea Life* was commissioned as a live radio broadcast by BBC Radio 4 as part of an evening of plays based on the lives of philosophers. Producer Sue Roberts worked with Julia on most of her radio plays.

Julia's last play was *A Manifesto for a New City*, which was produced by Northern Stage in 2005. The play, a poetic musical, was recorded by the original cast.

As well as her dramatic work Julia published a collection of short stories, *Bloodlines* (Panurge); two novels, *Crocodile Soup* and *The Taxi Driver's Daughter* (Penguin Books); and two collections of poetry, *Sudden Collapses in Public Places* and *Apology for Absence* (Arc Press).

With Cynthia Fuller, Julia edited *The Poetry Cure* (Bloodaxe), a collection of poetry about health.

A website devoted to Julia hosts her widely-read personal web-log, which charted both her creative and private life. At the time of her death, Julia was working on the innovative *First Aid Kit for the Mind* with artist Emma Holliday.

She was awarded a £60,000 Northern Rock Foundation Writer's Award in 2003, and was a fellow at the School of English Language and Linguistics at the University of Newcastle upon Tyne, where she worked to develop projects around poetry and health.

More information about Julia's life and work can be found at www.juliadarling.co.uk.

Julia Darling's plays

A Manifesto for a New City	Northern Stage
Sudden Collapses in Public Places	Live Theatre
Appointments	Woman's Hour, BBC Radio 4
Maud's Eye	Live Theatre
Attachments	Live Theatre*
Posties	Woman's Hour, BBC Radio 4
Doughnuts Like Fanny's	Quondam Theatre
The Last Post	Live Theatre
Sea Life	BBC Radio 4
Personal Belongings	Live Theatre
Venetia Love Goes Netting	Live Theatre
The Night Tom Jones Came to Barrow	The Ashton Group Contemporary Theatre
Newcastle Is Barcelona	Dog Leap Cabaret
The Women Who Painted Ships	Live Theatre
Eating the Elephant	Ashton Group Contemporary Theatre
Black Diamonds	Quondam Theatre
Head of Steel	Quondam Theatre
Rafferty's Café	Quondam Theatre
Victory Harvest	Chopwell Drama Group
Growing Pains	Tyne and Wear TIE
Mother of Invention	Wallsend Youth Theatre
Gone with the Lettuce	Wallsend Youth Theatre
Rites from Wrongs	Bruvvers Theatre Company

*A television version of *Attachments*, entitled *Cold Calling*, was published in *Live Theatre: Six Plays from the North East* (Methuen, ISBN 0413774090, 2003).

New Writing North

New Writing North is the writing development agency for the north east of England. We aim to create an environment in the north east of England in which new writing in all genres can flourish and develop. We are a unique organisation within the UK, merging as we do individual development work with writers across all media with educational work and the production of creative projects. We work with writers from different genres and forms to develop career opportunities, new commissions, projects, residencies, publications and live events.

We work in partnership with a broad range of organisations, universities, local authorities, regional development agencies, sponsors and media producers to develop opportunities for writers in our region. Recent projects in this area include the *Hawthorn Wordworks* public poetry project with One North East, the development of proposals for a Northern Writers' Centre with Newcastle University, the Yorkshire TV Writer's Bursary Scheme and a large-scale community project, *Writing Westpark*, sponsored by property developers Bussey and Armstrong in Darlington.

We manage the *Northern Writers' Awards* and the *Northern Rock Foundation Writer's Award* (currently the largest literary award in the UK and worth £60,000 to the winning writer) and support writers at all stages of their careers by career mentoring and by the creation of professional development training initiatives and projects such as the *Ignite Creative Radio Programme* which runs in conjunction with the BBC.

We work in partnership with writers, theatres and producers to develop new writing for the stage and have initiated work and new commissions with many of the theatre companies in our region and helped to set up initiatives such as the Dramaturg's post at Northern Stage/Newcastle University.

Through our international work we aspire to create partnerships and projects for writers from our region with international counterparts. We are currently developing projects in Bulgaria, Siberia and the Czech Republic.

We run a wide-ranging education and community programme which involves the development of creative projects with writers and young people both inside and outside of schools. We also train writers to work with young people and our writers in schools programme works with individual schools, Education Action Zones and Creative Partnership Programmes to undertake innovative work with young people.

With support from Orange, we develop activities for young writers aged 11-18 to help develop the next generation of creative writers in the region. In 2005 we set up www.wordmavericks.com, a creative website for young writers.

Our published work includes the CD-Rom *Book of the North*; *Hawthorn Wordworks*, edited by Linda France; *Bound*, a collection of short stories inspired by County Durham; *Kaput!* by Margaret Wilkinson; and *We Love You, Arthur* by Fiona Evans. Forthcoming published work includes *Writer-to-Writer*, new short stories emerging from the 2004 *Festival of Stories;* and *Magnetic North*, a collection of work from North East writers.

Claire Malcolm
Director
claire@newwritingnorth.com

Anna Summerford
Deputy Director
anna@newwritingnorth.com

Holly Hooper
Projects and Information Assistant
holly@newwritingnorth.com

For more information about our work:

www.newwritingnorth.com
www.literaturenortheast.co.uk
www.nr-foundationwriters.com
www.wordmavericks.com